Microsoft® Office 98 For Macs® For Dummies®

Cheat Sheet

Word 98 Standard and Formatting toolbars

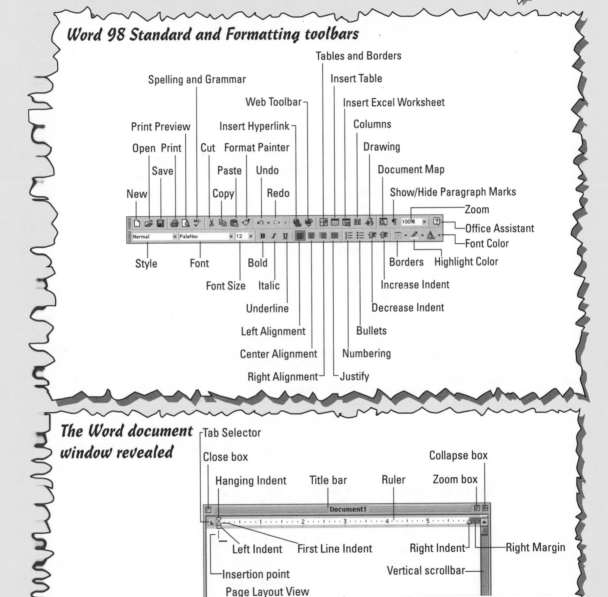

Tables and Borders

Insert Table

Spelling and Grammar

Web Toolbar

Insert Excel Worksheet

Print Preview

Insert Hyperlink

Columns

Open Print

Cut Format Painter

Drawing

Save

Paste Undo

Document Map

Copy Redo

Show/Hide Paragraph Marks

New

Zoom

Office Assistant

Font Color

Style

Font

Bold

Borders Highlight Color

Font Size

Italic

Increase Indent

Underline

Decrease Indent

Left Alignment

Bullets

Center Alignment

Numbering

Right Alignment

Justify

The Word document window revealed

Tab Selector

Close box

Collapse box

Hanging Indent Title bar Ruler Zoom box

Left Indent First Line Indent Right Indent Right Margin

Insertion point

Vertical scrollbar

Page Layout View

Outline View

Select

Online Layout View Text area Horiz

Normal View

D1404120

...For Dummies: #1 Computer Book Series for Beginners

Microsoft® Office 98 For Macs® For Dummies®

Cheat Sheet

PowerPoint 98 Standard and Formatting toolbars

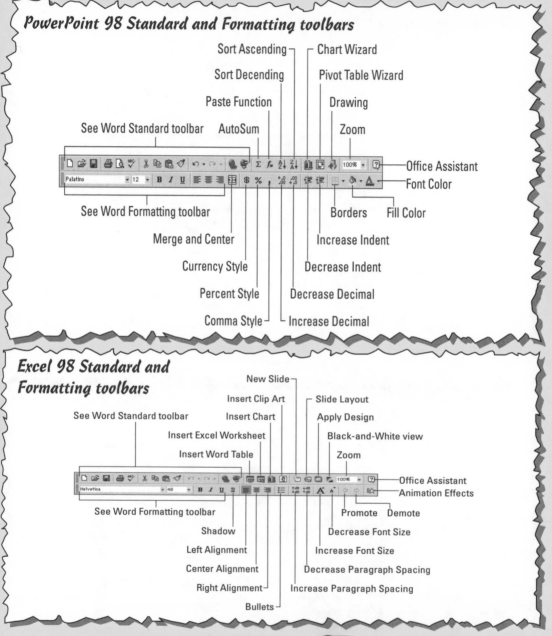

- Sort Ascending
- Sort Decending
- Paste Function
- See Word Standard toolbar
- AutoSum
- Chart Wizard
- Pivot Table Wizard
- Drawing
- Zoom
- Office Assistant
- Font Color
- See Word Formatting toolbar
- Borders
- Fill Color
- Merge and Center
- Increase Indent
- Currency Style
- Decrease Indent
- Percent Style
- Decrease Decimal
- Comma Style
- Increase Decimal

Palatino   12

Excel 98 Standard and Formatting toolbars

- New Slide
- Insert Clip Art
- See Word Standard toolbar
- Insert Chart
- Slide Layout
- Apply Design
- Insert Excel Worksheet
- Black-and-White view
- Insert Word Table
- Zoom
- Office Assistant
- Animation Effects
- See Word Formatting toolbar
- Promote
- Demote
- Shadow
- Decrease Font Size
- Left Alignment
- Increase Font Size
- Center Alignment
- Decrease Paragraph Spacing
- Right Alignment
- Increase Paragraph Spacing
- Bullets

Helvetica   48

IDG BOOKS WORLDWIDE™

...For Dummies: #1 Computer Book Series for Beginners

MICROSOFT®
OFFICE 98
FOR MACS®
FOR
DUMMIES®

MICROSOFT® OFFICE 98 FOR MACS® FOR DUMMIES®

by Tom Negrino

IDG BOOKS WORLDWIDE

IDG Books Worldwide, Inc.
An International Data Group Company

Foster City, CA ♦ Chicago, IL ♦ Indianapolis, IN ♦ New York, NY

Microsoft® Office 98 For Macs® For Dummies®

Published by
IDG Books Worldwide, Inc.
An International Data Group Company
919 E. Hillsdale Blvd.
Suite 400
Foster City, CA 94404
www.idgbooks.com (IDG Books Worldwide Web site)
www.dummies.com (Dummies Press Web site)

Library of Congress Catalog Card No.: 98-85683

ISBN: 0-7645-0229-8

Printed in the United States of America

10 9 8 7 6 5 4 3 2 1

IE/SS/QW/ZY/IN

Distributed in the United States by IDG Books Worldwide, Inc.

Distributed by Macmillan Canada for Canada; by Transworld Publishers Limited in the United Kingdom; by IDG Norge Books for Norway; by IDG Sweden Books for Sweden; by Woodslane Pty. Ltd. for Australia; by Woodslane Enterprises Ltd. for New Zealand; by Longman Singapore Publishers Ltd. for Singapore, Malaysia, Thailand, and Indonesia; by Simron Pty. Ltd. for South Africa; by Toppan Company Ltd. for Japan; by Distribuidora Cuspide for Argentina; by Livraria Cultura for Brazil; by Ediciencia S.A. for Ecuador; by Addison-Wesley Publishing Company for Korea; by Ediciones ZETA S.C.R. Ltda. for Peru; by WS Computer Publishing Corporation, Inc., for the Philippines; by Unalis Corporation for Taiwan; by Contemporanea de Ediciones for Venezuela; by Computer Book & Magazine Store for Puerto Rico; by Express Computer Distributors for the Caribbean and West Indies. Authorized Sales Agent: Anthony Rudkin Associates for the Middle East and North Africa.

For general information on IDG Books Worldwide's books in the U.S., please call our Consumer Customer Service department at 800-762-2974. For reseller information, including discounts and premium sales, please call our Reseller Customer Service department at 800-434-3422.

For information on where to purchase IDG Books Worldwide's books outside the U.S., please contact our International Sales department at 650-655-3200 or fax 650-655-3295.

For information on foreign language translations, please contact our Foreign & Subsidiary Rights department at 650-655-3021 or fax 650-655-3281.

For sales inquiries and special prices for bulk quantities, please contact our Sales department at 650-655-3200 or write to the address above.

For information on using IDG Books Worldwide's books in the classroom or for ordering examination copies, please contact our Educational Sales department at 800-434-2086 or fax 817-251-8174.

For press review copies, author interviews, or other publicity information, please contact our Public Relations department at 650-655-3000 or fax 650-655-3299.

For authorization to photocopy items for corporate, personal, or educational use, please contact Copyright Clearance Center, 222 Rosewood Drive, Danvers, MA 01923, or fax 978-750-4470.

About the Author

Tom Negrino is an author, a consultant, and a longtime contributor to *Macworld* magazine. His work has also appeared in *MacAddict, Digital Video, MacGuide,* and other magazines. He is a frequent speaker at Macworld Expo and other computer trade shows. He is also the president of the Los Angeles Macintosh Group, one of the largest Macintosh users' groups in the United States. You can find out more about LAMG at http://www.lamg.org.

Tom co-authored the best-selling *JavaScript Visual QuickStart Guide,* 2nd Edition. His other books for IDG Books Worldwide are *Macs For Kids and Parents, Macworld Web Essentials,* and *Yahoo! Unplugged.*

He lives in the Los Angeles area with his girlfriend, Dori, their son, Sean, Pixel the cat (you can visit Pixel's home page, at http://www.chalcedony.com/pixel/), nine computers, and (bliss!) a cable modem.

Please visit Tom's Web site, at http://www.negrino.com.

ABOUT IDG BOOKS WORLDWIDE

Welcome to the world of IDG Books Worldwide.

IDG Books Worldwide, Inc., is a subsidiary of International Data Group, the world's largest publisher of computer-related information and the leading global provider of information services on information technology. IDG was founded more than 25 years ago and now employs more than 8,500 people worldwide. IDG publishes more than 275 computer publications in over 75 countries (see listing below). More than 90 million people read one or more IDG publications each month.

Launched in 1990, IDG Books Worldwide is today the #1 publisher of best-selling computer books in the United States. We are proud to have received eight awards from the Computer Press Association in recognition of editorial excellence and three from *Computer Currents'* First Annual Readers' Choice Awards. Our best-selling *...For Dummies®* series has more than 50 million copies in print with translations in 38 languages. IDG Books Worldwide, through a joint venture with IDG's Hi-Tech Beijing, became the first U.S. publisher to publish a computer book in the People's Republic of China. In record time, IDG Books Worldwide has become the first choice for millions of readers around the world who want to learn how to better manage their businesses.

Our mission is simple: Every one of our books is designed to bring extra value and skill-building instructions to the reader. Our books are written by experts who understand and care about our readers. The knowledge base of our editorial staff comes from years of experience in publishing, education, and journalism — experience we use to produce books for the '90s. In short, we care about books, so we attract the best people. We devote special attention to details such as audience, interior design, use of icons, and illustrations. And because we use an efficient process of authoring, editing, and desktop publishing our books electronically, we can spend more time ensuring superior content and spend less time on the technicalities of making books.

You can count on our commitment to deliver high-quality books at competitive prices on topics you want to read about. At IDG Books Worldwide, we continue in the IDG tradition of delivering quality for more than 25 years. You'll find no better book on a subject than one from IDG Books Worldwide.

John Kilcullen
John Kilcullen
CEO
IDG Books Worldwide, Inc.

Steven Berkowitz
Steven Berkowitz
President and Publisher
IDG Books Worldwide, Inc.

VIII
WINNER
*Eighth Annual
Computer Press
Awards ≥1992*

IX
WINNER
*Ninth Annual
Computer Press
Awards ≥1993*

X
WINNER
*Tenth Annual
Computer Press
Awards ≥1994*

XI
WINNER
*Eleventh Annual
Computer Press
Awards ≥1995*

Dedication

To Patricia Negrino, for her love and her support of me as a writer. Sleep well, Sis.

Author's Acknowledgments

I'd like to thank a bunch of people for helping out with this book:

Christian Boyce, for his excellent work on the Excel section.

IDG Books Worldwide's Jill Pisoni, for her understanding and help while I dealt with a family tragedy. And for giving me the job in the first place.

Rebecca Whitney, my project editor, who spun straw into gold. Or at least ...*For Dummies* yellow.

The fine folks at StudioB, for agenting above and beyond the call: David Rogelberg, Brian Gill (thanks, pal; I'll miss you), and Sherry Rogelberg.

Kevin Browne, Deanna Meyers, Hillel Cooperman, and Dick Craddock, of Microsoft. Thanks also to Irving Kwong, at Waggener-Edstrom.

Dori Smith, just for being all that she is.

Sean Smith, who is still the World's Best Kid™.

Publisher's Acknowledgments

We're proud of this book; please register your comments through our IDG Books Worldwide Online Registration Form located at http://my2cents.dummies.com.

Some of the people who helped bring this book to market include the following:

Acquisitions, Editorial, and Media Development

Project Editor: Rebecca Whitney

Senior Acquisitions Editor: Jill Pisoni

Copy Editors: Kathy Simpson, Kelly Oliver, Bill McManus

Technical Editor: Greg Holden

Editorial Manager: Mary C. Corder

Editorial Assistant: Paul E. Kuzmic

Production

Project Coordinator: Cindy L. Phipps

Layout and Graphics: Lou Boudreau, Angela F. Hunckler, Jane E. Martin, Brent Savage, Kate Snell

Proofreaders: Christine Berman, Kelli Botta, Nancy Price, Christine Snyder, Janet M. Withers

Indexer: Liz Cunningham

Special Help

Suzanne Thomas

General and Administrative

IDG Books Worldwide, Inc.: John Kilcullen, CEO; Steven Berkowitz, President and Publisher

IDG Books Technology Publishing: Brenda McLaughlin, Senior Vice President and Group Publisher

Dummies Technology Press and Dummies Editorial: Diane Graves Steele, Vice President and Associate Publisher; Mary Bednarek, Director of Acquisitions and Product Development; Kristin A. Cocks, Editorial Director

Dummies Trade Press: Kathleen A. Welton, Vice President and Publisher; Kevin Thornton, Acquisitions Manager

IDG Books Production for Dummies Press: Michael R. Britton, Vice President of Production; Beth Jenkins Roberts, Production Director; Cindy L. Phipps, Manager of Project Coordination, Production Proofreading, and Indexing; Kathie S. Schutte, Supervisor of Page Layout; Shelley Lea, Supervisor of Graphics and Design; Debbie J. Gates, Production Systems Specialist; Robert Springer, Supervisor of Proofreading; Debbie Stailey, Special Projects Coordinator; Tony Augsburger, Supervisor of Reprints and Bluelines; Leslie Popplewell, Media Archive Coordinator

Dummies Packaging and Book Design: Robin Seaman, Creative Director; Jocelyn Kelaita, Product Packaging Coordinator; Kavish + Kavish, Cover Design

◆

The publisher would like to give special thanks to Patrick J. McGovern, without whom this book would not have been possible.

◆

Contents at a Glance

Cartoons at a Glance

By Rich Tennant

page 113

page 171

page 37

page 219

page 253

page 293

page 7

Fax: 978-546-7747 • **E-mail:** the5wave@tiac.net

Table of Contents

Introduction

· ·

*W*elcome to *Microsoft Office 98 For Macs For Dummies!*

If you've spent any time at all with Office 98, you've seen that it consists of three main programs (and two others): Word 98 is its word processor, Excel 98 is its spreadsheet program, and PowerPoint 98 is its presentation program. Office 98 also has a Web browser, Internet Explorer, and an e-mail program, Outlook Express.

All these programs add up to a great deal of power and a great deal of complexity. That's where this book comes in. When you're working in one of the Office programs and you ask yourself "How do I . . .?" or "How does this work?" just reach for this book. Chances are, you'll find the answers here.

A long time ago, I learned that there are two basic kinds of auto mechanics. One type is the mechanic who has been factory-trained and had every class under the sun; the other type learned everything from just tinkering with every car that passed by. The factory-trained mechanic has all the right tools and is the one you want to rebuild your engine. The tinkerer is the one you turn to when your car breaks down in the middle of nowhere — the one who can always get your car running long enough to get you to the shop. This book is more like the tinkerer: It helps you get the job done when you need it the most. When you have a question, just look up the answer, and then get back on the road.

How to Use This Book

I've written *Microsoft Office 98 For Macs For Dummies* so that you can skip around in it and read just the chapters that interest you. You don't have to read Chapter 1, for example, in order to understand and enjoy Chapter 15, though it would be nice if you got around to reading Chapter 1 sometime; that chapter has some stuff that I especially like. But there's no hurry — and no requirement that you read the chapters in a particular order. The *...For Dummies* books are written as reference books, not as tutorials.

Cheeky assumptions I've made

In writing this book, I've made the following assumptions about you: First and foremost, you're meeting the minimal requirements for running Office 98. You must have a Power Macintosh with Microsoft Office 98 installed on it. On that Power Macintosh, you have to be running Mac OS 7.5 or later (and in my not-so-humble opinion, you really should be using Mac OS 8.1 or later; the benefits of using Mac OS 8.1 make it a must-have). You should also have at least 32MB of RAM and a CD-ROM drive (virtually every Power Macintosh does).

I've also made the assumption that you're familiar with the basics of using a Macintosh. You don't need to be a Mac guru, although you shouldn't be stumped by concepts like selecting text, clicking and dragging, and using files and folders. If you need a refresher in the essentials, you may want to buy *Macs For Dummies,* by David Pogue (published by IDG Books Worldwide, Inc.); if you want detailed information about using the Mac OS, I suggest that you pick up a copy of Lon Poole's *Mac OS 8.1 Bible,* also published by IDG Books Worldwide.

Conventions

Throughout this book, I use some special codes to make reading the book easier. I'll often say things like "choose File⇨New." Whenever you see something like that, it means that I'm asking you to choose a command from a menu. When you see File⇨New, I'm really saying, "Click the File menu and drag down to select the New command."

You'll also see the ⌘ symbol throughout this book. Whenever I use this symbol, I'm talking about the ⌘ key on your keyboard. This key is usually referred to as the Command key, and longtime Mac users often refer to Command-key shortcuts when they talk about performing a task from the keyboard. When I tell you to use a shortcut key, such as ⌘+P, just hold down the ⌘ key and press the P key.

Icons Used in This Book

Throughout *Microsoft Office 98 For Macs For Dummies,* I use little pictures, called *icons,* next to the text to get your attention. Here are the icons I use:

This icon marks pieces of information that can be helpful and that you should remember.

If you're looking for the best way, the fast way, the you-can't-top-this way of doing things, this icon tips you off. The Tip icon always points out what you can do to make your Office 98 experience easier or faster.

 Watch out! You have to be careful and follow the advice given here, or else you can have some real trouble.

 You don't have to read this stuff. If you do, however, you get a deeper understanding of the subject being discussed. You may even be able to impress and amaze your friends with the depth of your incredible knowledge.

How This Book Is Organized

Microsoft Office 98 For Macs For Dummies is split into seven parts. Here's the lowdown:

Part I: Getting Started with Microsoft Office 98

Sensibly enough, I start out by introducing you to Microsoft Office 98. In this part, I show you what Office 98 can do for you, why Office 98 is a terrific Macintosh product (unlike some previous versions of Microsoft Office), and how the package stacks up against the competition.

This part also shows you how do some things that are common to all the Office 98 programs, such as start up and switch between the programs, open documents, and use the suite's help features. You also meet Max, the Office Assistant, a friendly, animated character who's great at answering your Office 98 questions.

Part II: Using Word 98

Microsoft Word 98 is a superb word processor, capable of handling everything from a quick note to Mom (though I think that handwritten notes to Mom are nicer, don't you?) to reports, books, and your doctoral thesis. Word 98 is chock-full of features to help you wrestle your words into shape. Because most people work with words more than anything else they do, this part of the book is the longest and most detailed part.

Part II starts you off easy with the basics of creating a Word document. Then you see how Word can help you out with automatic formatting and by checking your spelling and grammar. Because the look of your work is almost as important as its content, you see how to create professional-looking documents, including fancy pieces like reports, newsletters, and even Web pages.

Part III: Crunching Your Numbers with Excel 98

This part show you how to create your own spreadsheets with Microsoft Excel 98. You start out in Spreadsheet Boot Camp, and, after you know the basics, discover how to add your own formulas so that Excel 98 calculates results automatically. Excel knows how to make your spreadsheets look good, and you'll see how you can make your spreadsheets look spiffy with just a few clicks of the mouse. Because numbers can be dull, however (with apologies to our accountant friends), you discover how to use Excel 98 to create flashy charts and graphs. With the right arsenal of pie charts and bar graphs, you'll be certain to win friends, influence co-workers, and get in the running for that next Nobel prize.

Part IV: Getting Net Savvy with Internet Explorer and Outlook Express

In the early 1990s, only a few people were using the Internet, the worldwide data and information network. Only a few years later, being on the Internet and, specifically, having an electronic mail address are barely optional if you're in business. In this part, you discover how to use the two Office 98 programs that can help you master the Internet. The first is Internet Explorer, which enables you to browse and explore the World Wide Web and copy files from computers across the Net to your Macintosh. The other program, Outlook Express, enables you to compose, send, and receive e-mail and to read and participate on Usenet, the Internet's public bulletin board.

Part V: Putting on a Show with PowerPoint 98

Giving a presentation can be the scariest thing most people do in the office (aside from asking for a big raise, of course!). In this part, you meet PowerPoint 98, which makes creating snappy presentations a painless experience. After you see how simple it is to create a simple slide show, you find out how to improve your presentations with fancy graphics and slick animation and how you can add high-tech, interactive features to your shows. I haven't forgotten the human element, though: An entire section full of tips helps you deliver the presentation while simultaneously conquering stage fright.

Part VI: Working Well with Others

No man is an island, and your Mac isn't, either. You often need to share your work with other people, and Office 98 has a zillion tools that can help. This part shows you how you can make Word, Excel, and PowerPoint work together to create powerhouse documents that are more than the sum of their parts. You discover how to share your documents with co-workers to gather their comments and suggestions, and then you see how to ignore those suggestions (okay, and use them, too).

Because one of the best mediums for sharing work is the Internet, this part delves into how you can embed live Internet links in your documents; create Web pages from any of the Office 98 programs (especially from Word 98); and even how you can set up your own personal Web server (it takes only about two minutes — honest!).

Part VII: The Part of Tens

If you're hungry for hot tips and tricks to help you use Microsoft Office 98 better, The Part of Tens is the place for you. You find out how to tame your toolbars, you get a bunch of time-saving tips, and you read about some of the best ways to customize Office 98.

Onward and Upward!

You may want to start out by looking up something you've seen in one of the Office 98 programs. If you're completely new to Microsoft Office 98, start by browsing through Part I. You'll find the basics there.

Fasten your seat belt, and let's go!

Part I

Getting Started with Microsoft Office 98

The 5th Wave

By Rich Tennant

"YES, WE STILL HAVE A FEW BUGS IN THE WORD PROCESSING SOFTWARE. BY THE WAY, HERE'S A MEMO FROM MARKETING."

In this part . . .

Every journey begins with a single step, and your journey into the heart of Microsoft Office 98 is no exception. Part I gives you an overview of the Office 98 programs and shows you how Office compares to its most popular competition. Then you find out how to create documents with the Office programs and other basics common to the whole package.

One of the best features of Office 98 is also one of the most helpful: Max, the Office Assistant. Max can answer almost any question you have about using Office 98, and he's fun to have around too. You meet Max in this part and find out how he's the biggest and best key to getting help with Office 98 (except for this book, of course!).

Chapter 1

Why Office 98?

For many people, the days of job specialization are over. The average worker today, whether she works as an employee or as an entrepreneur, must do many things during the course of a day and needs many software tools to get the job done.

Imagine a typical day. You arrive at work and turn on your computer. Sipping your morning coffee, you log on to the Internet to read your electronic mail. One of the messages is a request from your boss for more details about your latest project. You start a word-processing program and write a short memo, explaining your approach. You launch your spreadsheet program and create a set of numbers to support your memo. Switching back to your e-mail, you send the memo and spreadsheet to your boss for approval. Then you go to lunch. When you get back, your boss has already replied (doesn't this guy ever take a lunch hour?), asking you to present your proposal at a meeting later that afternoon. You realize that handing copies of your memo around the table won't have the impact you want, so you fire up your presentation software and create a nice slide show.

After the smashing success of your presentation, your boss calls you into his office and offers you a huge raise. Beautiful women in evening dresses crowd around you, press bouquets of roses into your arms, and place a diamond tiara on your head. Music swells, and you begin your walk down the runway, waving to your cheering co-workers. Blinking away tears of joy, you say happily, "I owe it all to my software!"

Okay, maybe this isn't a *typical* day.

Introducing Microsoft Office 98

To deal with all the things that come up in your workday, you need software that can handle writing, number crunching, presenting, e-mail, and more. You could try to find all these functions in one mammoth program — the approach taken by *integrated software* packages such as ClarisWorks, and Microsoft Works. Or you can search for a few separate, powerful, expensive programs that have been put together in one box for a cut-rate price. That arrangement is called a *suite* of programs, which is what Microsoft Office is. The Office suite includes Microsoft Word, the word processor; Microsoft Excel, the spreadsheet; and Microsoft PowerPoint, the presentation program. Figure 1-1 shows the icons for these three powerhouse programs.

Figure 1-1:
The icons
for the
three main
Office 98
programs.

In addition to the three main programs, the Office 98 CD-ROM includes two Internet programs. Internet Explorer is the suite's Web browser, and Outlook Express is its electronic-mail program. Figure 1-2 shows the desktop icons for the Office 98 Internet duo.

Figure 1-2:
The Internet
Explorer
and Outlook
Express
icons.

Office 98 is all new and comes as a welcome break with the past. The preceding version of Microsoft Office, Office 4.2, included Microsoft Word 6, Excel 5, and PowerPoint 4, and was less than a resounding success. Word 6 in particular was widely condemned for providing slow performance, having rampant bugs, and being too much like a (shudder!) Windows program. Office 4.2 received almost universally bad press, and many people refused to upgrade, sticking with the 1992-vintage Word 5.1 and Excel 4.0.

As you can see, Microsoft had something to prove with a new version of Office, and with the release of Microsoft Office 98, the company has risen admirably to the occasion. The Office 98 programs have been completely rewritten to make them look better and to work faster, smarter, and easier, yet still providing more features than you'll likely ever use. The following sections describe the individual pieces of the Office 98 package.

Word 98

Nothing is more important than words. It's probably no surprise that a writer would say that, but it's still true. The words you write shape the way people think about you and may even change your career. If words are so important, the means of getting those words down is vital. You should look for a writing tool that helps you get more work done with less effort.

Microsoft Word 98 is an excellent writing tool for short memos or entire books, and it's smart: It checks spelling and grammar as you type. If you frequently type the same words, Word 98 can remember that text and spit it back the next time you start to type it. Word watches what you do, and it can automatically format your documents. If you type the salutation of a letter, for example, Word recognizes the "Dear Oswald" part and asks whether you're writing a letter and (if so) whether you want to format your document like a letter.

Word 98 comes with terrific online help (as do Excel and PowerPoint) that enables you to ask questions about the program in plain English.

Word 98 can create almost any type of document that contains words, from letters to Web pages and from books to newsletters. Figure 1-3 shows Word 98 being used to make a newsletter.

I could go on and on singing the praises of Word 98, but I get to do that in Part II of this book.

Excel 98

Excel is the premier spreadsheet for any computer platform, and the latest version is better than ever. What's a *spreadsheet?* Think of an accountant's ledger pad, with all the rows and columns ready to be filled in with numbers. Then imagine a pad that can do all the math for you. That's a spreadsheet. Although Excel is fine for accounting, it works well for any task that involves grinding through numbers: financial projections, statistical analysis, rocket trajectories (hey, it *is* rocket science) — you name it.

Figure 1-3:
Creating a
newsletter
in Word 98.

Figure 1-4 shows an expense report written in Excel. Writing a report may not be as exciting as going to the moon, but in the grand scheme of things, isn't being reimbursed for your travel expenses just as important?

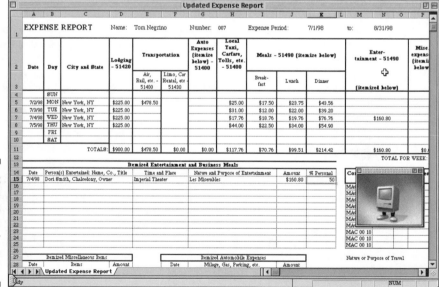

Figure 1-4:
Have
Excel 98
calculate
your
expense
report!

Spreadsheets also are the cannon fodder for charts and graphs. The numbers in a spreadsheet can be changed into cool graphs of just about every description. Looking to make a big splash at your next meeting? Two words: pie charts. Bosses love 'em; they can't resist a piping-hot pie chart. You can bake one yourself — with the help of Excel 98.

PowerPoint 98

When you need to persuade, you'll turn to PowerPoint 98. It's a presentation program that enables you to create slide shows that can be shown on a computer screen (or with a projector from a computer), printed, or even transferred to 35mm slides or overhead transparencies.

PowerPoint provides powerful tools that enable you to organize your thoughts and create presentations. The program's outline mode makes building a presentation easy, and the outline converts directly into slides. You can format your slides any way you want and add animated slide transitions (as well as add animation within slides). PowerPoint 98 also comes with dozens of templates, canned presentations, clip art, and Wizards that help you through the hassle of developing a presentation.

PowerPoint 98 is a great improvement over PowerPoint 4, its Mac predecessor in Office 4.2. The new features include easy presentation creation with the AutoContent Wizard, improved drawing capabilities, and more flexible presentation options. Check out Figure 1-5 to see a PowerPoint 98 presentation being created.

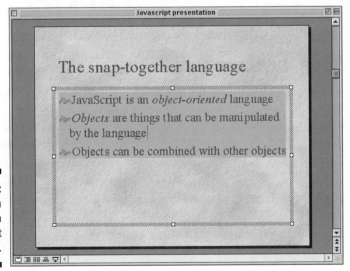

Figure 1-5: Building a slide with PowerPoint 98.

Internet Explorer 4.0

Surfing the World Wide Web has become a core requirement of every computing platform. The Web browser that comes with Office 98 (and that now is also the built-in browser for Mac OS, the Macintosh system software) is Microsoft Internet Explorer 4.0. Overall, Explorer is an excellent browser, although early versions were plagued by bugs (the result of a little too much haste in getting the product out the door). You should make sure that you're using Version 4.01 or later of Internet Explorer because many of the bugs have been fixed in recent versions. Internet Explorer can view Web sites, as shown in Figure 1-6, and download files from the Internet.

Figure 1-6:
Web surfing
with
Internet
Explorer.

Outlook Express 4.0

Outlook Express is the Office 98 electronic-mail and Usenet newsreading program. Considering that Outlook Express can be downloaded for free, it is a surprisingly complete program, with support for the latest e-mail standards, mail filtering, and much more. Figure 1-7 shows Outlook Express in action.

Usenet is the Internet's worldwide bulletin board. People post public messages about virtually every imaginable topic. For more information about Usenet, see Chapter 14.

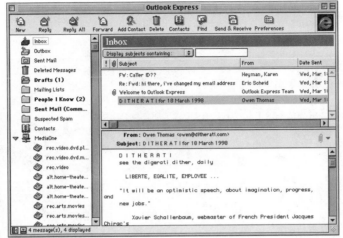

Figure 1-7:
Outlook
Express is
an excellent
electronic-
mail
program.

Microsoft Office 98 versus ClarisWorks Office

If you haven't already bought Microsoft Office 98, you owe it to yourself to compare Office 98 with its closet competitor. Although several Office-like suites are available for Windows, on the Mac side, ClarisWorks Office is practically the only choice. This package is a suite only by courtesy — instead of being several full-featured programs bundled together, ClarisWorks 5.0 consists mainly of ClarisWorks Office, an integrated program that includes a word processor, spreadsheet, database, drawing program, painting program, and rudimentary terminal program for using a modem. The package also includes Claris HomePage Lite (a stripped-down version of the company's Web-page editor) and a large bundle of templates for newsletters, spreadsheets, presentations, and Web pages.

Although ClarisWorks hasn't yet changed its name, it isn't made by Claris Corporation anymore. In early 1998, Apple Computer (which owned Claris) took into the Apple fold most of the Claris products, including ClarisWorks and Emailer. The remaining Claris products — FileMaker Pro and Claris HomePage — stayed behind, and Claris was renamed FileMaker, Inc. Although Apple has announced that ClarisWorks will eventually be renamed AppleWorks, the company hasn't set a date for the transition.

ClarisWorks 5.0 is a terrific product, with a more-than-adequate word processor and spreadsheet, and its drawing and painting modules are good, if not especially inspired. The database is basic but gets the job done for tasks such as mail merges and simple recordkeeping. Claris claims that ClarisWorks 5.0 has all the power most people ever need, for a fraction of the complexity and price of Microsoft Office. Figure 1-8 shows ClarisWorks 5.0 in action.

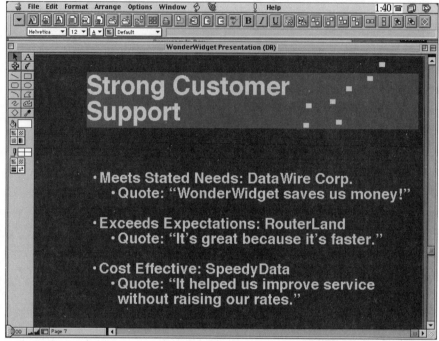

Figure 1-8:
Creating a
presentation
in the
ClarisWorks
5.0 drawing
module.

If you have an older Mac, ClarisWorks Office may be the better choice for you. Office 98 requires a Power Macintosh with at least 16 megabytes (MB) of RAM (although 32MB is a more realistic figure), whereas ClarisWorks Office runs on any Macintosh with a 68020 processor or later and requires only 8MB of RAM.

ClarisWorks Office is also much gentler on your pocketbook than Microsoft Office 98. A brand-new copy of Office 98 costs around $450, whereas ClarisWorks Office sets you back only about $100.

It's true that many people don't ever need more powerful software than ClarisWorks 5.0. If you do, however, you'll be frustrated when ClarisWorks runs out of steam. ClarisWorks 5.0 uses its drawing module to create presentations and newsletters, for example — a poor substitute for the capabilities of PowerPoint and Word, respectively. The capabilities of Word 98 far outshine those of the word processor inside ClarisWorks, and the differences are big enough that if your business depends on words (ultimately, most businesses do), Word 98 is well worth the extra investment. Also, although the ClarisWorks spreadsheet isn't bad, it doesn't hold a candle to Excel 98, the recognized world champion in spreadsheets.

Another issue you should consider is whether you need to share files with other people. ClarisWorks Office can read and write Microsoft Word files up to Version 5.1 (but not Word 6 or Word 98 files) and Microsoft Excel files up to Version 4.0 (but not Excel 5.0 or Excel 98 files). Because Office 98 files on the Mac and Office 97 files on the PC are interchangeable, if you use ClarisWorks Office, you have to ask people who work with Office 98 programs to resave their files in an earlier format so that you can use those files. (To be fair, no version of Microsoft Office can open any version of ClarisWorks files directly; at least Claris made the compatibility effort.)

You can use Office 98 (and Office 4.2 and Office 97) files in ClarisWorks Office, but you need to invest in the excellent MacLink Plus Translator Pro package from DataViz (about $95; you can get more information from the World Wide Web, at http://www.dataviz.com). MacLink Plus can convert almost any sort of word-processing or spreadsheet file to any other format. The program handles and converts files created in programs that have long since faded into the mists of time (such as the PC program MultiMate and the Apple II program AppleWorks) to modern Mac formats. MacLink Plus works well for converting recent Office files created on Macs and Windows 95 machines to ClarisWorks, and vice versa. MacLink Plus can also handle translations between some graphics formats. Whether or not you use ClarisWorks, MacLink Plus is still useful to have around for converting random PC files your friends send you.

Your decision to go with ClarisWorks Office or Microsoft Office 98 must be based on your unique circumstances, after balancing cost, hardware and software compatibility, and features. Some people are okay with tools that are adequate for their needs. I'm the kind of person, though, who wants to know that if I ever decide to squeeze the maximum amount of power from a program, that power will be there, with no compromises. That's why I use Office 98.

Chapter 2

Running Office 98

In This Chapter

▶ Using the Office 98 programs

▶ Opening documents

▶ Quitting Office 98 programs

*I*n this chapter, you find out how to do things that are common to all Office 98 programs, such as opening and closing programs and files, saving, and printing.

Installing Office 98

One amazing new feature of Office 98 is a throwback to the early days of using the Macintosh. Way back in prehistory (the 1980s), you never had to use any Installer programs to put programs on your Mac. You just slammed the program's floppy disk into your Mac and dragged the program's icon over to your hard disk. As time went on, programs got more complicated and required support files, called *extensions,* to be installed in your Mac's System Folder. Soon, so many of these support files were required that people couldn't keep track of them, and all programs came with Installer programs, which ensure that all the files required to make the program run are put in the right places on your hard disk.

Office 98 enables you to return to the old way of doing installations — with a modern twist. To install Office 98, you drag the Office 98 folder from the CD-ROM to your hard disk's icon, as shown in Figure 2-1. This action copies the main Office 98 programs (Word, Excel, and PowerPoint) to your hard disk.

Before you drag the Office 98 folder to your hard disk icon, make sure that you have enough available disk space. The Office suite is big: The standard installation takes a whopping 77 megabytes (MB) of space. To find out how much disk space you have available, look at the header of any Finder window, as shown in Figure 2-2. As long as you have at least 100MB free, you're fine.

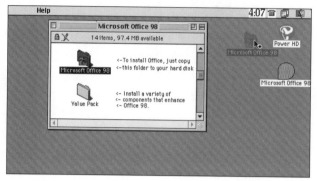

Figure 2-1:
Copying the
Office 98
folder to your
hard disk.

The amount of available disk space

Figure 2-2:
Checking your
disk space.

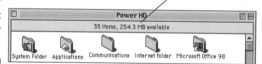

Running any Office 98 program for the first time takes a little extra time because Office 98 checks your disk and automatically installs any additional files it needs. Best of all, if you later accidentally throw away any of these files, Office 98 is smart enough to fix the installation for you. The next time you run any of the Office 98 programs, Office asks you to reinsert the CD-ROM and then copies the missing files back to your hard disk. This "self-healing" feature is a big improvement from previous versions of Office, which often required a bewildering amount of fiddling and saddled you with an intrusive Setup program.

Using Office 98 Programs

After you copy the Microsoft Office 98 folder to your hard disk, open the folder. You see the icons for the three main Office programs, plus several folders that hold additional support files. Decide which Office program you want to start, and double-click its icon. If you want to start Word, for example, just double-click the Microsoft Word icon.

Another way to start or launch any Macintosh program or document is to single-click the icon and then choose File⇨Open.

When an Office program starts, you see a brief introduction screen that displays the logo of the program; then you get a fresh new document, as shown in Figure 2-3.

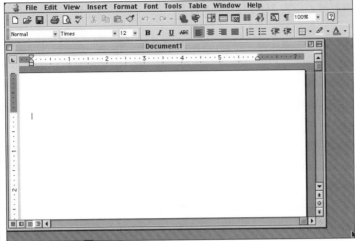

Figure 2-3:
A blank
Word 98
document.

Creating a new document

You always get a new document when you start one of the Office programs.
What happens, however, if you're already working in an Office program and
want to create a new document? You create it in the same way as you would
in any Macintosh program: by choosing File➪New. Unlike most other Mac
programs, though, Word and Excel act differently when you click the mouse
to choose the command than they do when you press the ⌘+N shortcut key.

When you press the shortcut key, Word and Excel create a new, blank
document based on the Normal template. When you choose File➪New,
however, you see the New dialog box, which enables you to choose from
among a variety of templates, as shown in Figure 2-4. (See Chapter 3 for
more information about using templates.)

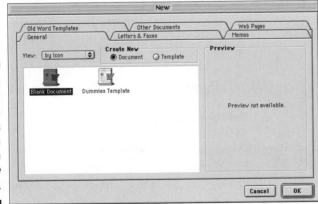

Figure 2-4:
The Word
New dialog
box displays
templates you
can use
for a new
document.

Saving a document

Type a line or two of text in the blank document so that you have something to save. Then follow these steps to save the document:

1. Choose File⇨Save.

The Save dialog box appears, as shown in Figure 2-5. The large scroll box shows you where the file will be saved.

Scroll box Pop-up navigation list

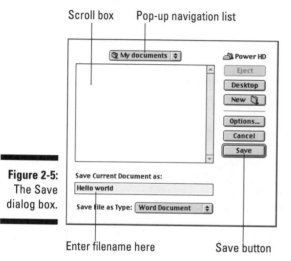

Figure 2-5:
The Save
dialog box.

Enter filename here   Save button

2. If you want to save the file in a different place, navigate to that place, by clicking the pop-up menu at the top of the scroll box.

Notice that Word has already suggested a name for the document, based on the first line of text. (Other Office programs do the same thing.)

3. If that name is acceptable, click the Save button.

If you prefer to give the document a different name, just start typing; the new name replaces the name Word gave the document.

Closing a document

You can close a document by using any of three methods:

✔ **Click the close box in the top-left corner of the document window.** This method is the easiest.

✔ **Choose File⇨Close:** Use this method if you prefer to use the mouse.

✔ **Press ⌘+W.** This method works well for people who prefer to work from the keyboard.

No matter how you close the document, if you have unsaved changes, you're asked whether you want to save them. After you click Save or Don't Save, the document closes.

People commonly confuse closing a document with quitting a program. When you want to switch from one document to another that was created in the same program, always close the document by using one of the preceding methods; then choose File⇨Open to locate and open the next document. What you don't want to do is quit the program, search for the next document in the Finder, and then double-click the document, because starting a program takes much longer than simply opening another document while the program is already running.

Opening an existing document

You can open an existing document in two ways: from the Finder (the terms *Finder* and *desktop* are used interchangeably in this book) or from inside any Office application. If you're working on the desktop, just find the icon for the document you want to work with and then double-click it. The program that created the document launches and opens the document.

If you're already working in one of the Office programs, choose File⇨Open or click the Open button (it looks like a little open folder) on the Standard toolbar. The Open dialog box appears, as shown in Figure 2-6. If the document you're looking for is in the folder displayed in the scroll box, select it and then click the Open button. Otherwise, navigate to the correct folder by using the pop-up navigation menu at the top of the dialog box; then open the file by clicking the Open button.

Figure 2-6:
The Open
dialog box.

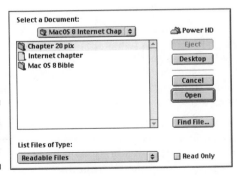

Printing a document

To print a document that is open on-screen, all you normally have to do is choose File➪Print and then click OK in the resulting Print dialog box. If you're trying to print for the first time, however, making sure that you have selected a printer in the Chooser is a good idea. Follow these steps:

1. **Choose Apple➪Chooser.**

   The Chooser window appears, as shown in Figure 2-7.

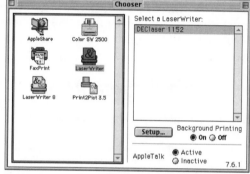

Figure 2-7: Be sure to pick a printer in the Chooser.

2. **In the left pane of the window, click the icon that corresponds to your printer.**

   Don't be surprised if what's on your screen isn't exactly the same as what's shown in Figure 2-7; different computers display things differently.

   The software that tells your Macintosh how to use a particular printer is called a *printer driver*. By clicking one of these icons in the Chooser, you are really selecting a printer driver.

   After you click a printer icon in the left pane of the Chooser window, the right pane changes. The type of change depends on whether you're using a networked printer or a directly connected printer. If you're using a networked printer, such as a LaserWriter, the right pane of the Chooser window displays a list of the printers on your network. Click to select the name of the printer you want to use.

   If you're choosing a networked printer and no names are listed in the right pane of the Chooser window, no printers of that type are available on the network — usually because somebody switched the printer off. Or, your Mac may have been disconnected from the network. Check your network connections (the wires on the back of your Mac that connect it to the network), and then try choosing the printer again. You should also make sure that the AppleTalk Active radio button is selected at the bottom of the Chooser.

If you choose an icon for a directly connected printer, such as a Style Writer, the Chooser displays the ports to which the printer can be connected (usually, the printer and modem ports). Choose the appropriate port by clicking it in the right pane of the Chooser window.

Figure 2-8 shows you how to choose the port for a directly connected printer.

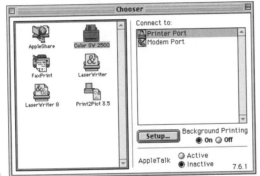

Figure 2-8:
Choosing a
directly
connected
printer.

Chapter 3

Help Is Everywhere You Turn

In This Chapter

▶ Using the Office Assistant

▶ Using the other Help files

*T*he Office 98 package is big and powerful, enabling you to do just about anything you can imagine (within limits; it's just software, after all!). Powerful software means complex software, which in turn means that figuring out just how to make the programs do what you want can take some doing. Fortunately, Microsoft includes a boatload of online help that can show you how to solve even the thorniest problems.

By clicking the Help icon on the Macintosh menu bar, Office 98 also provides on-screen Help files, which is similar to having the Office 98 manuals inside your computer. Using the on-screen Help system to find information is much easier than digging through the printed manuals. The Help system has an electronic index that enables you to enter a keyword. After you enter the keyword, the Help system searches thousands of pages and presents a list of (usually) relevant topics. The Office Assistant is the friendly face of the Help system; when you ask the Office Assistant a question, it displays the right topics in a Help file.

Office 98 also provides on-screen Help files, which is similar to having the Office 98 manuals inside your computer. Using the on-screen Help system to find information is much easier than digging through the printed manuals. The Help system has an electronic index that enables you to enter a key-word. After you enter the keyword, the Help system searches thousands of pages and presents a list of (usually) relevant topics. The Office Assistant is the friendly face of the Help system; when you ask the Office Assistant a question, it displays the right topics in a Help file.

If you need even more help, Office 98 also includes the Apple-standard Balloon Help. One common Help system that Office doesn't have is Apple Guide; the Office Assistant serves much the same purpose.

Getting to Know the Office Assistant

The idea behind a big, integrated package such as Office 98 is to enable people to do virtually anything they can imagine doing with a word processor, spreadsheet, or presentation program. For this reason, Microsoft has added virtually every feature that has ever been requested. Then the people in charge of Microsoft Office development noticed an odd fact: A large percentage of enhancement requests they received were for features that were already in the programs! Because the company realized that people needed an easier way to discover just what the programs can do, the Office Assistant was born.

The Office Assistant provides help in both an active and passive manner. It watches what you do (I'm not joking; the Assistant character actually turns and looks at the document while you are working on it) and offers tips, when appropriate. You can also ask the Assistant for help at any time by clicking the Assistant window. The Assistant tries to make sure that it doesn't get in your way. When you haven't used the Assistant's window for a while, it gets smaller, and if you need to type or click where the Assistant window is, it scoots out of your way.

The Macintosh version of Office 98 has a unique Office Assistant named Max. Max looks like the original all-in-one Macintosh, from the Macintosh Plus era, except that he has feet (made of two computer mice!), as shown in Figure 3-1.

Figure 3-1:
Max, the
Office
Assistant.

Max has a variety of whimsical behaviors, including snoring and falling over with a crash when you haven't touched the mouse or keyboard for a while. I suspect that you may get tired of Max in a hurry, but I like the little guy.

Asking the Assistant for help

To get help from the Office Assistant, follow these steps:

1. **Click the Office Assistant window.** (If the Assistant window isn't visible, activate it by clicking the Help button on the Standard toolbar — the one that looks like a cartoon balloon with a question mark in it.)

   A yellow balloon pops up, as shown in Figure 3-2.

2. **Type a question, such as** How do I make an outline?, **and then click the Search button.**

Another balloon pops up, displaying a list of topics related to your question, as shown in Figure 3-3.

3. **Click the button that matches the appropriate topic.**

If the balloon has a See More button, more topics are available, although they don't fit in the balloon. Click the down arrow to see the rest of the topics.

A Help window appears, displaying information about the selected topic, as shown in Figure 3-4.

Search button

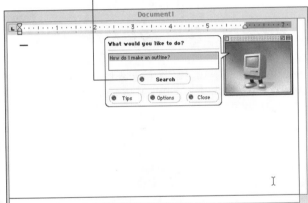

Figure 3-2:
The Office
Assistant
asks you
what you
want to do.

Topic buttons

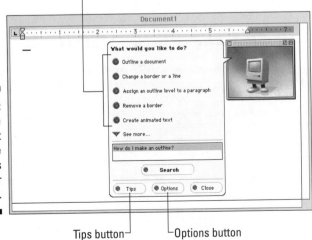

Figure 3-3:
The Office
Assistant
shows the
Help topics
for your
question.

Tips button ⌐ ⌐Options button

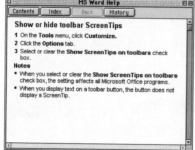

Figure 3-4:
The
detailed
Help
information
you
requested.

4. **When you finish reading the Help information, close the Help window by clicking the close box in the top-left corner of the Help window.**

Picking up tips from the Assistant

The Office Assistant pays attention to you as you're working, and when it sees an easier way of performing a particular task, it tells you so. When you see the lightbulb in the Assistant window, you can click the window to get the tip, as shown in Figure 3-5.

Figure 3-5:
A tip from
the Office
Assistant.
You've been
warned!

Installing and changing Assistants

In addition to Max, Office 98 comes with 13 Assistants, as shown in Figure 3-6. You can find them in the Value Pack folder on the Office 98 CD-ROM. Each Assistant has a different personality and displays a different set of behaviors in response to your actions. All Assistants are helpful, however.

You can choose from among these Assistants:

- ✔ Bosgrove, the butler
- ✔ The Genius, who looks and acts like a relatively famous mathematician
- ✔ Will, the bard of the group
- ✔ Earl, the high-strung cat
- ✔ PowerPup, the dog to the rescue
- ✔ Rocky, the faithful canine companion
- ✔ Scribble, the paper cat
- ✔ F1, a robot
- ✔ Hoverbot, another robot
- ✔ Clipit, the standard Assistant from the Windows version of Office 97
- ✔ Dot, a happy face
- ✔ Mother Nature, an Earth figure
- ✔ Office Logo, for corporate types

The standard installation of Office 98 installs only Max, although you can easily install other Assistants. Just run the Value Pack Installer inside the Value Pack folder on the Office 98 CD-ROM. To install all the additional Assistants, click the Assistants check box in the Installer. To install individual Assistants, click the disclosure triangle next to the Assistants option so that it points down, and then select the Assistants you want.

Bosgrove
The Genius
Will

Earl
PowerPup
Rocky
Scribble

F1
Hoverbot
Clipit
Dot

Figure 3-6:
The Office
Assistants.

Mother Nature
Office Logo

To change installed Assistants, follow these steps:

1. **Click the Office Assistant window.**

   The Assistant's yellow cartoon balloon appears.

2. **Click the Options button.**

   The Office Assistant dialog box appears, as shown in Figure 3-7.

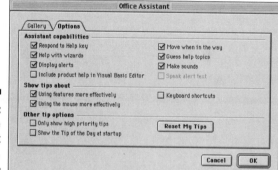

Figure 3-7:
The Office
Assistant
dialog box.

3. **Click the Options tab (if it isn't already displayed).**

   This tab enables you to fine-tune the Assistant's reactions; feel free to experiment with the settings to see which ones work best for you.

   Because the Office Assistant is shared by all the Office programs, any changes you make in the Assistant options affect the Assistant in all the Office programs.

4. **Click the Gallery tab.**

   The screen changes as shown in Figure 3-8, displaying a description and a brief animation of each Assistant.

5. **Click the Back and Next buttons to flip through the Assistants until you find the one you want to use.**

6. **Click the OK button.**

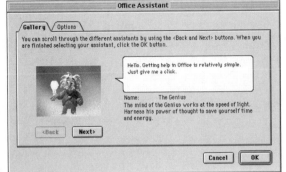

Figure 3-8:
Browsing
the choices
in the Office
Assistant
Gallery.

Using the Other Help Files

Using the Office Assistant is one way to get to the Help files, although you
can get to them directly too. To go straight to the Help files, follow these
steps:

1. **Choose Help⇨Contents and Index.**

   (If you use any version of Mac OS 7, you should use the menu with the
   question-mark icon, which was changed to Help in Mac OS 8.)

   The Help contents window appears, as shown in Figure 3-9.

2. **Click one of the book icons to display a list of subtopics.**

   The book icon changes to an open book with the subtopic document
   icons marked with question marks.

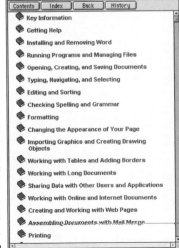

Figure 3-9:
Choose
from a
wealth of
information
on the Help
contents
screen.

3. **Click the icon of a subtopic that interests you.**

   A detailed Help window appears, as shown in Figure 3-10.

4. **When you're done reading the Help window, close it by clicking the close box in the top-left corner.**

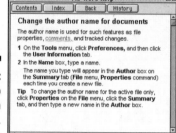

Figure 3-10:
A Help
window in
Word 98.

You can use the Back button in the Help window to step back a level, and you can click the Contents button to get back to the top level.

Getting to the Help index

Sometimes, searching for keywords in an index is faster than drilling down through several topic levels. To search the Help file by keyword, follow these steps:

1. **Choose Help⇨Contents and Index.**

   The Help contents window appears.

2. **Click the Index button.**

   The alphabetical index list appears.

3. **Type the first few letters of the topic you're looking for.**

4. **Click the topic you want.**

5. **Click the Show Topics button.**

   A list of appropriate topics appears at the bottom of the index window, as shown in Figure 3-11.

6. **Click the Go To button.**

7. **Read the Help topic that appears.**

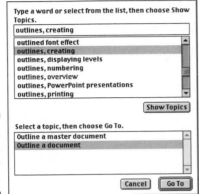

Figure 3-11:
Choosing a
topic in the
index.

Using Balloon Help

Compared with the Office Assistant, Balloon Help seems to be somewhat quaint and old-fashioned. Still, it can be useful for reminding you what toolbar buttons mean, because it gives you a more detailed explanation than the ScreenTips feature does. It displays only the name of the button, whereas Balloon Help provides a description.

To use Balloon Help, follow these steps:

1. **Choose Help⇨Show Balloons.**

2. **Point at an area on-screen that you want to know more about.**

   An information balloon appears, as shown in Figure 3-12.

Finding Help on the Web

In addition to providing all the Help files that come with Office 98, Microsoft makes assistance available on its Web site. Office 98 comes with a Web file that has links to the Microsoft Web help page. To access this page, choose Help⇨Help on the Web in any Office program. Your Web browser opens, as shown in Figure 3-13.

Click the appropriate links to get to the Help areas on the Microsoft Web site.

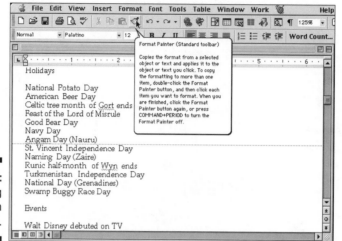

Figure 3-12:
Using
Balloon
Help.

Figure 3-13:
Finding the
Microsoft
online Web
Help page.

Part II
Using Word 98

The 5th Wave — By Rich Tennant

"HE SAID 'WHY BUY JUST A WORD PROCESSOR WHEN YOU CAN GET ONE WITH A MATH AND GRAPHICS LINK CAPABLE OF DOING SCHEMATICS OF AN F100 AIRCRAFT ENGINE?' AND I THOUGHT, WELL, WE NEVER BUY TOASTEMS WITHOUT BRAN ..."

In this part . . .

No matter what you do for a living, you can do it better if you write clearly and effectively. Microsoft Word 98 is a full-featured word processor (one of the best in the world) that lets you type and revise your work, check your spelling and grammar, expand your vocabulary with a built-in thesaurus, mix your text with graphics images, and work with colleagues to revise and improve your documents.

In this part of the book, you see how to use Word 98 to get your words on-screen (and on paper); how to format your words so that they look great; and how to create terrific reports and newsletters that get your point across. This part of the book tells you everything you need to know to begin using Word 98 effectively.

Chapter 4

Getting Friendly with Word 98

· ·

In This Chapter

▶ Creating a new document

▶ Opening existing documents

▶ Navigating your document

▶ Working with toolbars

▶ Formatting documents

▶ Saving your files

▶ Printing

▶ Backing up your files

· ·

Microsoft Word 98 is the part of Office 98 that enables you to work with words. With Word 98, you can write letters, memos, books, newsletters, Web pages, and virtually any other document that depends on words. You can use Word to write your dissertation. You can use Word to create brilliant ad copy. You can use Word to write down your list of nonnegotiable demands. After several revisions, Microsoft has given Word 98 an amazing amount of power, and chances are that you'll never use more than a fraction of that power. Who cares? Getting your work done with Word 98 is all that counts.

Creating a New Document

To write in a document, you first must create one. In Word 98, you create a document in one of these four ways:

✓ Start Word 98. Doing so automatically creates a blank document, ready for you to begin typing.

✓ Choose File➪New.

✓ Press ⌘+N.

✓ Click the New button on the Standard toolbar.

Opening an Existing Document

Most people work with documents that they've already created even more than they create new documents, and Word 98 provides four ways to open an existing document:

  ✔ Choose File➪Open.

  ✔ Press ⌘+O.

  ✔ Click the Open button on the Standard toolbar.

  ✔ Choose from the bottom of the File menu one of the last four files you opened, as shown in Figure 4-1.

Figure 4-1:
The bottom
of the
File menu
shows the
last four
files you've
worked on.

You can increase or decrease the number of files Word 98 displays on the File menu. Choose Tools➪Preferences to display the Preferences dialog box; then click the General tab. In the text box labeled Recently Used File List, type a number ranging from 0 through 9.

No matter which method you use to open a file, you see the standard Macintosh Open dialog box, as shown in Figure 4-2. Navigate the folders until you find the file you want; then click the Open button.

Navigating Your Document

After you open a document, take a minute to give it a good look. Although the document looks a little confusing at first, you soon get used to it. Figure 4-3 gives you a rundown of the parts of the Word 98 screen.

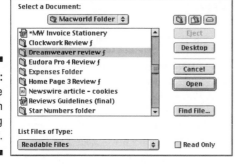

Figure 4-2:
The
Macintosh
Open dialog
box.

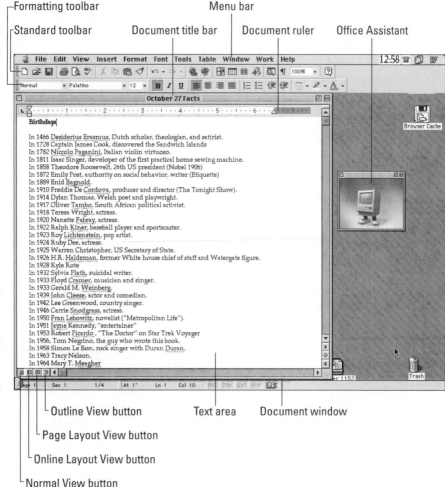

Figure 4-3:
The
Word 98
document
window.

Formatting toolbar

Standard toolbar

Menu bar

Document title bar   Document ruler   Office Assistant

Outline View button   Text area   Document window

Page Layout View button

Online Layout View button

Normal View button

Taking a different view

Word 98 enables you to view your document in four ways. Each view gives you a different perspective of the organization and appearance of your document. To change the view of your document, choose one of these options from the View menu:

- ✔ **Normal:** The standard view you work in most of the time, providing the cleanest screen and the fewest distractions. Just click in the document area and type.

- ✔ **Online Layout:** Changes the layout of the document in an effort to make it easier to read on-screen. Text is larger and wraps to fit the window rather than as it would actually print. The headings you use in your document are used by the Document Map, a separate pane in the document window. When you click headings in the Document Map, you jump to the corresponding area in the document. Online Layout view is also the only view that displays certain features (such as background colors and textures) you use when you create Web pages.

- ✔ **Page Layout:** Shows the document exactly as it will appear when you print it, including headers, footers, and page numbers.

- ✔ **Outline:** Outline view shows you the document's structure. Each heading in your document is a topic or subtopic. Subtopics are indented below topics. Outline view is a good way to organize your thoughts before you begin writing the body of the document. (Some people love working with outlines; others hate it. Me, I'm an outline kind of guy.)

The other way to switch views is to click the View buttons on the horizontal scrollbar (refer to Figure 4-3).

Zooming in and out

Although the views Word 98 provides are useful, sometimes you need to see your document closer — or farther away. You may want to use the 12-point Times font for your letter, for example, because it looks good when you print the document. For many people, however, 12-point Times is not a good screen font because it's a little too small. Word 98 enables you to magnify the document for greater comfort. In the same manner, you can shrink the document to get an overview of the document's structure or just to fit more words on your screen.

To zoom in or out of your document, follow these steps:

1. **Choose View⇨Zoom.**

   The Zoom dialog box appears, as shown in Figure 4-4.

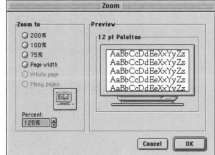

Figure 4-4:
The Zoom
dialog box.

2. **Click the radio buttons to set the document magnification you want.**

   If you don't like one of the button choices, you can type any number you want (between 10 and 500) in the Percent box.

 Clicking the Page Width radio button is a fast way to get the document to zoom up to fit comfortably in the document window, no matter how you may have resized that window.

3. **Click the OK button.**

 You can also zoom in or out of your document by using the Zoom pop-up menu at the right end of the Standard toolbar. Because the menu provides more preset magnification choices, using it may be more convenient for you than using the Zoom dialog box.

Much Ado about Toolbars

The Office 98 programs try, whenever possible, to give you multiple ways to accomplish a task so that you're not forced to memorize one particular way to get your work done. Quite often, you have three ways to do something: You can choose a command from a menu, press a shortcut key, or click a button on one of the many toolbars.

Although Word 98 has 18 preset toolbars, most of the time you use only two of them: the Standard and Formatting toolbars. These toolbars appear when you start Word 98; as with any of the other toolbars, you can hide or display these two toolbars whenever you want.

Hiding and showing toolbars

To hide or show a toolbar, follow these steps:

1. Ctrl+click any visible toolbar.

The Toolbar pop-up menu appears, as shown in Figure 4-5.

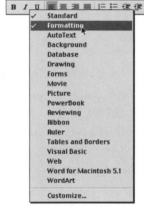

Figure 4-5:
Hiding or showing toolbars with the Toolbar pop-up menu.

2. Click the name of the toolbar you want to hide or show.

You can also hide or display toolbars by choosing View⇨Toolbars and then choosing a toolbar from the hierarchical menu. If you prefer to work with dialog boxes, you can choose Tools⇨Customize to display the Customize dialog box and then put a check in the appropriate check boxes to activate certain toolbars.

Introducing the Standard toolbar

The Standard toolbar enables you to control the core features of Word 98 — the ones you'll probably use most often. Figure 4-6 shows the Standard toolbar.

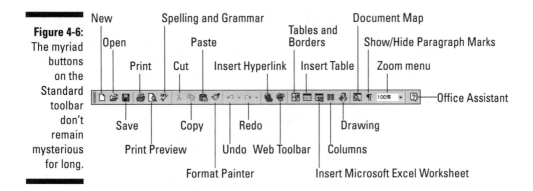

Figure 4-6:
The myriad
buttons
on the
Standard
toolbar
don't
remain
mysterious
for long.

From left to right, here's what each of the buttons on the Standard toolbar does:

- ✔ **New:** Creates a new blank document

- ✔ **Open:** Opens an existing document

- ✔ **Save:** Saves the current document to disk

- ✔ **Print:** Prints the current document to whatever printer is selected in the Chooser

- ✔ **Print Preview:** Shows you what your document will look like when you print it

- ✔ **Spelling and Grammar:** Checks and corrects the spelling and grammar in your document

- ✔ **Cut:** Moves the selected text to the Clipboard

- ✔ **Copy:** Copies the selected text to the Clipboard

- ✔ **Paste:** Puts the contents of the Clipboard in the current document, where the insertion point is blinking

- ✔ **Format Painter:** Copies the formatting of the selected text and enables you to apply that formatting to whatever text you next select

- ✔ **Undo:** Reverses your last action; click this button to recover from mistakes

- ✔ **Redo:** Reverses an Undo action; click this button to repeat your mistakes

- ✔ **Insert Hyperlink:** Creates a link to a Web page, a different file on your hard disk, or another place in the current document

- ✔ **Web Toolbar:** Shows the Web toolbar

- ✔ **Tables and Borders:** Shows the Tables and Borders toolbar

- ✔ **Insert Table:** Inserts a table into your document, at the insertion point
- ✔ **Insert Microsoft Excel Worksheet:** Inserts, at the insertion point, a Microsoft Excel worksheet into the current document
- ✔ **Columns:** Formats your text in one to four columns
- ✔ **Drawing:** Shows the Drawing toolbar
- ✔ **Document Map:** Switches to Online Layout view
- ✔ **Show/Hide Paragraph Marks:** Shows or hides the characters for tabs, spaces, carriage returns, and hidden text
- ✔ **Zoom menu:** Changes the screen magnification of your document
- ✔ **Office Assistant:** Activates the Office Assistant

To activate any function, just click a button. The buttons on toolbars require only a single click.

If you're wondering, "How will I ever remember what all those little toolbar buttons mean?" — don't worry. Point at any button and hold the mouse still for a moment. A small yellow label, called a ScreenTip, pops up, showing you the name of the button.

Whipping text into shape with the Formatting toolbar

In an ideal world, the content of your document would be all that matters. The look and format of the document would be of only secondary importance, if they were noticed at all. Welcome to the real world. Looks matter, and you have to make sure that your document is pretty as well as shining with inner brilliance.

Your chief weapon for making your documents look good is the Formatting toolbar, which contains buttons for commands that change the style, font, font size, and alignment of the type in your document. Figure 4-7 shows the Formatting toolbar.

Here's what each of the buttons on the Formatting toolbar does:

- ✔ **Style:** Sets the *style* — the predefined blueprint, including font, font size, type style, paragraph spacing, and so on — for the paragraph the insertion point is in.
- ✔ **Font:** Sets the *font* — the type style — of the selected text.
- ✔ **Font Size:** Sets the size of the selected text. The numbers are in *point sizes,* which are common measurements printers use.
- ✔ **Bold:** Makes selected text **bold.**

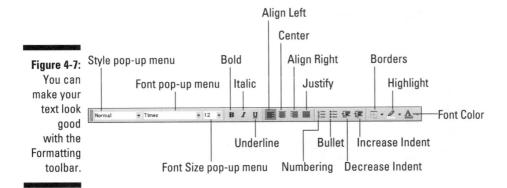

Figure 4-7:
You can
make your
text look
good
with the
Formatting
toolbar.

Align Left
Center
Style pop-up menu   Bold   Align Right   Borders
Font pop-up menu   Italic   Justify   Highlight
Font Color
Underline   Bullet   Increase Indent
Font Size pop-up menu   Numbering   Decrease Indent

✔ **Italic:** Makes selected text *italic.*

✔ **Underline:** <u>Underlines</u> selected text.

✔ **Align Left:** Makes the lines of text even on the left side. (The right margin of the text is *ragged,* or uneven.)

✔ **Center:** Centers a line of text horizontally on the page.

✔ **Align Right:** Makes the lines of text even on the right side. (The left margin of the text is ragged.)

✔ **Justify:** Makes the lines of text even on both the left and right sides. If a line is not long enough, Word 98 stretches the line to fit horizontally by adding extra spaces between words.

✔ **Numbering:** Adds automatic numbering to or removes automatic numbering from paragraphs.

✔ **Bullet:** Adds or removes bullets from paragraphs.

✔ **Decrease Indent:** Moves selected paragraphs one tab stop to the left.

✔ **Increase Indent:** Moves selected paragraphs one tab stop to the right.

✔ **Borders:** Adds borders to or removes borders from paragraphs.

✔ **Highlight:** Accents text with a different-color background (like an electronic felt-tip marker).

✔ **Font Color:** Changes selected text to a different color.

Formatting Documents with the Ruler

The *ruler* shows you the margins, indents, and tab stops in your document. You can use the ruler to set any of these features, and if you have multiple columns in your document, the ruler can also set column width.

Setting tabs

Word 98 enables you to set four kinds of tabs, as shown in Figure 4-8:

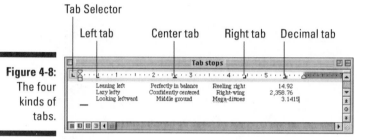

Tab Selector

Left tab   Center tab   Right tab   Decimal tab

Figure 4-8:
The four
kinds of
tabs.

Word 98 had four types of tabs; you use the Tab Selector to switch between them:

- **Left Tab:** The regular tab stop. Text is aligned at the stop on its left edge.
- **Right Tab:** Pushes text out to the left of the tab stop so that the right edge of the text lines up with the tab stop.
- **Center Tab:** Centers text on the tab stop.
- **Decimal Tab:** Perfect for columns of numbers; lines up the decimal points of the numbers at the tab stop.
- **Tab Selector:** Clicking the button switches between the four tab types.

To put a tab on the ruler, follow these steps:

1. **Click anywhere in the paragraph in which you want to insert a tab.**
2. **Click the Tab Selector button on the ruler until it shows the kind of tab you want to use.**
3. **Click the marker on the ruler where you want to put the tab.**

To move an existing tab, follow these steps:

1. **Click anywhere in the paragraph in which you want to modify a tab.**
2. **On the ruler, drag the tab marker to its new location.**

To remove a tab, follow these steps:

1. **Click anywhere in the paragraph in which you want to modify a tab.**
2. **Drag from the ruler the tab you want to delete.**

Indenting paragraphs

You also use the ruler to indent paragraphs. Four controls on the ruler help you set indents, as shown in Figure 4-9:

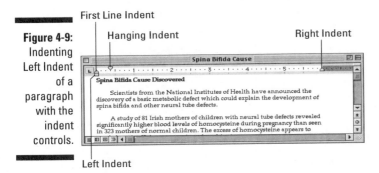

Figure 4-9: Indenting Left Indent of a paragraph with the indent controls.

To indent paragraphs by using the First Line Indent, Left Indent, Right Indent, or Hanging Indent controls, follow these steps:

1. **Select the paragraphs you want to indent.**

2. **On the ruler, drag the indent control you want to use to where you want to indent the paragraph.**

Don't Lose It: Saving Your Files

If you've gone to all the time and trouble of creating a document, you're going to want to save it. Word 98 gives you four ways to save a file by yourself, and it provides two other ways to save your files automatically. Get the impression that saving is *really* important?

Saving your file

To save the document that's on your screen, use any of these methods:

- Choose File⇨Save.
- Click the Save button on the Standard toolbar.
- Press ⌘+S.

When a computer crashes, it almost always does so without warning. Anything you've written since the last time you saved the document in Word 98 is lost. To be on the safe side, get into the habit of frequently saving your files. Learn to love the shortcut key combination for saving, which is ⌘+S. Then teach your left hand to press ⌘+S at every opportunity. If you take a momentary break from typing, press ⌘+S. If you sneeze, press ⌘+S. If you stop for a moment to gather your thoughts while writing, press ⌘+S. Ingrain this habit; you'll be happy that you did.

The first time you save a file, Word 98 asks you to give the file a name. Macintosh filenames can be as long as 31 characters and must not contain a colon (:) or begin with a period (.).

Saving a file under another name

The Save As command, which is available in almost all Macintosh programs, saves a copy of the current document under a different name. You want to do that when you base a new document on an existing document. You start the older document, make any changes you need, and then save the edited document under a new name.

To save a file under a different name, choose File⇨Save As; then give the new file a name in the Save As dialog box.

Saving a file in a different format

As great as Office 98 is, you probably have many co-workers who haven't upgraded, who are using Windows 95 machines, or who simply prefer to use other products. The Office 98 programs enable you to open and save files in other file formats, including older Macintosh Office files and most Microsoft PC document formats.

To save a Word 98 document in a different file format, choose File⇨Save As; then choose a file format from the Save File As Type pop-up menu in the Save As dialog box, as shown in Figure 4-10.

If you don't find on the pop-up menu the file format you need, don't despair. You can always save a file in either of two almost universally supported formats: RTF (Rich Text Format) or plain text. Virtually any word processor running on any kind of computer can read files saved in one of these two formats. Using RTF preserves most of your document's text formatting, such as font, size, and character styles. Plain text is the lowest common denominator, and you have to reformat your document — but that's still better than having to type the entire thing again.

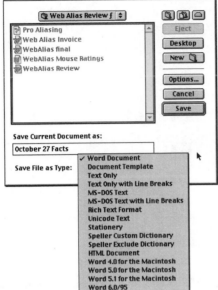

Figure 4-10:
Choosing a
different file
format.

Saving a file automatically

Few computer events are more frustrating than realizing immediately after your computer crashes that the last time you saved your document was about two hours ago. With older versions of Word, you could pretty much wave happy trails to all the work you had done since the last save. Word 98, on the other hand, is determined to be smart, even if you weren't. The program has two ways to rescue you: automatic file backup and AutoRecover.

Automatic file backup is just what it sounds like: Word 98 saves a copy of your document at preset intervals. AutoRecover tries to resurrect your document in the event of a system crash or power failure.

To have Word 98 save your files for you automatically, follow these steps:

1. **Choose Tools⇨Preferences.**

   The Preferences dialog box appears.

2. **Click the Save tab.**

   The Save tab appears, as shown in Figure 4-11.

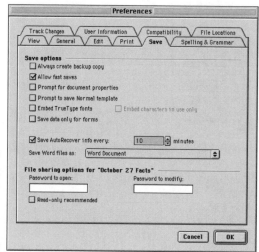

Figure 4-11:
The Save
tab in the
Preferences
dialog box.

3. **If you want to have Word 98 save a backup copy of your document, click the Always Create Backup Copy check box.**

Automatically saving a backup copy has one drawback: You end up with twice as many files on your hard disk as you need. You have your original file (World Domination Plan, for example) and the extra backup file (Backup of World Domination Plan).

4. **To have Word 98 protect you against crashes, click the Save AutoRecover Info Every check box and fill in the number of minutes you want to wait between saves.**

5. **Click the OK button.**

Printing a Document

Even in this brave new world, in which we all live in the paperless office (ha — we have more paper than ever in the office at the end of the second decade of the personal computer; so much for pompous prognostications by the so-called "experts"), you want to print your documents. Before committing your masterpiece to paper, however, looking at it in the Word 98 Print Preview window is a good idea. If the document needs to be tweaked to look right, you can change it before you print it. You have little reason to print a document before it's really done.

Previewing before you print

To preview a document with Print Preview, follow these steps:

1. **Choose File⇨Print Preview.**

   Word 98 displays a miniature view of your document, as shown in Figure 4-12.

2. **To view your document in full size, click the magnifying glass any-where on the document; to zoom back out again, click the mouse again.**

   You can change the margins of your document in Print Preview mode. Just click the margin markers in the rulers and drag them to set the margins you want.

3. **Click Close to exit Print Preview mode.**

Printing

To print a document, follow these steps:

1. **Choose File⇨Print or press ⌘+P.**

   The Print dialog box appears.

2. **Specify how many copies you want to print.**

3. **Click the Print button.**

   The main pop-up menu in the Print dialog box has a Microsoft Word 98 option. Choosing this option shows you the Word 98 special print options. You can choose to print the document, document properties, comments, styles, AutoText entries, or shortcut-key assignments. You can also choose to print just the odd-numbered pages or just the even-numbered pages in your document. The Range button enables you to print different ranges of pages, as shown in Figure 4-13.

Creating a Backup Strategy

Here's a hard fact of life: Computers crash. Although they don't crash that often, it happens. In fact, they always seem to happen at the worst possible times, such as when you're almost ready to print — a scant ten minutes before your deadline — the report on which your entire future career rests.

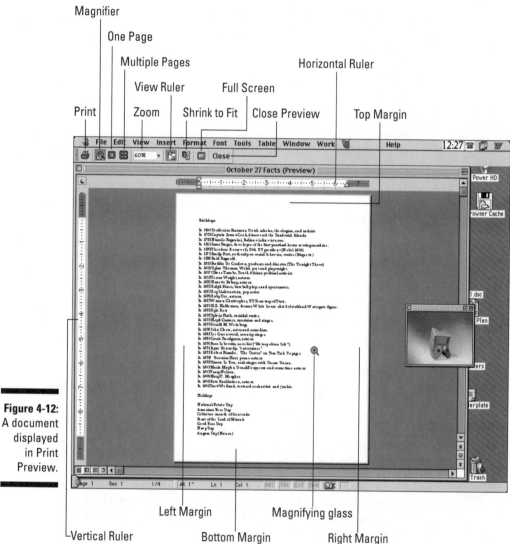

Magnifier

One Page

Multiple Pages

View Ruler   Full Screen   Horizontal Ruler

Print   Zoom   Shrink to Fit   Close Preview   Top Margin

Figure 4-12:
A document
displayed
in Print
Preview.

Vertical Ruler   Left Margin   Magnifying glass

Bottom Margin   Right Margin

More often, your computer doesn't crash, but a document file does become
corrupted and unreadable. This situation can occur for any number of
reasons: a hardware failure, a problem with your system software, or other
software incompatibilities.

Computer problems aren't the only reason that you should be thinking
about backups. Plenty of other things can go wrong, including fires, floods,
theft, earthquakes, hurricanes, plagues of locusts, and — well, you get the idea.

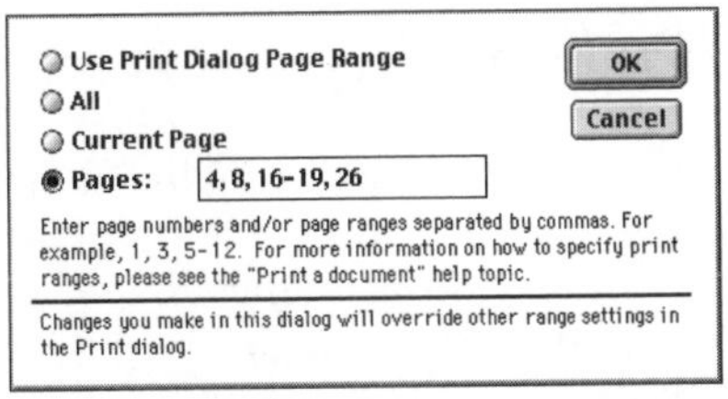

Figure 4-13:
The Print
Range
dialog box.

○ Use Print Dialog Page Range
○ All
○ Current Page
● Pages: `4, 8, 16–19, 26`

Enter page numbers and/or page ranges separated by commas. For
example, 1, 3, 5–12. For more information on how to specify print
ranges, please see the "Print a document" help topic.

Changes you make in this dialog will override other range settings in
the Print dialog.

[OK]
[Cancel]

One possible solution is to pray nightly to the Computer Gods, but this
approach has a spotty success rate. A better idea is to keep backups of your
files. A *backup* is a recent copy (or better yet, multiple copies) of your documents. You can copy the files to floppy disks, removable cartridge disks
(such as the Iomega Zip or Jaz disks), or to a second hard disk, or you can
buy a specialized backup device called a *tape drive*.

For many people, the Iomega Zip disk is the perfect balance between cost
and convenience. The disk holds 100MB (megabytes) of data and costs less
than $20, and the drive usually costs less than $150. Those prices are
relatively economical, especially if you back up only your documents, which
don't take up much space on your hard disk compared with your applications and the System software. Although having a full backup of your entire
hard disk is nice, these days, when computers come with 4GB (gigabyte)
hard disks, you would need almost 40 Zip disks. You're better off to back up
only your documents, which shouldn't take more than a few Zip disks, if that
many. If the worst happens, you can restore your system software and
applications from their original disks and then restore your documents from
your backup disks.

Depending on how much money you want to spend on backing up, you can
make your backup chore easier. You can get an Iomega Jaz drive, which has
a removable cartridge that holds as much as 2GB worth of data. Two
cartridges could back up your entire hard disk.

The ultimate in backup convenience — and cost — is a tape drive. Tape
backups are fast, backing up your data at as much as 70MB per minute.
Because the tapes themselves hold at least 8GB worth of data, you don't
have to worry about changing tapes very often. Tape drives come with
backup software that enables you to back up your hard disk automatically,
even if you're not around. The drawback is that a good tape drive costs $600
or more.

Following a Backup Strategy

No matter which backup medium you choose, you should get into the habit of backing up regularly. Have a schedule. Get into the habit of backing up your files before you shut down your Mac, for example. If you keep all your documents in a single folder on your desktop, dragging that folder to a Zip disk and copying the files is a simple matter.

Having multiple backup copies is the extra-safe way to go. You can easily rotate your backup copies so that you always have three good backups of your work. Many people use the idea of a "family" of backups. You start on Monday with a backup disk and copy your files to it. On Tuesday, you take a fresh, second disk and back up all your files again. On Wednesday, you repeat the process with a third new disk. Now you have three backup disks, each with a progressively older set of backed-up files. Wednesday's disk is the child disk. Tuesday's disk is the parent disk. Monday's backup — the oldest backup — is the grandparent disk. On Thursday, rotate the grandparent disk back to the front of the lineup (making it the new child disk), and use it to back up your files. Keep repeating the process, and you'll always have three days' worth of backups.

For even more protection, keep an extra backup off the premises in a safe place, such as a safe-deposit box. Bring in that backup and update it periodically — once per month, for example. Then take the backup off-site again. Having multiple backups does you no good if all your backup disks are destroyed along with your computer.

Chapter 5
Working with Words

. . . .

In This Chapter

▶ Selecting and editing text

▶ Searching for text

▶ Using the spelling and grammar checkers

▶ Using the built-in thesaurus

▶ Correcting mistakes automatically

▶ Useful stuff to know

. . . .

*W*riting well is difficult, and a good word processor makes it easy to deal with drudgery such as checking your spelling and grammar, formatting your words correctly, and moving text around.

Word 98 has intelligence under the hood that automates some of these tasks, and it gets others done with the least amount of effort.

Selecting and Editing Text

Word 98 can't do anything with your text until you select it. Selecting text tells Word 98 that whatever you do next, this text is what you want to do it to. You select text by using either the mouse or the keyboard.

Selecting text with the mouse

Selecting text with the mouse is a basic Macintosh skill — and one you probably already have. Just click at the beginning of the text you want to select, hold down the mouse button, and drag to the end of the text, which highlights everything in between. When you get to the end of the text you want to select, release the mouse button. This list describes a few text-selection tips:

- ✔ Double-click a word to select it.
- ✔ Select an entire sentence by holding down the ⌘ key and clicking anywhere in the sentence.
- ✔ Triple-click inside a paragraph to select the entire paragraph.
- ✔ If you want to select a large block of text, clicking and dragging it can be difficult to do. Instead, click at the beginning of the selection, scroll to the end of the selection, and then hold down the Shift key and click. All the text between the two clicks is then selected.
- ✔ To select a line of text, place the mouse pointer to the left of the line of text until the mouse pointer changes to a right-pointing arrow; then click.
- ✔ Double-click when the mouse pointer is a right-pointing arrow to select an entire paragraph.
- ✔ Triple-click when the mouse pointer is a right-pointing arrow to select the entire document.
- ✔ Cancel a selection by clicking anywhere other than on the selected text in the document window, or press any arrow key.

Selecting text with the keyboard

Yeah, I know: Mac users are mouse-oriented. We want to do *everything* with the mouse. Mouse, mouse, mouse. Well, here's my secret shame as a Mac user since 1984: I like to use the keyboard. Lots of times, using the keyboard is just faster. I like using shortcut keys, using keyboard macro programs such as QuickKeys and Keyquencer, and even selecting text with the keyboard. Try it a few times, and you probably will too. The keyboard shortcuts listed in Table 5-1 get you started, but the list is not exhaustive; if you want to know more, ask the Office Assistant.

Table 5-1	Shortcut Keys for Selecting Text
Shortcut Key	*Selects*
Shift+→	One character to the right of the insertion point
Shift+←	One character to the left of the insertion point
⌘+Shift+→	To the end of the word
⌘+Shift+←	To the beginning of the word
Shift+↓	One line down
Shift+↑	One line up
⌘+Shift+↓	To the end of the paragraph
⌘+Shift+↑	To the beginning of a paragraph
⌘+A	The entire document

Moving and copying text

To move or copy text from one place in a document to another, follow these steps:

1. **Select the text.**

2. **Cut or copy the selected text.**

   To cut the text, choose Edit⇨Cut, press ⌘+X, or click the Cut button on the Standard toolbar. To copy the text, choose Edit⇨Copy, press ⌘+C, or click the Copy button on the Standard toolbar.

3. **Click where you want the text to go.**

4. **Paste the text by choosing Edit⇨Paste, pressing ⌘+V, or clicking the Paste button on the Standard toolbar.**

Wonder where the text goes when you cut or copy it? It goes to an invisible holding area called the *Clipboard.* Because the Clipboard can hold only one item at a time, cutting or copying a second item replaces the contents of the Clipboard.

Dragging and dropping

Rather than cut and paste text, you can move text easily by dragging and dropping it with the mouse.

One of the big improvements in Microsoft Office 98 is that all the programs are now compatible with the Macintosh Drag-and-Drop feature. You can now drag items (including formatted text and graphics) from any Office program to any other Macintosh program that is compatible with Macintosh Drag-and-Drop. Because one of those programs is the Finder, you can now drag text clippings to and from the desktop into your Office 98 document.

To drag and drop text to a new location, follow these steps:

1. **Select the text, and hold down the mouse button.**

   The mouse pointer now has a small dashed box above it, and a dotted vertical line shows you where the text will end up when you release the mouse button.

2. **Drag the text to its new location.**

3. **Release the mouse button.**

To copy the text rather than move it, hold down the Option key as you drag the text.

Deleting text

Not much can be said about deleting text. Just select the offending text and press the Delete key on your keyboard. (Some keyboards call this key Backspace.) You can also select the text and choose Edit⇨Clear, although that technique is more work than it's worth, if you ask me.

You don't have to delete text before you begin replacing it with new text. Just select the text and begin typing. The new text replaces the old.

Searching for Text

When your company changes the name of its main product from Whizbang-Thing to WonderWidget and you have to make the changes in the 200-page annual report, you'll be glad that Word 98 can search for text throughout a document and replace it with other text.

Finding text

To find a bit of text in your document, follow these steps:

1. Choose Edit⇨Find or press ⌘+F.

The Find and Replace dialog box appears, set to the Find tab, as shown in Figure 5-1.

Figure 5-1:
The Find tab in the Find and Replace dialog box.

Find and Replace
Find / Replace / Go To
Find what: neural
Options: Search Down, Whole Words
Find Next
Cancel
More ⅔

2. In the Find What box, type the text you want to find.

3. Click the Find Next button.

Word 98 finds the text and highlights it in your document.

4. **To find the next occurrence of the text, click the Find Next button again.**

5. **When you're done finding text, click the Cancel button.**

Finding and replacing text

To find a word or a phrase and replace it with other text, follow these steps:

1. **Choose Edit⇨Replace or press ⌘+H.**

   The Find and Replace dialog box appears, set to the Replace tab, as shown in Figure 5-2.

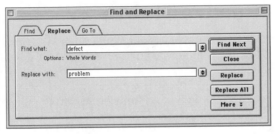

Figure 5-2:
The Replace
tab in the
Find and
Replace
dialog box.

2. **In the Find What box, type the word or phrase you want to find.**

3. **In the Replace With box, type the word or phrase you want to substitute for the found text.**

4. **Click the Find Next button.**

   Word 98 finds and selects the next instance of the text you're searching for.

5. **Click the Replace button.**

   Word 98 inserts the replacement text and then finds the next instance of the search text.

   To replace all instances of the search text with the replacement text in one step, click the Replace All button instead.

6. **When you're done replacing text, click the Close button.**

Using the Spelling and Grammar Checkers

Even if you are a good speller, using the Word 98 spelling checker is a good idea because it usually catches typographical errors in addition to true spelling mistakes. The grammar checker tries to find mistakes in sentence structure and capitalization as well as misused words.

Word 98 points out a potential spelling error by putting a wavy red line below the suspect text. Suspected grammar problems get a wavy green underline.

Checking as you type

If you prefer, Word 98 can watch your typing and immediately point out a possible mistake. When the telltale wavy red or green underline appears, you can fix the problem right away.

To fix a spelling error that Word 98 flags, follow these steps:

1. **Control+click a word that has a wavy red underline.**

   A pop-up menu appears, as shown in Figure 5-3. The pop-up menu contains suggestions for the spelling error.

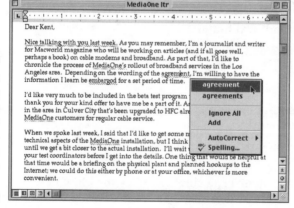

Figure 5-3:
Fixing spelling on the fly with the spell-checking pop-up menu.

2. **If the correct spelling appears on the pop-up menu, choose it.**

   The incorrect version is replaced by the correct version.

If the suspect word is spelled correctly, the word may simply not be in the built-in dictionary. You can add the word to your own custom dictionary by choosing Add from the pop-up menu. If the word is correct but you don't want to add it to your custom dictionary, choose Ignore All from the pop-up menu.

To check grammar as you type, follow these steps:

1. **Control+click a word or phrase that has a wavy green underline.**

   A pop-up menu appears, containing suggested corrections for the grammar error.

2. **If you like one of the suggestions, choose it from the pop-up menu.**

   The text is replaced by a Word 98 suggestion.

   If you complete this step, you can skip the remaining steps.

3. **If you need more information about the grammar error, choose Grammar from the pop-up menu.**

   The Grammar dialog box appears, as shown in Figure 5-4. The top box shows you the error in context, labeled with the type of error it is. The bottom box contains suggestions for replacement.

Figure 5-4:
The
Grammar
dialog box.

4. **Click the Ignore or Replace button to deal with the grammar error.**

5. **Repeat Steps 1 through 4 as necessary until you deal with all the grammar errors.**

6. **Click the Cancel button to dismiss the Grammar dialog box.**

Some people think that it's kind of creepy to have your word processor always looking over your shoulder for mistakes. If you're in that camp, follow these steps to turn off this feature:

1. **Choose Tools⇨Preferences.**

   The Preferences dialog box appears.

2. **Click the Spelling and Grammar tab.**

3. **Clear the check boxes labeled Check Spelling As You Type and Check Grammar As You Type.**

4. **Click the OK button.**

Checking everything at the same time

To check the spelling and grammar of your document at the same time, follow these steps:

1. **Choose Tools⇨Spelling and Grammar or click the Spelling and Grammar button on the Standard toolbar (it's the one that looks like a check mark with the small letters *ABC* above it).**

   Word 98 displays the Spelling and Grammar dialog box, as shown in Figure 5-5, and begins to check the document.

Figure 5-5:
The
Spelling
and
Grammar
dialog box.

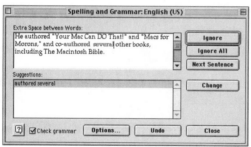

2. **Do one of the following things (remember that because Word is just a software program, it could be wrong):**

   - Click Ignore to skip this instance of the error.

   - Click Ignore All to skip all instances of the error.

   - Click one of the suggestions displayed in the Suggestions box; then click Change or Change All.

   When all the errors have been dealt with, the Office Assistant pops up a message to tell you that the spelling and grammar check is complete.

   You can also fix errors in the top box of the Spelling and Grammar dialog box and then click the Change button.

3. **Click the OK button to go back to your document.**

The other buttons in the Spelling and Grammar dialog box give you other options:

- ✔ The Add button adds the flagged word to your custom dictionary, which is shared by Microsoft Excel, Microsoft PowerPoint, and Outlook Express. Use this button when the word is spelled correctly yet not recognized by Word 98, such as a proper name or a technical word.

- ✔ The AutoCorrect button adds the word to the AutoCorrect list — a list of errors that Word 98 fixes automatically (see the section "Correcting mistakes with AutoCorrect," later in this chapter).

This fact will come as a shock to fourth-grade teachers everywhere, but many people don't like to use a grammar checker. To turn off grammar checking (without turning off spell checking), follow these steps:

1. **Choose Tools⇨Preferences.**

   The Preferences dialog box appears.

2. **Click the Spelling and Grammar tab.**

3. **Clear the check box labeled Check Grammar with Spelling.**

4. **Click the OK button.**

If you want to turn off grammar checking for just the current check, clear the Check Grammar check box in the Spelling and Grammar dialog box (refer to Figure 5-5).

Using the Built-In Thesaurus

A huge difference exists between the right word and the wrong word for any occasion, and Word 98 has a tool that helps you pick the right word at the right time. The thesaurus provides synonyms for words you select. To use the thesaurus, follow these steps:

1. **Select a word for which you want to find a synonym.**

2. **Choose Tools⇨Language⇨Thesaurus.**

   The Thesaurus dialog box appears, as shown in Figure 5-6.

3. **In the Meanings box, click the desired meaning of the word you selected.**

   A list of synonyms appears in the box on the right.

Using Quick Thesaurus

Word 98 has a faster way to pick synonyms: the Quick Thesaurus. The Quick Thesaurus first lived in the early Jurassic period, when he spent most of his time dodging the larger, slower thesauruses. A Quick Thesaurus that wasn't quick enough became, of course, a Dead Thesaurus. After millions of years, the Quick Thesaurus became an employee of Microsoft, where he happily lives inside Office 98 for the Macintosh. (Sadly, no similar feature exists for our friends who use Office 97 on the PC.)

To use the Quick Thesaurus, follow these steps:

1. **Control+click a word for which you want to find a synonym.**

   A pop-up menu appears.

2. **Choose Synonyms.**

   You see a hierarchical menu of synonyms.

3. **If you like one of the synonyms, choose it from the pop-up menu.**

   The original text is replaced by a Word 98 suggestion.

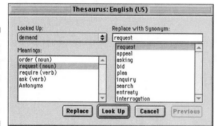

Figure 5-6:
Finding synonyms with the thesaurus.

Was the Thesaurus dialog box empty when it appeared? If so, you forgot to select some text first. Just click the Cancel button to dismiss the Thesaurus dialog box; then try again.

4. **In the box on the right, click the synonym you want to use.**

5. **Click the Replace button.**

   Word 98 replaces the original word with the selected synonym.

Having Word 98 Do the Work for You

If you've read the first part of this chapter, you've seen the ways you can get Word 98 to correct your mistakes. Microsoft built more intelligence into Word 98, however, so that the program can actively seek out and fix some errors. Word 98 can also help you by remembering standard or repeatedly used text and then spilling it out on command.

Correcting mistakes with AutoCorrect

AutoCorrect is already programmed with a list of common spelling mistakes and typographical errors. When you make one of these mistakes (such as typing *teh* rather than *the* or *compair* rather than *compare*), AutoCorrect automatically replaces the misspelling immediately. Often, you don't even realize that you made a mistake.

You can add your personal list of typing annoyances to the AutoCorrect list. I tend to type *instread* for *instead,* for example, but the mistake never reaches my documents anymore.

To add your own entries to the AutoCorrect list, follow these steps:

1. Choose Tools⇨AutoCorrect.

The AutoCorrect dialog box appears, as shown in Figure 5-7.

Figure 5-7:
The
AutoCorrect
dialog box.

2. In the Replace box, type a word you often misspell.

You can also type a shortcut word to represent a longer phrase. You could type **NYC**, which would be replaced by *New York City,* or you could use your initials, which would expand to your entire name.

3. In the With box, type the correct spelling of the word or type the phrase you want AutoCorrect to use to replace the shortcut word.

4. Click the Add button.

5. Click the OK button.

Removing a word from AutoCorrect

To remove a word from the AutoCorrect list, follow these steps:

1. **Choose Tools⇨AutoCorrect.**

   The AutoCorrect dialog box appears.

2. **Select the word you want to remove from the list.**

3. **Click the Delete button.**

4. **Click the OK button.**

Turning AutoCorrect off

If AutoCorrect bugs you, you can turn it off. Follow these steps:

1. **Choose Tools⇨AutoCorrect.**

   The AutoCorrect dialog box appears.

2. **Clear the check box labeled Replace Text As You Type.**

3. **Click the OK button.**

Inserting text automatically with AutoText

Although AutoCorrect is cool, AutoText can really save you some time. If you think about your writing for a moment, you'll probably realize that many of the words and phrases you use are common to many of your documents. Elements such as salutations and signatures in letters and the formats of headers and footers tend to be standardized. Some people regularly use the same paragraphs or groups of paragraphs in their writing. This type of standard text is called *boilerplate*. You can store it in AutoText and insert it by choosing a single menu command, without having to copy and paste it from older documents.

Word 98 comes with several AutoText entries, and you can easily add your own. You may well be able to create entire letters by using AutoText.

Because AutoText can handle graphics as well as text, you can also use it to store the images you use most often. You could save your company logo as an AutoText entry, for example, and then squirt it into your document in a flash.

In previous versions of Word, AutoText was called the Glossary. The feature has gained the capability to hold more boilerplate text and has also garnered its own toolbar. AutoText is now more like glossaries on steroids.

To create your own AutoText entry, follow these steps:

1. **Select the text or graphic you want to save as AutoText.**
2. **Choose Insert⇨AutoText⇨New.**

   The Create AutoText dialog box appears. Word 98 proposes a name for the AutoText entry.
3. **Accept the name or enter your own.**
4. **Click the OK button.**

To insert an AutoText entry into your document, follow these steps:

1. **Click where you want to insert the AutoText.**
2. **Choose Insert⇨AutoText.**

   A submenu appears.
3. **Choose the category you want.**
4. **From the appropriate submenu, choose the AutoText entry you want to use.**

AutoText entries can contain virtually any formatting, including paragraph styles. To include the style of your selected text in the AutoText entry, first click the Show/Hide Paragraph Marks button on the Standard toolbar to display paragraph marks in your document. Select the paragraph mark at the end of the text you want to use as an AutoText entry. (The paragraph mark contains the formatting information for the paragraph.) Then choose Insert⇨AutoText⇨New.

Useful Stuff to Know

Hey, it's Word 98 Grab Bag time! Although the topics in this section don't exactly belong in this chapter, I think that they're important things to know how to do in Word 98, so they ended up here. You'll want to perform each of these tasks sooner or later, so here they are, sooner.

Printing envelopes

Word 98 has a nifty built-in envelope-printing utility, which actually works! You can use this utility to print almost any kind of envelope that fits into your printer.

To print a single envelope, follow these steps:

1. **Choose Tools⇨Envelopes and Labels.**

    The Envelopes and Labels dialog box appears.

2. **Click the Envelopes tab (see Figure 5-8).**

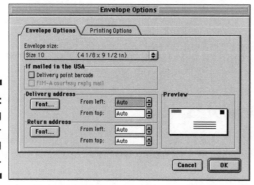

Figure 5-8: The Envelopes tab of the Envelopes and Labels dialog box.

3. **In the Delivery Address box, type the recipient's address.**

4. **In the Return Address box, type your address.**

    To create a default return address — one that always appears in the Return Address box — choose Tools⇨Preferences to display the Preferences dialog box; click the User Information tab; and then type your name and address in the Mailing Address box.

5. **Click the Options button.**

    The Envelope Options dialog box appears, as shown in Figure 5-9.

Figure 5-9: Setting envelope-printing options.

6. **Set the necessary options.**

   The most important option is the envelope size; choose one from the pop-up menu.

7. **Click the Printing Options tab, and set the correct envelope-feeding directions for your printer.**

   After you get this setting correct, you don't have to do it again.

8. **Click the OK button to return to the Envelopes and Labels dialog box.**

9. **Click the Print button to print your envelope.**

Printing mailing labels

Word 98 handles the printing of mailing labels and envelopes in a similar manner. To print mailing labels, follow these steps:

1. **Choose Tools⇨Envelopes and Labels.**

   The Envelopes and Labels dialog box appears.

2. **Click the Labels tab, as shown in Figure 5-10.**

Figure 5-10: The Labels tab in the Envelopes and Labels dialog box.

3. **Click the Options button.**

   The Label Options dialog box appears, as shown in Figure 5-11.

4. **In the Printer Information box, select Dot Matrix or Laser and Inkjet.**

5. **Use the Product Number pop-up menu and text box to specify the kind of label you plan to use.**

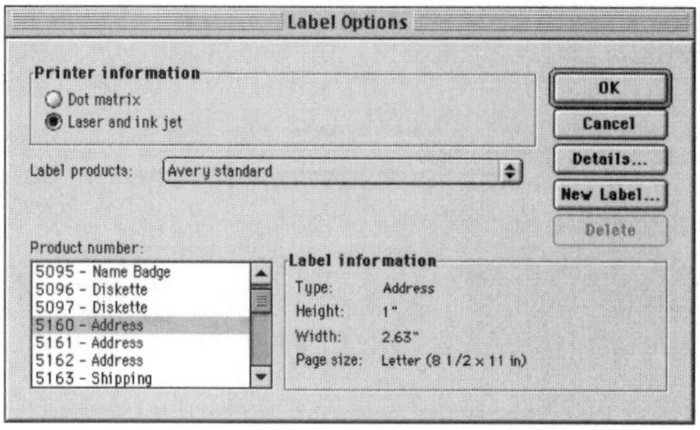

Figure 5-11:
Setting
mailing-
label
options.

6. **Click the OK button to return to the Envelopes and Labels dialog box.**

7. **To print an entire page of labels that contain the same text (such as return-address labels), click the Full Page of the Same Label button, type the address in the Address box, and then skip to Step 9.**

8. **To print a single label from a sheet of labels, click the Single Label button and then set the row and column numbers of the next free label on your sheet.**

9. **Click the Print button.**

To print a bunch of different names on mailing labels, you have to have a data source that contains the names. This data source can be the Word 98 internal Address Book, an Excel spreadsheet, another Word document, or the Contacts List from Outlook Express.

Counting your words

For some people (especially professional writers!), counting the number of words in a document is a useful capability. Word 98 counts the pages, words, paragraphs, characters, and number of lines in your document.

To count the words in your document, choose Tools⇨Word Count. The Word Count dialog box appears, as shown in Figure 5-12. When you're done looking at the statistics, click the Close button to dismiss the dialog box.

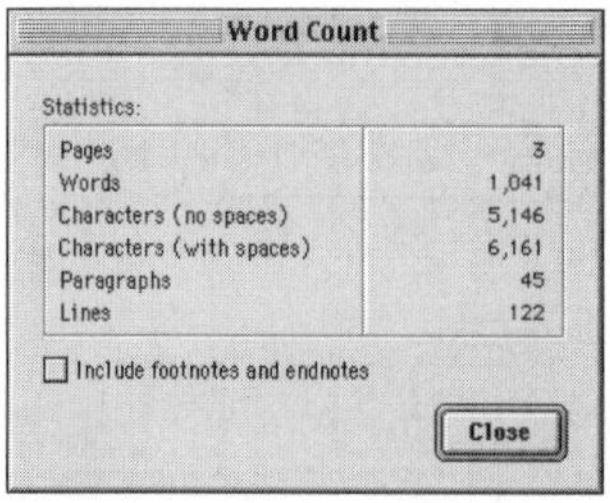

Figure 5-12:
The Word
Count
dialog box.

If you select some text before you choose Tools⇨Word Count, Word 98 counts just the words in the selection.

Inserting the date or time into your document

Can't remember what the date is? Word 98 can (at least, it can if the Mac's clock is set correctly). To insert the date or time into your document, choose Insert⇨Date and Time; then choose one of the many date and time formats. If you want the date or time to change whenever the document is opened or printed, click the Update Automatically check box. If you prefer that the date remain the one you put in when you wrote the document, clear that check box.

Numbering pages

To add page numbers, follow these steps:

1. **Choose Insert⇨Page Numbers.**

   The Page Numbers dialog box appears, as shown in Figure 5-13.

Figure 5-13:
Setting page numbering.

Page Numbers
Position:
Bottom of page (Footer)
Alignment:
Right
☐ Show number on first page
Preview
Format...   Cancel   OK

2. **Choose the page-number position and alignment from the appropriate menus.**

3. **Click the OK button.**

Chapter 6

Looks Matter: A Guide to Attractive Formatting

· ·

In This Chapter

▶ Formatting text

▶ Using Wizards and templates

▶ Setting up styles

▶ Using AutoFormat

▶ Creating tables

· ·

A well-written document is like a good musical performance. In music, the singer delivers the meaning of the song, and backup musicians provide the context that lets you appreciate the singer. In a document, the meaning of your words is enhanced by the format of the document. Just as people appreciate a singer more if she's backed by a good band, your audience is more receptive to your words if they are presented attractively.

Making Text Look Good

Word 98 provides many tools to change the appearance of your text. You can control the fonts and font sizes, styles, text colors, and character spacing. Word 98 lets you apply any of these controls on a character-by-character basis so that you have complete mastery over the look of your document.

On the other hand, restraint is important too. Just because you *can* make every character look different doesn't mean that you *should*. Documents with too much formatting look amateurish, so find a happy medium.

Choosing fonts and font sizes

Because the Macintosh was the first personal computer to come with a variety of fonts, having (and using) many fonts is practically the birthright of a Macintosh user. Every Macintosh is shipped with a variety of attractive fonts, and most Mac users quickly add more. Installing Office 98 adds even more fonts to your Macintosh.

To change the font of some text, follow these steps:

1. **Select the text you want to change.**

2. **From the Font menu, choose the new font.**

   If you prefer, you can use the Font menu on the Formatting toolbar (it's quicker).

To change the font size of text, follow these steps:

1. **Select the text you want to change.**

2. **Choose a new size from the Font Size menu on the Formatting toolbar.**

Picking character styles

Character styles add emphasis to your words. Words in *italics,* **boldface,** UPPERCASE, and <u>underlined</u> words draw the reader's attention.

Try to avoid underlining text. Underlining is a technique left over from the use of typewriters, which didn't have italics. Use italics for emphasis or to denote things like the titles of books. Another problem with underlined words in the age of the World Wide Web is that they are easily mistaken for hyperlinks. Likewise, when uppercase letters are used to emphasize text, they aren't as readable as lowercase letters, and uppercase letters break up the visual flow of a document.

To add character styles to text, follow these steps:

1. **Select the text you want to change.**

2. **Choose one or more of the following:**

   • Click the Bold button on the Formatting toolbar or press ⌘+B.

   • Click the Italic button on the Formatting toolbar or press ⌘+I.

   • Click the Underline button on the Formatting toolbar or press ⌘+U.

If you need to make many changes to text, you can do it all in one step by using the Font dialog box, as shown in Figure 6-1. You can change the font, font style, font size, color, and several other text attributes.

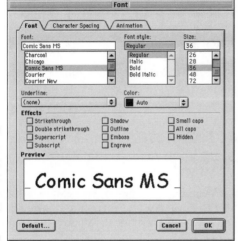

Figure 6-1: The Font dialog box lets you control text styles.

A sense of style

The difference between a good-looking document and an amateurish-looking one is in both the broad strokes and the details. Type is used in both good and bad ways. The following list includes a few tips to help you improve your documents — all the fonts mentioned are either part of the standard Macintosh complement or installed with Office 98:

✔ A formal message requires a formal font. If you're writing a report for the board of directors, for example, use an authoritative font, such as Times or Palatino. If you're writing an invitation to a beach party, a fun font like Comic Sans MS is appropriate.

✔ Try not to use more than two different fonts per page. The use of a sans serif font like Helvetica for headlines and a serif font like Times for body text is common. *Serifs* are the small, decorative strokes that are added to the end of a letter's main strokes; *sans serif* text doesn't have the decorative strokes.

✔ Left justification (the lines of text are lined up on the left) is usually easier to read and doesn't look as formal as full justification.

✔ Use headings and subheadings to help your readers easily find information in your document.

✔ Keep your document simple and clean. Visual clutter is the enemy of readability.

To make many changes at a time to text, follow these steps:

1. **Choose Format⇨Font.**

   The Font dialog box appears.

2. **Make the changes you want.**

   You can see the effects of your changes in the Preview box at the bottom of the Font dialog box.

If you apply any character formatting without selecting text first, Word 98 applies that formatting to the next text you type.

Copying character formats with Format Painter

After you format a text block the way you like it, you can use the terrific Word 98 tool Format Painter to copy the text format and apply it to other text. Using Format Painter saves you time because you have to format a text block only once.

To use Format Painter, follow these steps:

1. **Select the text that is formatted the way you like it.**

2. **Click the Format Painter button (the one that looks like a paintbrush) on the Standard toolbar.**

   The insertion point turns into an I-beam with a plus sign next to it.

3. **Select the text to which you want to apply the formatting.**

   The text changes to the formatting of the text you selected in Step 1.

To copy the selected formatting to more than one location, double-click the Format Painter button. This action "locks on" the button. Click the button again after you finish formatting.

Changing case

If you've ever typed an entire sentence without realizing that the Caps Lock key on your keyboard was accidentally turned on, you'll appreciate the Word 98 Change Case feature. You can use it to change the capitalization of selected text in the following five ways:

- ✔ **Sentence case:** The selected text has an initial capital letter.
- ✔ **Lowercase:** The selected text has no capital letters.

✔ **Uppercase:** The selected text has all capital letters.

✔ **Title case:** Each word in the selected text begins with a capital letter.

✔ **Toggle case:** Each letter in the selected text is reversed from normal, sentence case (upper-/lowercase) capitalization; for example, i LIVE IN lOS aNGELES.

To change case, follow these steps:

1. **Select the text you want to change.**

2. **Choose Format⇨Change Case.**

   The Change Case dialog box appears.

3. **Choose the capitalization option you want.**

4. **Click OK.**

Using Wizards and Templates to Jump-Start a Document

One of the key goals of the Microsoft team that created Microsoft Office 98 was to make programs that would save you time by doing as much work for you as possible. What could be more helpful than documents that format themselves? The Office 98 programs have two features that give you preformatted documents. *Wizards* ask you a series of questions and then create a document based on your responses. *Templates* are documents that Microsoft provides with formatting already in place; you simply fill in the templates with your own text.

Besides the Wizards and templates that come with the usual installation of Office 98, more Wizards and templates are included in the Value Pack folder on the Office 98 CD-ROM.

We're off to see the Wizard

Wizards are amazing. When you use a Wizard, Word 98 presents you with dialog boxes that ask you questions about the document you want to create. The Wizard then uses your answers to create a custom document. Word 98 comes with Wizards that help you create agendas, newsletters, envelopes, faxes, letters, mailing labels, memos, Web pages, and more.

The following example uses the Memo Wizard, and other Wizards work in much the same way.

To create a document with the Memo Wizard, follow these steps:

1. **Choose File➪New.**

   The New dialog box appears.

   To make the New dialog box appear, you must choose use File➪New with the mouse rather than use the ⌘+N shortcut key.

2. **Click the Memos tab.**

   Now you can see the Memo Wizard icon, as shown in Figure 6-2.

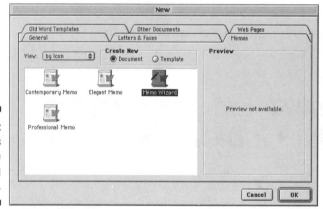

Figure 6-2:
The Memos
tab in the
New dialog
box.

3. **Click the Memo Wizard icon.**

4. **Click OK.**

   The first of the Memo Wizard dialog boxes appears. This first screen is a title screen that tells you what the Wizard does.

5. **Click Next.**

   The Style screen appears, as shown in Figure 6-3.

Figure 6-3:
Picking a
style for
your memo.

6. **Pick one of the three memo styles (Professional, Contemporary, or Elegant), and then click Next.**

   The Memo Title screen appears.

7. **Type a title for your memo, and then click Next.**

   The Header screen appears, as shown in Figure 6-4. The Date and From boxes are already filled in.

Figure 6-4:
Choosing
the items in
the memo's
header.

8. **Choose whether you want to include entries for the Date, From, Subject, or Priority fields in the header of the memo, and then click Next.**

   The Recipient screen appears.

9. **Fill in the To and cc fields with the names of the recipients of the memo, and then click Next.**

   The Closing Fields screen appears.

10. **Choose whether you want to include the writer's initials, the typist's initials, or notations for enclosures and attachments, and then click Next.**

    The Header and Footer screen appears.

11. **Choose which items you want to appear in the header and footer, and then click Next.**

12. **Click Finish.**

    Word 98 creates the memo form, as shown in Figure 6-5.

13. **Click the memo form where it says "Click here and type your memo text," and then type your own text for the memo.**

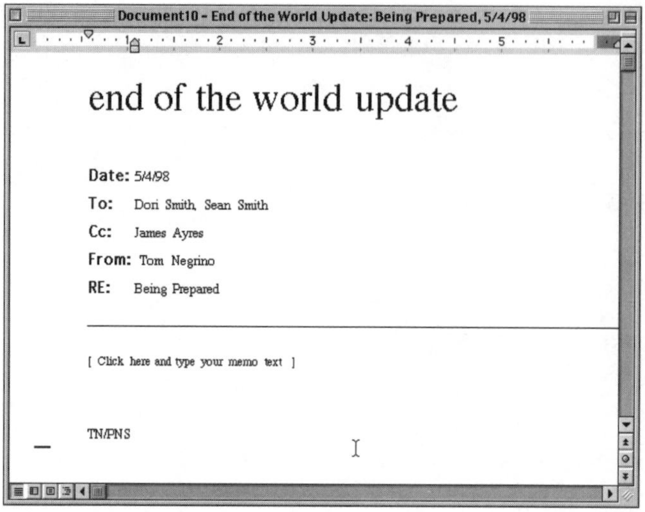

Figure 6-5:
The to-be-completed memo form, ready for text entry.

Using templates

Unlike with Wizards, when you use a template, you don't have to answer any questions. Microsoft creates the document template for you, and it comes complete with appropriate character formatting, styles, and sometimes even graphics. You only have to fill in the template with your own words.

The following example uses one of the letter templates; the other templates work in a similar manner.

To use a template to start a document, follow these steps:

1. **Choose File⇨New.**

   The New dialog box appears.

2. **Click one of the tabs and find a template you want to use.**

3. **Click the icon for the template you're using, and then click OK.**

   Word 98 creates the document, based on the template you chose, as shown in Figure 6-6. Placeholder text is included in the fields where you enter your information.

4. **Click the fields on the new document and enter your own text where the placeholder text is.**

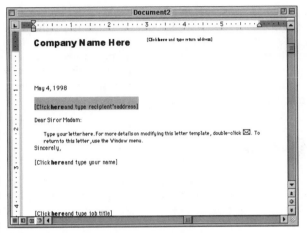

Figure 6-6:
A new
document,
fresh
from the
template.

Do It with Styles

Of all the candidates for the prize of Most Underused Word 98 Feature, I give the nod to *styles,* which define the appearance of text in your document. You can store a whole set of character and paragraph formats under a style name. After a style is created, you can select a paragraph and use that style to apply its set of formats in one step.

Suppose that you want the headlines in your document to be Helvetica 14-point boldface, centered on the page. You can format your headline manually just once and then assign the formats to a style you name Heading 1. When you want to apply that formatting to other parts of your document, you can select the text you want to format and apply the Heading 1 style by using the Formatting toolbar. Boom! — the selected text gets formatted in the same style as the original text.

One of the nicest things about styles is that when you want to change the formatting of all the text in a particular part of your document, you can simply change the style definition. If you decide, for example, that your headlines look better in Times 18-point font and left-justified, just change your Heading 1 style definition, and all the text in your document that is formatted as Heading 1 also changes. This feature is incredibly cool because formatting is the dog work of word processing. The longer a document is, the better the use of styles is. Imagine having a 100-page document with lots of pictures and your boss telling you to change the typeface of all the picture captions. You could go through and change each caption separately, or, if you defined a Caption style, you could use just one dialog box to change the Caption style, which would then ripple throughout the entire document.

Word 98 has two kinds of styles. A *character style* is a combination of any of the character formats in the Font dialog box that is then given a style name. A *paragraph style* is a set of character formats and paragraph formats (including justification, indents, and line spacing) stored under a single name. Paragraph styles tend to be used more than character styles because styles are most useful for formatting the structure of a document, and that structure is made up of paragraphs.

Creating styles

The fastest way to create a new paragraph style is to format a paragraph in your document the way you like it and then store that formatting as a style by using the Formatting toolbar. Follow these steps:

1. **Select some text you want to use as an example for a style.**

2. **If necessary, format the text the way you want.**

3. **Make sure that the text is still selected.**

4. **On the Formatting toolbar, click the Style box.**

   The style name in the Style box is highlighted, as shown in Figure 6-7.

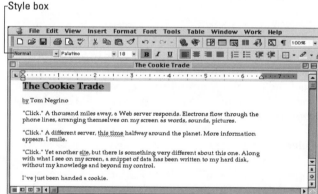

Figure 6-7:
Giving the
new style a
name.

5. **Type over the existing style name to create your new style name.**

6. **Press Return.**

Applying styles

To apply a different paragraph style, follow these steps:

1. **Select the text you want to change.**

2. **Select from the Style pop-up menu on the Formatting toolbar the style you want to apply, as shown in Figure 6-8.**

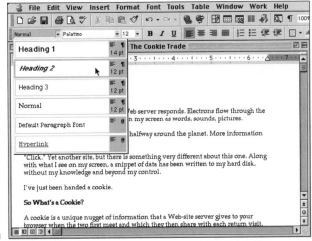

Figure 6-8: Using the Style pop-up menu on the Formatting toolbar to apply a new style.

3. **Press Return.**

Paragraph styles almost always include character attributes, such as bold or italic. You can apply the character attributes of a paragraph style to specific text within a paragraph, without changing the style of the entire paragraph the text is in: Simply select a portion of text in a paragraph, and then apply the paragraph style. The selected text changes to the character attributes of the newly applied paragraph style, and the rest of the paragraph retains the original paragraph style. If you select the entire paragraph and apply the paragraph style, the entire paragraph changes, of course, to the new style definition.

Modifying styles

Sometimes you want to change a style you've already defined or modify a style predefined in an Office 98 template. To change or modify a style, follow these steps:

1. Choose Format⇨Style.

The Style dialog box appears, as shown in Figure 6-9. Notice that the Style dialog box contains preview areas that show how the paragraph will look and how characters in the paragraph will look.

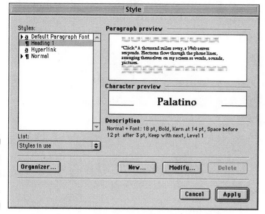

Figure 6-9:
The Style
dialog box.

2. In the Style dialog box, click the style you want to modify.

The preview of that style appears in the Paragraph Preview and Character Preview boxes.

3. Click Modify.

The Modify Style dialog box appears, as shown in Figure 6-10.

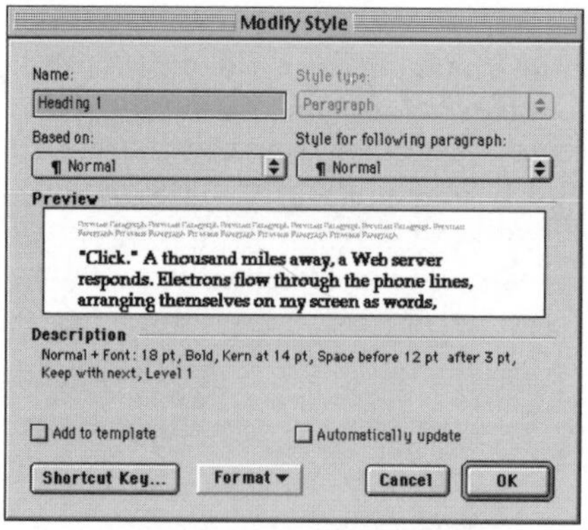

Figure 6-10:
The Modify
Style dialog
box.

4. **Click Format, and then choose from the pop-up menu the attribute you want to change (such as Font, Paragraph, or Tabs).**

   The dialog box for the attribute you chose appears.

5. **Make whichever changes you want, and then click OK.**

   You return to the Modify Style dialog box.

6. **Continue choosing from the Format pop-up menu the attributes to change.**

7. **When you're done changing attributes, click the OK button in the Modify Style dialog box.**

8. **If you want to apply the modified style, click the Apply button. Otherwise, click the Close button.**

   The modified style is saved in the style template of the current document.

AutoFormat Steps In

The Word 98 AutoFormat feature makes formatting your documents even easier by doing the work for you. AutoFormat analyzes your document and then applies paragraph styles to make your document look good. AutoFormat works in two main ways:

- ✔ The AutoFormat command formats your entire document in one pass.
- ✔ The AutoFormat As You Type feature watches what you're typing and automatically formats headings, numbers, symbols, and bulleted and numbered lists.

AutoFormatting entire documents

When you use the AutoFormat command, Word 98 first scans your document and tries to figure out which parts of your document are headings, which are body text, and so on, and then it applies paragraph styles. You can choose to have AutoFormat make all the changes at one time, or you can review each change as it is made. To automatically format an entire document, follow these steps:

1. **Choose Format⇨AutoFormat.**

   The AutoFormat dialog box appears, as shown in Figure 6-11.

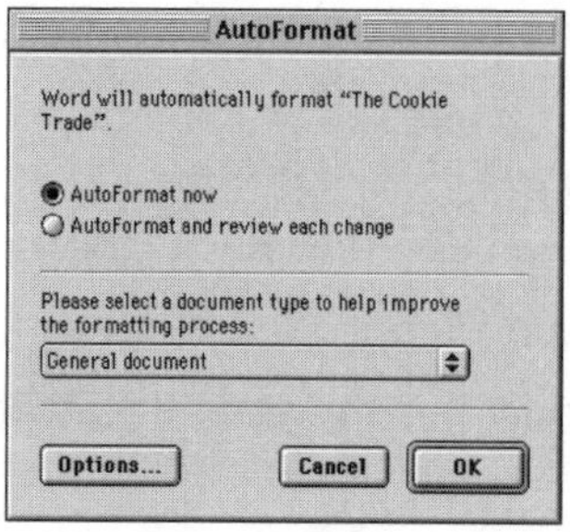

Figure 6-11:
The
AutoFormat
dialog box.

2. **Choose either AutoFormat now or AutoFormat and review each change.**

3. **Select a document type from the pop-up menu.**

   AutoFormat uses this document type as a starting point for the formatting process.

4. **(Optional) Click the Options button to set AutoFormat options.**

   The AutoCorrect dialog box opens, set to the AutoFormat tab, as shown in Figure 6-12.

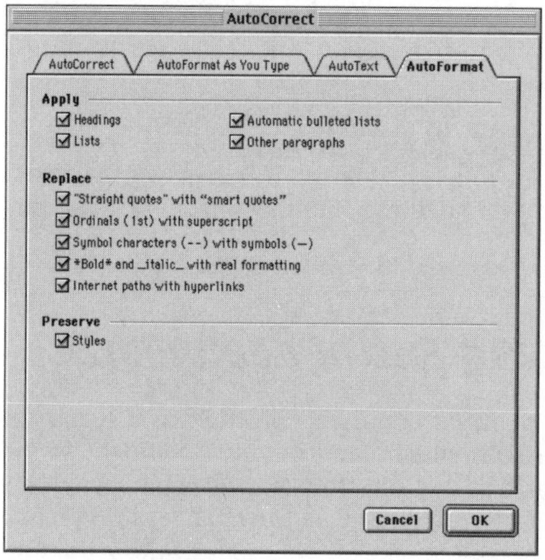

Figure 6-12:
Setting
AutoFormat
options.

5. **(Optional) Turn on or off any AutoFormat options, and then click OK.**

6. **Back in the AutoFormat dialog box, click OK.**

AutoFormatting as you type

To have the Word 98 AutoFormat feature help you format your document as you write it, follow these steps:

1. **Choose Tools⇨AutoCorrect.**

   The AutoCorrect dialog box appears.

2. **Click the AutoFormat As You Type tab.**

   The dialog box now looks like Figure 6-13.

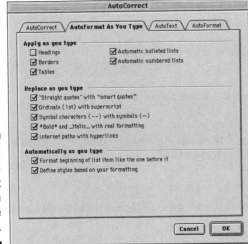

Figure 6-13:
Setting the
AutoFormat
As You
Type
options.

3. **Set the AutoFormat options you want.**

4. **Click OK.**

You need to set these options only once; after you do so, Word 98 remembers your settings and automatically formats your text as you type it.

To turn off all automatic formatting, clear all the options on the AutoFormat As You Type tab in the AutoCorrect dialog box.

Using AutoFormat for numbered and bulleted lists

AutoFormat As You Type makes creating numbered or bulleted lists easy. You simply start the list with a bullet or number and then press Return. AutoFormat inserts the next number or bullet for you.

Here's an example of a numbered list:

1. **Call florist**

2. **Buy candy**

3. **Beg forgiveness**

This list is a bulleted list:

✔ **Call lawyer**

✔ **Serve papers**

✔ **Move out**

To have Word 98 format your lists for you, follow these steps:

1. **Choose Tools⇨AutoCorrect.**

   The AutoCorrect dialog box appears.

2. **Click the AutoFormat As You Type tab.**

   Refer to Figure 6-13.

3. **Make sure that the Automatic Bulleted Lists and Automatic Numbered Lists options are checked.**

4. **Click OK.**

To stop the automatic numbering or bulleting, press the Return key twice.

Word 98 creates a numbered list when you type a number followed by a period, hyphen, closing parenthesis, or greater-than sign (>) followed by a space or a tab and then text. A bulleted list is created when you type an asterisk, one or two hyphens, or a greater-than sign followed by a space or a tab and then text.

If you don't like the format of the numbered or bulleted list Word 98 creates, you can change it by following these steps:

1. **Select the numbered or bulleted list you want to change.**

2. **Choose Format⇨Bullets and Numbering.**

   The Bullets and Numbering dialog box appears, as shown in Figure 6-14.

3. **Click either the Bulleted or Numbered tab.**

4. **Choose one of the eight styles of bullets or numbers.**

5. **Click OK.**

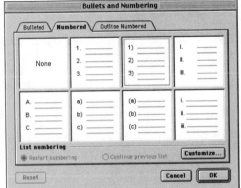

Figure 6-14:
Changing
your
document's
bullet or
numbering
format.

By using the Bullets and Numbering dialog box, you can change a bulleted list to a numbered list or vice versa. You can also turn a group of selected paragraphs into a bulleted or numbered list.

Instant hyperlinks

AutoFormat can also help you create instant hyperlinks in your documents. *Hyperlinks* are colored and underlined text you click to jump to a file or a particular location in a file on your hard disk, to an e-mail address, or to a page on the World Wide Web.

To automatically format hyperlinks, follow these steps:

1. **Choose Tools⇨AutoCorrect.**

   The AutoCorrect dialog box appears.

2. **Click the AutoFormat As You Type tab.**

   Refer to Figure 6-13.

3. **In the Replace As You Type section, make sure that the option labeled Internet Paths with Hyperlinks is checked.**

4. **Click OK.**

Whenever you type an e-mail or Web address, Word 98 now automatically converts it into a hyperlink.

Hyperlinks can also take you to FTP sites, newsgroups, Telnet sites, and Gopher sites.

Using the Style Gallery

After you use AutoFormat to apply styles throughout your document, you can then apply a style template to change the entire look of your document in one step. Because Word 98 includes many style templates, giving your document a facelift is easy. Follow these steps to apply a style template:

1. **Choose Format⇨Style Gallery.**

   The Style Gallery dialog box appears, as shown in Figure 6-15.

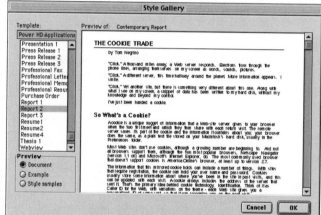

Figure 6-15: Choosing a new document format from the Style Gallery.

2. **In the Template area on the left, click the name of a template.**

   The Preview area shows what your document will look like if you apply the template you've selected.

3. **Click OK.**

Working with Tables

Tables are great for presenting complicated information in simple ways. Tables enable you to organize columns of numbers, produce forms, and format reports.

Tables consist of rows and columns. *Rows* are the horizontal divisions of the table; *columns* are the vertical divisions. A row and a column intersect to form a *cell*. You can put either text or a graphics image into a cell. When you type text in a cell, the text wraps within the cell, and the cell enlarges as you enter more text.

When you add a table to your document, you need to define the number of rows and columns in the table. After the table is added, you can modify the table and its contents by formatting the text, adding borders, and changing the size of the table.

Creating a table

Word 98 gives you three ways to create tables:

- ✔ Use the Insert Table button on the Standard toolbar.
- ✔ Use the Insert Table dialog box from the Table menu.
- ✔ Use the new Draw Table feature.

Using the toolbar

The fastest way to create a table is from the Standard toolbar, by following these steps:

1. Click the Insert Table button on the Standard toolbar.

A table appears below the toolbar, as shown in Figure 6-16.

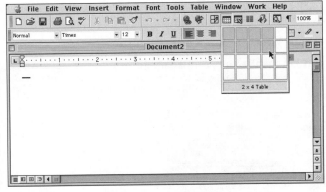

Figure 6-16:
Building a table with the Insert Table button.

2. Drag the mouse down and to the right to choose the height and width of your table.

3. Release the mouse button.

Word 98 draws the table.

Using the Insert Table dialog box

Using the Insert Table dialog box to create a table isn't as quick as using the Standard toolbar, although the dialog box gives you a little more control. Follow these steps to create a table with the Insert Table dialog box:

1. **Choose Table⇨Insert Table.**

   The Insert Table dialog box appears, as shown in Figure 6-17.

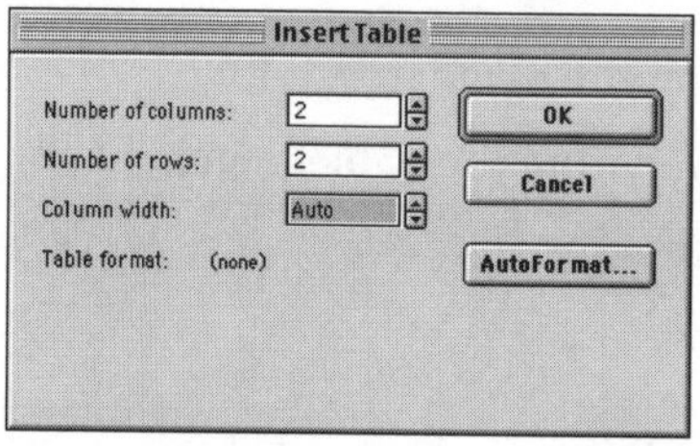

Figure 6-17:
The Insert Table dialog box.

2. **In the box labeled Number of Columns, enter the number of columns you want in the table.**

3. **In the box labeled Number of Rows, enter the number of rows you want in the table.**

4. **Leave the box labeled Column width set to Auto, or click the up and down arrow to set the column width.**

5. **(Optional) Click the AutoFormat button.**

   If you don't want to use AutoFormat for your table, skip to Step 8.

   The Table AutoFormat dialog box appears, as shown in Figure 6-18.

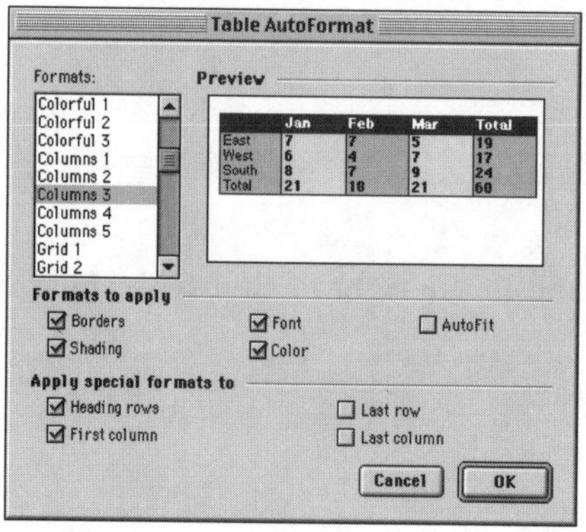

Figure 6-18:
The Table AutoFormat dialog box.

6. **Click one of the predefined table formats in the Formats list.**

   Experiment with the different formats and formatting options available in the dialog box. The Preview area shows what your table will look like.

7. **Click OK.**

   The Insert Table dialog box reappears (refer to Figure 6-17).

8. **Click OK.**

Using the Draw Table feature

Using the Draw Table feature to create a table is brand-new to Word 98. This feature enables you to create complex tables just by drawing rows and columns with a pen tool. Follow these steps to use the new Draw Table feature:

1. **Click the insertion point where you want to create the table.**

2. **Click the Tables and Borders button on the Standard toolbar.**

   The Tables and Borders toolbar appears, and the mouse pointer turns into a pen.

3. **Drag diagonally to create the outer borders of the table.**

4. **Draw horizontally and vertically with the pen tool to create the rows and columns of your table.**

5. **To erase a line, click the Eraser tool and drag over the offending line.**

   The drawing method enables you to create complicated tables, as shown in Figure 6-19.

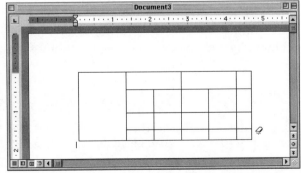

Figure 6-19: The result of drawing a table.

While you're drawing a table, pressing the Shift key toggles between the pen and eraser tools.

Changing table size

After you work with a table, you may realize that you made a mistake and want to change the number of rows or columns in the table. You can add or delete rows or columns and change the height and width of cells.

To add a row or column, follow these steps:

1. **Put the insertion point in any row or column.**

2. **Choose Table⇨Select Row (or Select Column).**

   Word 98 highlights the row or column.

3. **Choose Table⇨Insert Rows (or Insert Column).**

   Word 98 inserts the new row above the row the insertion point is in or adds a new column to the left of the column where the insertion point is.

To delete a row or column, follow these steps:

1. **Put the insertion point in any row or column.**

2. **Choose Table⇨Select Row (or Select Column).**

   Word 98 highlights the row or column.

3. **Choose Table⇨Delete Rows (or Delete Columns).**

   Word 98 wipes out the row or column that is selected.

To change the height or width of a table's cells, follow these steps:

1. **Put the insertion point over the column line or row line you want to move.**

   The insertion point turns into a two-headed arrow.

2. **Drag the column line or row line to where you want it located.**

Merging and splitting table cells

You may want to join one or more cells (or split them apart). The heads of columns often stretch across more than one column, for example.

To merge table cells, follow these steps:

1. **Select the cells you want to join.**

2. **Choose Table⇨Merge Cells.**

To split table cells, follow these steps:

1. **Select the cells you want to split.**

2. **Choose Table⇨Split Cells.**

Cleaning up your tables

If you've drawn a table or moved row or column lines around, your table may not look as neat as you want because the spacing is usually off between row or column lines. Word 98 has two tools to deal with this problem: the Distribute Rows Evenly and Distribute Columns Evenly buttons. Follow these steps to clean up your tables:

1. **Click multiple rows or columns inside a table.**

2. **On the Tables and Borders toolbar, click either the Distribute Rows Evenly or Distribute Columns Evenly button (or click both of them).**

   Word 98 evens out the amount of space between rows or columns.

Sorting a table

Although Word 98 doesn't have the data-manipulation capabilities that Excel 98 does, you can still do some simple sorts and calculations on the data in tables.

To sort the data in a table, follow these steps:

1. **Select the columns or rows you want to sort.**

   The data is highlighted, as shown in Figure 6-20.

Figure 6-20:
The table
before
sorting.

Asset	Date Acquired
Condo in Maui	4/97
Santa Monica Duplex	6/92
Cabin – Santa Fe	3/95
Brentwood estate	7/90
Redondo Beach Bungalow	5/91

2. **Choose Table⇨Sort.**

   The Sort dialog box appears.

3. Choose the sort options you want.

4. Click OK.

Word 98 sorts the table, with results similar to those shown in Figure 6-21.

Asset	Date Acquired
Brentwood estate	7/90
Cabin – Santa Fe	3/95
Condo in Maui	4/97
Redondo Beach Bungalow	5/91
Santa Monica Duplex	6/92

Figure 6-21:
The sorted
table.

Deleting a table

To delete a table (and its contents), follow these steps:

1. Click anywhere inside the table.

2. Choose Table⇨Select Table.

Word 98 highlights the entire table.

3. Choose Table⇨Delete Rows.

To delete the contents of the table (but not the table itself), follow these steps:

1. Click anywhere inside the table.

2. Choose Table⇨Select Table.

3. Press the Delete key.

Chapter 7

Creating Reports and Newsletters

. . . .

. . . .

*O*ver the years, Microsoft Word has gained more and more of the features previously found only in desktop publishing programs. With Word 98, you can create complicated documents such as newsletters and reports with a high degree of control.

In this chapter, you find out how to use Word 98 to create longer and more complex documents. You also see that although Word 98 won't be replacing Adobe PageMaker or QuarkXPress (the big-name desktop publishing programs designers use to make books, brochures, reports, and so on) on professional designers' desktops, it's more than capable enough for most of us.

Creating Reports

Reports come in many varieties: financial reports, reports to the board of directors, reports to your boss, and even your kids' book reports for school, for example.

Reports can seem like deceptively simple documents when you first look at them. But a closer look shows that many longer reports have quite a bit of complex formatting, including the following:

- A title page
- Multiple sections, each with its own format
- Headers and footers, which may or may not be different on even and odd pages
- Footnotes or endnotes

Pat yourself on the back: Adding a title page

Title pages have formatting that is usually different from the rest of your document. Typically, a title page has the title of the document centered vertically on the page and the author's byline either directly below the title or in a block of text at the bottom of the page.

The best way to create a title page in Word 98 is to first type all the text you want on the page, tell Word to set the page apart from the way the rest of the document is formatted (by adding a section break), and finally format the text on the title page the way you want.

To create a title page, follow these steps:

1. **Press ⌘+N to create a new blank document.**

2. **Type the text you want to appear on the title page.**

   In this example, I use a document title and an author's byline, but you can type as much or as little on the title page as you want.

3. **Choose Insert⇨Break.**

   The Break dialog box appears, as shown in Figure 7-1.

Figure 7-1:
Adding a section break with the Break dialog box.

4. **In the Section Breaks area, click the Next page radio button.**

   Clicking the Next page radio button tells Word that the next page is the beginning of a new *section*. Sections in Word can have entirely different formats. (For more about sections, see the section called "Using sections" later in this chapter.)

5. **Click OK.**

6. **Select the title that you typed in Step 2.**

7. **Format the title to your satisfaction. (Refer to Chapter 6 if you need help with formatting the text.)**

   Titles are usually in a large point size and are often centered on the page.

8. Format any other text on your title page.

After formatting, you could have a title page that looks like Figure 7-2.

If you want to center a title vertically on a page, you don't have to do it by pressing the Return key a bunch of times. Instead, choose Format⇨ Document, click the Layout tab, and select Center from the Vertical Alignment pop-up menu.

Using sections

Sections are extremely useful in formatting longer documents because each section of a Word document can have entirely different formatting. For example, one section can have a single column of text, and the next section can have multiple columns. The margins, headers, and footers of one section can differ from the next. Different sections can have opposite page orientations, so you can mix both portrait and landscape pages in the same document.

To tell Word that you are about to create a different section, you must insert a section break into your document. Word 98 has four types of section breaks:

- ✔ **Next page:** Inserts the section break, breaks the page, and starts the new section on the next page.

- ✔ **Continuous:** Inserts a section break and starts the new section on the same page.

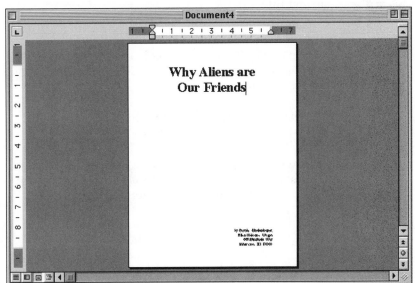

Figure 7-2: The formatted title page.

Why Aliens are Our Friends

by Sumb Klobulopus
Bklu Ukkas Whjs
685 Shubub Way
Whis son XI 87000

✔ **Odd page:** Inserts a section break and starts the new section on the next odd-numbered page.

✔ **Even page:** Inserts a section break and starts the new section on the next even-numbered page.

To insert a section break, follow these steps:

1. **Click where you want to insert the section break.**

2. **Choose Insert⇨Break or press ⌘+Enter.**

   The Break dialog box appears (refer to Figure 7-1).

3. **Choose the sort of section break you want.**

4. **Click OK.**

Using headers and footers

A *header* is an area of text at the top of each page that repeats itself on every page of your document. Similarly, a *footer* is an area of text at the bottom of the page that also repeats itself.

Typical things to put in a header or footer are

✔ The date

✔ Page numbers

✔ The document's title

✔ A chapter title

✔ Your name

When deciding what information to put in the header and footer, keep in mind that you probably don't want to put the same information in both the header and the footer.

To add a header or a footer, follow these steps:

1. **Choose View⇨Header and Footer.**

   Word 98 switches to Page Layout view, displays the Header and Footer toolbar, and displays Header and Footer text boxes, where you insert the text you want to appear (see Figure 7-3).

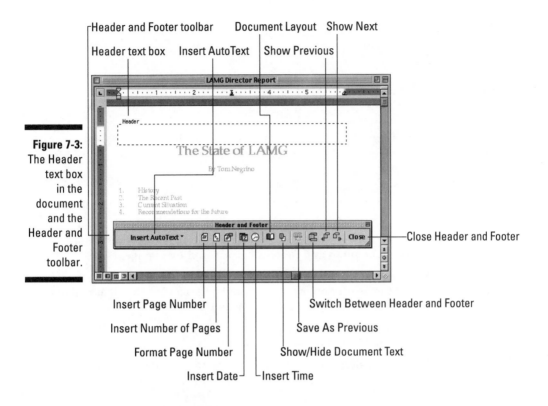

Header and Footer toolbar
Header text box   Insert AutoText   Document Layout   Show Next
Show Previous

Figure 7-3:
The Header
text box
in the
document
and the
Header and
Footer
toolbar.

Insert AutoText

Insert Page Number
Insert Number of Pages
Format Page Number
Insert Date   Insert Time

Switch Between Header and Footer
Save As Previous
Show/Hide Document Text
Close Header and Footer

2. **Type your header text in the Header text box (or if you're creating a footer, type in the Footer text box), or click a toolbar button to insert the page number, the date, or the time.**

If you want the word *Page* to appear before the page number, type the word **Page** and leave a space before you click the Insert Page Number button on the toolbar.

If you want to have one bit of information appear at the left end of the header, one in the center, and one on the right end, press Tab between them. The header and footer have separate paragraph formatting from the rest of your document, and you can change the tabs and other formatting to adjust the appearance of the header and footer as you like.

3. **Click the Document Layout button on the Header and Footer toolbar.**

The Document dialog box appears, set to the Layout tab, as shown in Figure 7-4.

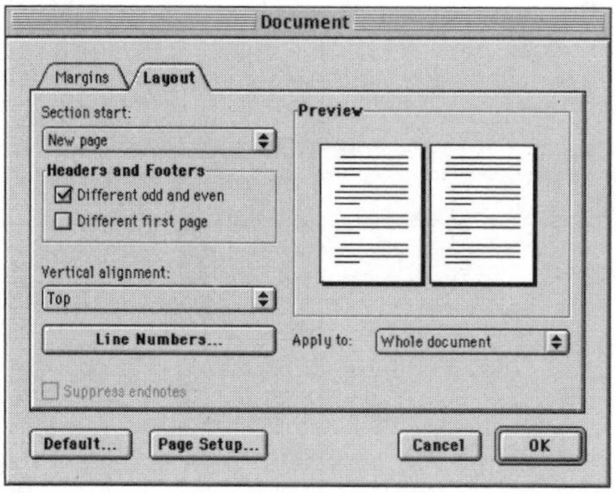

Figure 7-4:
Setting
Header and
Footer
layout
options.

4. **Click the Different odd and even check box if you want to have different headers and footers for odd and even pages.**

For example, you may want to have page numbers appear at the left end of the header on even-numbered pages and at the right end of the header on odd-numbered pages, as in this book.

5. **Click the Different first page check box if you want a different header or footer for your first page.**

You usually don't see page numbers on the first page in a document. You probably want to leave the header and footer blank on the first page.

6. **Click OK.**

The Document dialog box disappears.

7. **Click Close on the Header and Footer toolbar to leave Page Layout view.**

Adding footnotes and endnotes

Word 98 lets you bolster your arguments with footnotes and endnotes. A *footnote* appears at the bottom of a page and contains snippets of text citing sources of information, comments, explanations, or other references. *Endnotes* are similar, except that they appear at the end of your document. If you want, you can have both footnotes and endnotes in the same document; for example, you may use footnotes for comments and endnotes to cite your references.

A footnote or endnote consists of two linked parts — the note itself and the *note reference mark*. You can number note reference marks yourself, but Word can do it for you automatically. Word also automatically renumbers the marks if you delete, move, or add new ones.

To add a footnote or endnote, follow these steps:

1. **Choose View⇨Normal.**

   Word 98 requires you to be in Normal view; you can't insert footnotes or endnotes in Page Layout view (or any of the other views).

2. **Click in your document where you want to insert the note reference mark.**

3. **Choose Insert⇨Footnote.**

   The Footnote and Endnote dialog box appears, as shown in Figure 7-5.

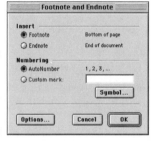

Figure 7-5:
Adding a footnote or endnote.

4. **In the Insert area, choose either Footnote or Endnote.**

5. **In the Numbering area, choose AutoNumber or Custom mark.**

6. **Click OK.**

   The document window splits to show a Footnotes pane, as shown in Figure 7-6.

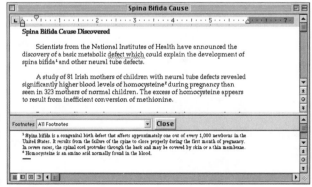

Figure 7-6:
Entering the footnote.

7. **Type your footnote or endnote text into the Footnotes pane.**

8. **Click back into the document pane to continue writing your document.**

    If you don't want to keep the Footnotes pane open, click the Close button.

A Nose for Newsletters

Before the introduction of the Macintosh launched the desktop publishing revolution, newsletters were produced by ink-stained wretches and paste-up artists. Now, anyone can create a newsletter with a word processor, and Word 98 has some great tools that help you get your newsletter done in a jiffy (okay, maybe two or three jiffies).

Newsletters can have almost any layout you want, from simple single-column pages to complex multicolumn behemoths with tables of contents, continued-on-page-12 text runs, and embedded images on the page.

Starting with the Newsletter Wizard

Rather than try to lay out the newsletter yourself, I suggest that you let the Word 98 Newsletter Wizard do the heavy lifting. This Wizard lets you choose from three basic styles of newsletters, and the results are just fine for most people.

 The Newsletter Wizard isn't installed with the basic installation of Microsoft Office 98; it's part of the Value Pack on the Office 98 CD-ROM. Take a minute to run the Value Pack Installer. Under the Templates section in the Value Pack Installer, choose Additional Word Templates.

To create a newsletter with the Newsletter Wizard, follow these steps:

1. **Choose File⇨New.**

    The New dialog box appears.

2. **Click the Other Documents tab.**

3. **Click the Newsletter Wizard icon.**

4. **Click OK.**

    A new document window opens, as does the opening screen of the Newsletter Wizard, explaining what the Wizard does.

5. Click Next.

The Style & Color window of the Wizard appears, as shown in Figure 7-7.

Figure 7-7: Choosing the style and color of your newsletter.

6. Select one of the three styles (Professional, Contemporary, or Elegant), and select whether you will print the newsletter on a black-and-white or color printer.

7. Click Next.

The Title and Content window appears.

8. Type the title of your newsletter in the Title box.

If you want to include a date at the top of your newsletter, click the Date check box and enter the newsletter's date. Similarly, if you want to include the Volume and Issue information, click that check box and enter that information.

9. Click Next.

The Mailing Label screen appears and asks whether you want to leave room for a mailing label on the back.

10. Click either the Yes or No button.

11. Click Finish.

Word creates the newsletter, as shown in Figure 7-8.

The newsletter consists of a headline, several text boxes where your stories will go, and a few pictures. Notice that the pre-inserted text in the text boxes tells you what to put in each of the text boxes. All you need to do is select the text and replace it with your own headlines, bylines, and stories.

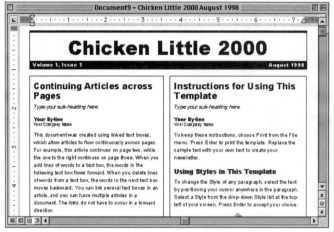

Figure 7-8:
The
completed
newsletter
template, as
created
by the
Newsletter
Wizard.

Working with text boxes

For newsletters, Word 98 uses *linked text boxes* to contain the text in columns. Linked text boxes allow articles to flow continuously across pages. For example, you can have a text box on the first page of your newsletter with the beginning of the story that is linked to another text box on the fourth page that continues and ends the story.

When you add words to the text box, any words in the following text box flow forward. When you delete words from a text box, the words in the following text box move backward.

Think of the text boxes as pipes and the words as water in the pipe. When you add more water to the beginning of the pipe, the water that's already in the pipe flows farther down the pipe.

Creating text boxes

To create a text box, follow these steps:

1. **Choose Insert⇨Text Box.**

   The cursor changes into a crosshair.

2. **Click and drag in the document window to draw a text box.**

   The text box appears, with a thick border and square white handles (the white squares that appear at the corners and the sides of the text box).

3. **Type inside the text box to use it.**

Linking text boxes

To link two text boxes, you must already have two existing text boxes. Follow these steps to link the two boxes:

1. **Click the border of the first text box to select it.**

   A thick border and handles appear around the text box.

2. **Choose View⇨Toolbars⇨Text Box.**

   The Text Box toolbar appears, as shown in Figure 7-9.

3. **Click the Create Text Box Link button on the Text Box toolbar.**

   The cursor changes into a pitcher.

4. **Click in the text box that you want the text to flow to.**

5. **Type in the first text box.**

   As your text fills the box, the excess text flows into the second box.

Deleting text boxes

To delete a text box, click inside the box to select it, and then press the Delete key. The box disappears, along with any text it contains. Deleting a text box that is the destination for a link also deletes that link.

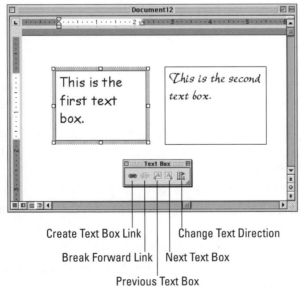

Figure 7-9:
Linking two text boxes with the Text Box toolbar.

Create Text Box Link | Change Text Direction
Break Forward Link | Next Text Box
Previous Text Box

Sizing and moving text boxes

To resize a text box that you've drawn, follow these steps:

1. **Click inside the text box you want to resize.**
2. **Click and drag one of the text box handles until the text box is the size that you want.**
3. **Release the mouse button.**

To move a text box, follow these steps:

1. **Click inside the text box that you want to move to select it.**
2. **Click and drag on the gray border of the text box, dragging the box to where you want to move it.**

   When you're moving a text box, the cursor becomes a four-headed arrow. If it is a two-headed arrow, it means that the mouse is over one of the text box handles. If you drag a text box handle, you resize the text box. Make sure that you see the four-headed arrow on-screen.

3. **Release the mouse button.**

Adding pictures to your newsletter

Newsletters have more impact with pictures, and Word 98 allows you to use several kinds of pictures:

- ✔ A picture from the clip art gallery that comes with Office 98
- ✔ Scanned photographs
- ✔ Any GIF, JPEG, or PICT file

To add a picture to your document, follow these steps:

1. **Choose Insert⇨Picture.**
2. **Choose one of the following:**
   - **Clip Art:** Lets you choose a picture from the Office 98 clip art gallery.
   - **From File:** Inserts a graphic from your hard disk.
   - **AutoShapes:** Lets you choose from the shapes found on the Word 98 Drawing toolbar.
   - **WordArt:** Lets you add special effects to text.
   - **Chart:** Inserts a chart, such as a pie or bar graph.

   Word inserts the picture.

Wrapping words around the pictures

By default, Word inserts pictures as *inline graphics,* which means that the pictures take up space just as lines of text would. You may sometimes want the text near the picture to wrap around the picture rather than have the picture breaking up the text.

To wrap words around pictures, follow these steps:

1. **Put the cursor over the picture around which you want to wrap text.**

2. **Ctrl+click the picture.**

   A pop-up menu appears.

3. **Choose Format Picture from the pop-up menu.**

   The Format Picture dialog box appears, as shown in Figure 7-10.

4. **Click the Wrapping tab.**

5. **Click one of the options in the Wrapping Style area.**

6. **Click one of the options in the Wrap To area.**

7. **Click the Top, Left, Bottom, or Right boxes, and set the amount of distance between the picture and the text that is wrapped around it.**

8. **Click OK.**

   The Format Picture dialog box disappears, and text now wraps around your picture.

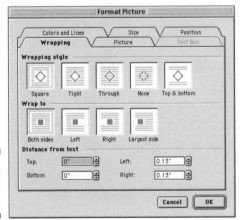

Figure 7-10:
Formatting
a picture.

Using drop caps

Drop caps are large, initial capital letters you often see in the first word of a paragraph. Drop caps are used for emphasis and to set apart the text on a page. For example, the first letter of the regular text in this chapter is a drop cap.

To create a drop cap, follow these steps:

1. **Click in the paragraph in which you want to create a drop cap.**

2. **Choose Format➪Drop Cap.**

   The Drop Cap dialog box appears, as shown in Figure 7-11.

3. **Choose a style for the drop cap.**

4. **Click OK.**

   Word creates the drop cap, as shown in Figure 7-12.

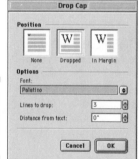

Figure 7-11:
The Drop Cap dialog box.

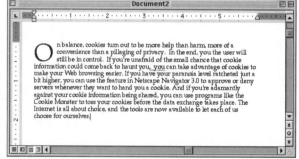

Figure 7-12:
The completed drop cap.

Part III
Crunching Your Numbers with Excel 98

"...AND TO ACCESS THE PROGRAM'S 'HOT KEY,' YOU JUST DEPRESS THESE ELEVEN KEYS SIMULTANEOUSLY. HERB OVER THERE HAS A KNACK FOR DOING THIS THAT I THINK YOU'LL ENJOY — HERB! GOT A MINUTE?"

In this part . . .

Whether it's filling in your expense report or finding out that your long-lost Uncle Sydney has left you a seven-figure gift in his will, you need to deal with numbers. Microsoft Excel 98 is just the ticket. You can use Excel to track your budget, follow the stock market, project financial results, figure out baseball averages, or just about anything else you can imagine doing with numbers.

After you have crunched the numbers, Excel 98 helps you turn your spreadsheets into cool-looking pie, bar, column, and line charts, which can tell you at a glance what your numbers really mean.

Chapter 8

Spreadsheets 101: Behind the Rows and Columns

This chapter explains what spreadsheets are and how to use them in a basic sense. Read Chapter 9 to learn how to make Excel 98 do the math in spreadsheets for you.

What the Heck Is a Spreadsheet?

This question is a good one to start with. It shows that you're paying attention.

Spreadsheets are pages from an electronic ledger pad — rows and columns of little boxes just waiting to be filled in, as shown in Figure 8-1. The Office 98 program that creates spreadsheets is Excel 98.

You can put anything you want in the boxes: words, numbers, pictures, whatever. As you see in this chapter, spreadsheets are most handy for working with numbers because (unlike "real" ledger pads) *spreadsheets can do the math for you.* Imagine typing a bunch of numbers and having them automatically totaled at the bottom of the page or typing a bunch of numbers and having them automatically averaged. Or think of what it would be like to type a bunch of numbers and have the largest one automatically highlighted in green or picture how a spreadsheet may keep you from ever needing to haul out your calculator again.

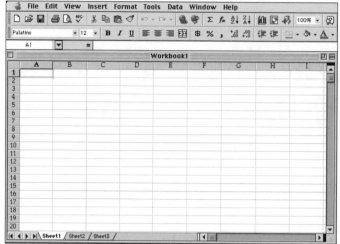

Figure 8-1:
An empty
spreadsheet.

Parts of the spreadsheet

Excel 98 spreadsheets have lots of parts, and, taken all together, those parts can be intimidating. Fortunately, you can ignore many things for now and concentrate on the basics. This section makes you familiar with cells, rows and columns, and the formula bar. That information is enough to get you started.

Cells

Cells are the basic building blocks of a spreadsheet. Every cell in a spreadsheet starts out the same way: blank. You get to put things (such as numbers, formulas, and words) into cells and control the way they appear. Figure 8-2 shows some cells with different types of information in them.

Notice that because Excel 98 cells can be sized to fit the stuff you enter into them, you don't have to worry about staying within the lines. Cells can be widened and deepened (and de-widened and de-deepened) at your command.

Rows and columns

Look down the left side of an Excel 98 spreadsheet, and you see a bunch of numbers. These *row labels* help you tell Excel 98 which row you're interested in. Look across the top of an Excel 98 spreadsheet, and you see letters rather than numbers. These letters — the labels of the columns — help you tell Excel 98 which column you're interested in. Figure 8-3 shows the rows and columns in a spreadsheet.

Cells

	Workbook1	

Figure 8-2:
Some cells
and their
varied
contents.

City | Altitude | Temperature
Davis | 52 | 90
Austin | 0 | 95
Santa Monica | 0 | 78

Name | Age
Jeff | 35
Pete | 35
Christian | 35

Artist | Title
Willie Nelson | Me and Paul
Johnny Cash | Folsom Prison Blues
Merle Haggard | Big City
Buck Owens | Streets of Bakersfield

Date | Weight
1/1/98 | 190
2/1/98 | 189
3/1/98 | 188
4/1/98 | 188
5/1/98 | 189
6/1/98 | 187

Excel 98 limits you to 65,536 rows and 256 columns. Naturally, most spread-sheets never get anywhere near that big. When Excel 98 runs out of letters for columns, it doubles up and the lettering goes X, Y, Z, AA, AB, AC, and so on.

Notice that each cell is the intersection of a row and a column. Thus, you can (and do) refer to the cell in the top-left corner of the spreadsheet as A1. Likewise, the cell at the intersection of Row 2 and Column B is B4, and the cell at the intersection of Row 6 and Column C is C6. Figure 8-4 shows some representative cells.

For some obscure reason, the Excel 98 cell references are column first, even though most people prefer row first. Thus, although you may expect the cell at the intersection of Row 2 and Column B to be 2B, it's B2.

The formula bar

The term *formula bar* is rather misleading because it is used for much more than just formulas. In fact, you use the formula bar every time you enter something into a cell, whether that something is a formula, a number, or a word. Figure 8-5 shows the formula bar.

When you click a cell, the formula bar displays the cell's contents. When you type something inside a cell, the formula bar displays what you type. You find out how to create formulas in Chapter 9; for now, however, it's worth knowing that when you want to create a formula (something that means, for example, "This cell equals that cell minus that other cell"), you do it on the formula bar.

Row labels   Column labels

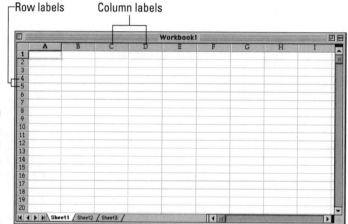

Figure 8-3:
An Excel 98
spreadsheet
has row
and column
labels.

Cell A1

Cell B4

Cell C6

Figure 8-4:
Representa-
tive cells
and the
notation
Excel 98
uses to
describe
them.

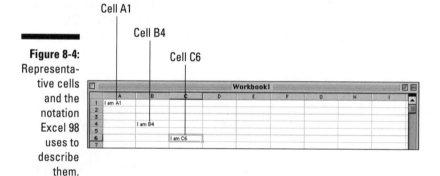

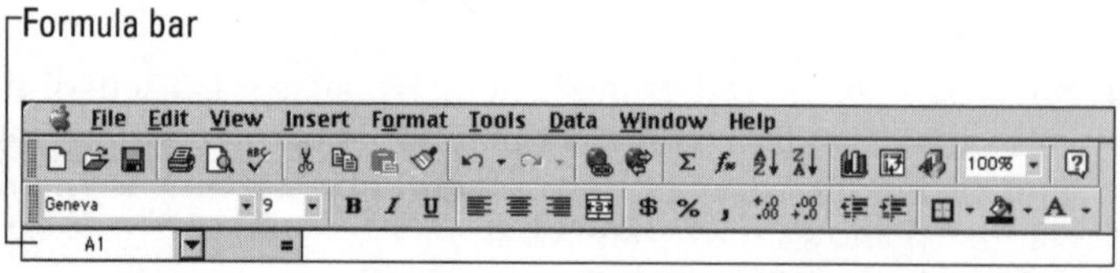

Formula bar

Figure 8-5:
The formula
bar.

What spreadsheets are good for

Spreadsheets excel (pardon the pun) at handling numbers. Spreadsheets are good, therefore, for doing math-type things you may always have done on paper, such as tracking your checks, stocks, and net income. Figure 8-6 shows a spreadsheet that tracks all these items. Notice that the math is done by Excel 98, not by you. All you do is enter the words and numbers and set up the formulas. Excel 98 gives you the answers.

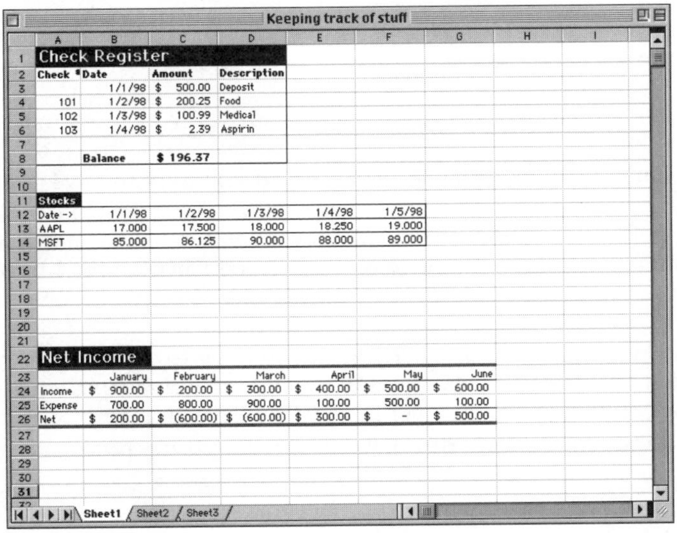

Figure 8-6: Checks, stocks, and net income tracked in a spreadsheet.

Things that spreadsheets don't do well

Back home, they have a saying: "When all you know is a hammer, everything looks like a nail." Roughly translated, that saying means "Use the right tool for the job." Spreadsheets are the right tools for many jobs, but not for all jobs. Spreadsheets are terrible word processors, for example. (Here's some advice: Use Word 98.) Spreadsheets are also terrible *food* processors (More advice: Use a Cuisinart). Do you want to make presentations, draw a floor plan, or maintain an address book? Although you can use Excel 98 for all three tasks, using it would be a great deal of trouble, and you would really have to work. Why bother, when other programs are better suited to these tasks? Take it from me (I ruined a number of wood screws when I was ten years old) — easier ways exist.

Cruising through a Worksheet

Before you go any further in this book, getting some terms straight is important. The discussion earlier in this chapter describes spreadsheets in general terms. This section, however, focuses on Excel 98, which has a few terms of its own:

- The basic Excel 98 document is called a *workbook*.
- A workbook can have multiple pages, which are called *worksheets*.
- Each worksheet is really just a *spreadsheet,* and you already know what a spreadsheet is.

Now you're ready to move ahead.

Right out of the box, Excel 98 assumes that you want to have three worksheets per workbook. Three pages may not be enough for you, but don't worry — the number of worksheets you can have in a workbook is unlimited. (You find out how to add worksheets in Chapter 10, so stay tuned.)

Excel 98 is literal: It does exactly what you tell it to do and, just as important, does so exactly *where* you say to do it. In this section, you find out how to move around in a worksheet so that you have an easier time of telling Excel 98 what tasks to perform and where to perform them.

Selecting cells with the mouse

You select cells to show Excel 98 which cells you're talking about. If you click a cell, Excel 98 highlights it with a little border and displays the name of the cell to the left of the formula bar, as shown in Figure 8-7.

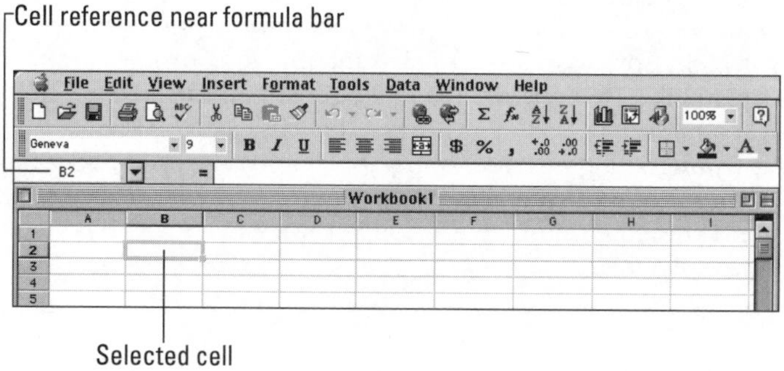

┌Cell reference near formula bar

Figure 8-7:
Someone
clicked Cell
B2, and
Excel 98 put
a border
around it.

Selected cell

If you click a cell, hold down the mouse button, and drag the mouse pointer toward some other cell, you select all the cells between those two cells. This technique is handy for quickly selecting a chunk, or a *range,* of the spreadsheet.

Figure 8-8 shows a range of selected cells. Notice that if you drag past the edge of the worksheet, Excel 98 scrolls automatically, so even if you can't see all the cells you want to select, you can do so by dragging. Just click where you want to start the selection and drag in the direction of the final cell.

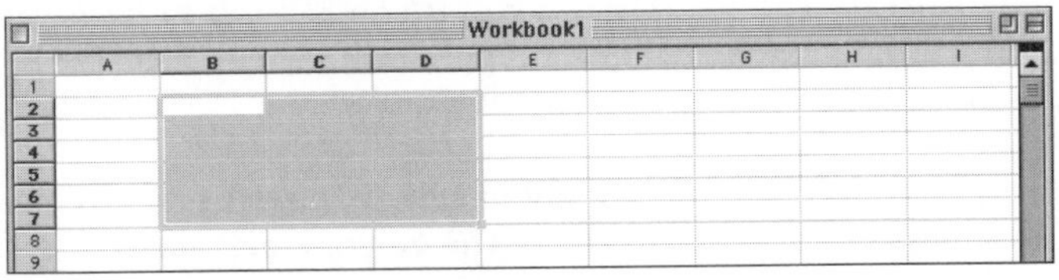

Figure 8-8:
Selecting a
range of
cells.

> If you're selecting a range and go too far, don't panic. Just keep holding down the mouse button and move back the other way. Everything's cool as long as you hold down the mouse button.

Variations on this theme exist, of course. If you select a cell, hold down the Shift key, and then click another cell, for example, Excel 98 selects everything between the two cells. This technique is one of the fastest ways to select a large group of cells, especially if they are widely separated. If you keep holding down the Shift key and continue to click cells, Excel 98 continues to adjust the highlighted range accordingly. The key to the technique, really, is choosing a good cell to start in and a good cell to stop in.

If you select a range of cells, hold down the Shift key, and click another cell, Excel 98 selects everything between where you originally clicked and where you Shift+clicked. In effect, Excel ignores the dragging you did.

If you select a range of cells and hold down the ⌘ key while selecting a different range of cells in another part of the spreadsheet, Excel 98 does *not* select everything between the first and second selections; rather, it highlights just what you dragged through the cells you selected, leaving the cells between unselected. This method of making a selection, called *discontiguous selection,* is extremely handy because it enables you to skip cells you want to leave alone.

If you click a cell, you select the cell. You knew that. If you click the name of a column or a row (the number or letter label), however, you select the entire column or row, all the way to the end! If you click the name of a column or a row and drag to another column's or row's label, you select all the columns or rows between them. If you click one column or row label, hold down the Shift key, and click another column or row label, you select everything between them; if you substitute the ⌘ key for the Shift key, you select just the columns or rows you clicked. This technique is definitely worth trying.

Using the keyboard

Using the mouse to select cells is easy and more or less intuitive. The technique isn't all that fast, however, and you can easily make mistakes by clicking the wrong places. You're much better off using the keyboard to select cells.

The arrow keys do the same thing you can do with the mouse, but in one-cell increments. If you want to select the cell one cell above the selected cell, press the up-arrow key one time. Want to move up two cells? Press the up-arrow key twice. Want to zoom around the worksheet? Press an arrow key and hold it down. Pretty elementary. But wait — there's more!

When you hold down the Shift key while you press an arrow key, something nice happens: You select cells, just like you do when you drag the mouse. If you hold down the Shift key, press the right-arrow key three times, and then (still holding down the Shift key) press the down-arrow key four times, you select a range of cells three cells wide and four cells deep.

If you go too far, don't worry. Keep holding down the Shift key and then press the arrow key that goes back the other way. If you accidentally select an extra row because of pressing the down-arrow key one too many times, just press the Shift key and then the up-arrow key. Voilà!

Hold down the ⌘ key while you press an arrow key, and you zip to an edge of the spreadsheet. Which edge depends on which arrow key you press. If you're way over in Column Z and want to get back to Column A, therefore, just hold down the ⌘ key and press the left-arrow key. If you're way down in Row 200 and want to get back to Row 1, hold down the ⌘ key and press the up-arrow key. Easy.

While you're at it, give the Home, Page Up, and Page Down keys a try too. Pressing Home zips you back to the first cell in the row you're in. Pressing Control+Home takes you back to Cell A1 — the first cell in the spreadsheet. Pressing Control+End takes you to the last cell in your spreadsheet (the last cell you used, not the geographic last cell). Pressing Page Up scrolls up a screen's worth of data, and pressing Page Down scrolls down a screen.

Naming cells and ranges

If you read the section "Parts of the spreadsheet," earlier in this chapter, you know that Excel 98 refers to its cells with row and column identifiers. You can go straight to a cell by telling Excel 98, "I want to go to Cell B4:"

1. **Choose Edit⇨Go To.**

   The Go To dialog box appears.

2. **In the Reference box, type** B4.

3. **Click OK.**

   B4 becomes the active cell.

When you use this technique, you have one big problem, and you've probably already guessed what it is: Remembering the row and column descriptions for more than a couple of cells is close to impossible. If you're trying to zip to a section of a worksheet and you can't remember whether it starts at Z99 or Y78, the Edit⇨Go To command doesn't do you much good. Enter the concept of naming cells and ranges.

Naming a cell or a range means giving it a name that makes sense to you. Suppose that your spreadsheet looks like the one shown in Figure 8-9.

Figure 8-9: Baseball standings.

Being able to quickly jump to the National League West section, for example, and selecting the cells you want may be handy. Follow these steps:

1. **Select the cell or range you want to name.**

2. **Choose Insert⇨Name⇨Define.**

   The Define Name dialog box appears.

3. **In the Names in Workbook box, type a name that describes the selected cell or range.**

4. **Click OK.**

You have to follow the Excel 98 rules for naming things. You can't use spaces in a name, you can't use apostrophes, and you can't use numbers. The name in the preceding example, therefore, could be NationalLeagueWest, but it couldn't be National League West or even Nat'lWest. Stick with one-word names, and you'll be okay.

To use a named range, start by selecting something else, away from the range. Choose Edit⇨Go To, choose your named range (it ought to be in the Go To dialog box), and click OK. Presto — you're in the right place, and the proper cells are selected. Very slick.

One amazingly cool feature of Excel 98 is its capability to select all cells of a certain kind. Suppose that you want to select in the spreadsheet shown in Figure 8-10 all the cells that contain words. (Perhaps you want to make them bold or green or something else along those lines.)

Figure 8-10:
You want to select the words but not the numbers.

	A	B	C	D	E	F	G	H	I	J
1										
2										
3	Baseball leaders									
4		Hitting			Pitching					
5		Player	Average		Player	ERA				
6		McGuire	0.398		Clemens	2.11				
7		Griffey	0.399		Nomo	2.31				
8		Mondesi	0.378		Abbot	3.01				
9		Piazza	0.350		Johnson	1.99				
10		Boyce	0.406		Rosenberg	1.75				
11										
12										

It would be a drag, as it were, if you had to select all these cells by hand. Excel 98 is up to the task. To select cells of a particular type, follow these steps:

1. **Choose Edit⇨Go To.**

   The Go To dialog box appears.

2. **Click the Special button.**

   3. Make your choices.

   4. Click OK.

   All the words are selected.

Remember this technique; you're sure to use it sooner or later.

Entering Information into a Worksheet

Even though you may know how to move around in a worksheet, you may not know how to put stuff into one. That situation will change — and fast. Master this section, and you're on your way to Spreadsheet 101 graduation ceremonies, with honors.

Putting information in a cell

As usual, you have a bunch of ways to put information in a cell. The simplest way is to select a cell, type something, and then press the Return key. This technique works with words and numbers, and you'll use it often.

Rather than press Return to tell Excel 98 that you're done typing, you can click the green check mark next to the formula bar. Although this method is slower, it has the advantage of being harder, which means that you're less likely to make mistakes when you're just starting. Clicking the red X next to the check mark means "Never mind; I liked things better the way they were before I started typing."

Again, as usual, variations on the theme exist. If you select a cell, type something, and press the Return key, the information is entered into the selected cell and the next cell down is selected. (When you press the Enter key, on the numeric keypad, the selected cell doesn't change.) If you select a cell, type something, and then press the Tab key, the information is entered in the selected cell and the cell to the right is selected. You can press the right-arrow key rather than Tab. The rest of the arrow keys work as you may expect, entering information and selecting the neighboring cell in whichever direction.

When you're working with numbers, the easiest method is to type them from the numeric keypad on the right side of most keyboards. You don't have to type decimal points if the numbers don't have them (if the number is 100.00, for example, you can just type **100**), and you don't have to type dollar signs, even if the numbers do have them. (Excel 98 has a way of automatically putting them in for you, as you see later in this chapter.)

You can, of course, copy the information in a cell or range and paste it somewhere else. Just select the cell (or cells) you want to copy, choose Edit⇨Copy, click where you want to begin pasting, and choose Edit⇨Paste. This technique puts the information in two places, which may not be what you want. If you simply want to move the information, choose Edit⇨Cut rather than Edit⇨Copy.

In the olden days (about three years ago), cutting and pasting was about as good as it got. Nowadays, the drag-and-drop technique enables you to cut your steps in half.

Suppose that your spreadsheet looks like the one shown in Figure 8-11.

Figure 8-11:
A spread-
sheet with
stuff in
wrong
places.

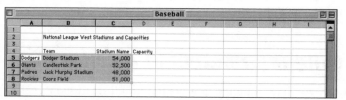

Now suppose that you want to move the selected stuff one cell to the right. You can cut and paste, of course, although the drag-and-drop method enables you to simply plop the selection into a new home:

1. **Click and hold the mouse button on any edge of the selection.**

   You know that the mouse pointer is in the right place when it changes from the standard Excel 98 cross to an arrow.

2. **Drag the selection anywhere you want.**

3. **When the selected cells are in the right place, release the mouse button.**

When you drop cells over cells that already contain data, Excel 98 assumes that you want to replace the old contents with the ones you are about to drop. Excel 98 displays a warning message every time this replacement is about to happen.

You see special effects when you hold down certain keys. If you hold down the Option key while dragging a range of cells to a new location, for example, you don't move them; you copy them.

How do you like that? You just finish reading that Excel 98 warns you when you are about to replace the contents of cells by dropping something on them, and now you find an exception — namely, if you use the Option-key technique to drag a copy of the cells, you do *not* see the warning. You simply replace whatever you drop on the cell. Be careful.

If you hold down the Control key while dragging, you get a slew of options, as shown in Figure 8-12. The figure shows an example of the Excel 98 contextual menus, which you see again later.

If you drag from a special place (the bottom-right corner, which is also known as the *fill handle*), Excel 98 doesn't move the cells. What it *does* do depends on the contents of the selected cells. If a cell contains the word *Monday,* for example, and you drag its bottom-right corner to the right, you fill the cells to the right with the days of the week as far as you like. Just drag to the right and release the mouse button, and you see how it works. Dragging down works as well.

When you fill cells in this way, you are creating a *series.* Excel 98 recognizes a bunch of series, including

- **Days of the week:** Full and abbreviated (Mon–Tues–Wed)

- **Months of the year:** Full and abbreviated (Jan–Feb–Mar)

- **Hours:** 10:00, 11:00, 12:00, and so on

- **Quarters of the year:** Full and abbreviated (1st Qtr–2nd Qtr–3rd Qtr)

- **Positional numbers:** 1st–2nd–3rd)

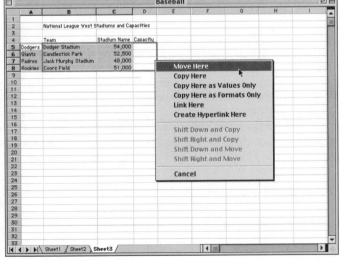

Figure 8-12:
You have options galore when you drag with the Control key.

Excel 98 can also figure out numeric series based on what you select. If you select two cells — one containing 10 and the other containing 20, for example — and then drag the fill handle further, Excel 98 guesses that the next number ought to be 30; the next number after that, 40; and so on. For this technique to work, select at least two cells; otherwise, Excel 98 can't figure out what you're trying to do.

Editing or deleting the contents of a cell

Unless you're always perfect, you may want to change the contents of a cell. Maybe you weren't looking when you typed things; maybe someone else did the typing; maybe you really were right the first time, and now you want to change something. No problem. Excel 98 enables you to make changes whenever you want.

Editing a cell's contents is as easy as selecting the cell and typing. The stuff you type replaces the stuff that used to be in the cell. Press Return (or click the green check next to the formula bar), and you're done.

Don't care for this method? Do you think that typing on the formula bar is awkward, especially when the cell you're editing is a long way from the formula bar? You're not alone, and Excel 98 knows that, so it gives you the option of editing cell contents *directly in the cell!* Simply double-click a cell, and you can type all over it, in much the same way as you would in a word processor. Feel free to use both the formula bar and the edit-in-cell methods in the same worksheet; Excel 98 doesn't care one whit.

Deleting the contents of a cell isn't rocket science: Click a cell and press the Delete key. Alternatively, click a cell, choose Edit⇨Clear, and then choose Contents from the pop-up menu. You can also click a cell and then choose Edit⇨Cut. Whichever method you use — poof! — the cell contents are gone.

Deleting the contents of a cell is not the same as deleting the cell itself. You may want to read that sentence again. *Deleting the contents of a cell clears it out but leaves the cell itself alone.* Deleting a cell creates a hole in your spreadsheet, and Excel 98 doesn't like holes, so it immediately asks how you want to close the hole — slide cells over from the right or up from the bottom. Make sure that you know what you're doing when you start deleting cells, because deleting is one of the easiest ways to louse up a good spreadsheet.

Making Your Worksheet Look Good

Nothing says "raise" to the boss louder than a smartly formatted spreadsheet. Excel 98 enables you to dress up your otherwise plain spreadsheet with colors, fonts, sizes, and even pictures. This section shows you how to format text and numbers — first, the easy AutoFormat way and then the harder, but more controllable, manual way. (You find out how to add pictures in the following section.)

Using AutoFormat

As its name suggests, AutoFormat performs automatic formatting. Excel 98 looks at the cells you selected, guesses which have headings and which have numeric data, and presents a bunch of ready-made formatting choices. In a jiffy, you can turn a general-issue spreadsheet like the one shown in Figure 8-13 into a snappy, income-adjusting masterpiece like the one shown in Figure 8-14:

1. **Select the cells you want to format.**

2. **Choose Format⇨AutoFormat.**

   The AutoFormat dialog box appears.

3. **Choose a format from the list.**

   When you click the name of a format, representative samples appear to the right of the dialog box. You can click the Options button and refine your choice (though I don't recommend doing that until you've tried doing things the Excel 98 way first because you can easily ruin a good formatting scheme).

4. **Click the OK button.**

   Excel automatically formats your spreadsheet.

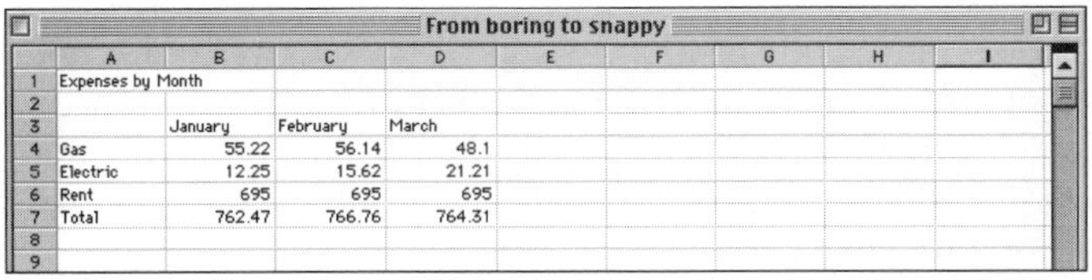

Figure 8-13:
A dull,
general-
issue
spreadsheet.

Figure 8-14:
A snappy,
income-
adjusting
spreadsheet.

	A	B	C	D	E	F	G	H	I	J	
							From boring to snappy				
1	Expenses by Month										
2											
3		January	February	March							
4	Gas	55.22	56.14	48.1							
5	Electric	12.25	15.62	21.21							
6	Rent	695	695	695							
7	Total	762.47	766.76	764.31							
8											
9											

If you don't like the way things turn out, don't worry; you can go straight back to the AutoFormat dialog box and choose another format. You can also modify the formatting that was applied automatically. Finally, remember that the Undo command is available until you do something else.

Information in your spreadsheet can look a little weird when you use AutoFormat. That's just the way things are when your cells are still selected. Click outside the cells you just formatted, and they'll probably look better.

Formatting numbers and text

AutoFormatting is great as long as you like the Excel 98 choices. For most people, AutoFormatting is a start, not a finished product. You have to do the rest of the formatting by hand if you're after a gorgeous spreadsheet. Fortunately, formatting is not hard, and you have options galore. This section starts by explaining number formatting and then moves on to text formatting.

Number formatting in Excel 98 is unbelievably powerful and, with this version of the program, is fairly easy to control. You can tell Excel 98 how many decimal places to use, whether to format numbers as dollars and cents, whether to use commas in long numbers, whether to display negative numbers in red or in parentheses, whether to format numbers as percentages, and on and on and on. Best of all, after you decide exactly what you want your numbers to look like, you can save the complete formatting instructions in a *style* and apply that style to numeric cells anywhere in your spreadsheet.

Applying formatting via a style is much faster than choosing countless options from the Excel 98 menus. Take a little extra time to set up some styles: Your work goes faster in the long run, and your spreadsheets have a consistent, professional look. Also, because number formatting is done on a cell-by-cell basis, some cells can be formatted one way and others can be formatted another. It's all up to you, although formatting is easiest when you use styles.

The spreadsheet shown back in Figure 8-14 isn't a bad-looking spreadsheet, but you may want to display dollar signs before every number. Follow these steps:

1. **Select the cells you want to format.**

2. **Choose Format⇨Cells.**

   The Format Cells dialog box appears.

3. **Click the Number tab.**

4. **Choose Currency from the Category list on the left side of the tab.**

5. **Choose dollar formatting with parentheses from the Negative Numbers list at the bottom of the tab.**

   You can choose currencies other than dollars, if you want.

When you choose the dollar formatting with parentheses, you tell Excel 98 to put parentheses around negative numbers. You have options here too: Rather than parentheses, negative numbers can be colored red, just have a minus sign in front of them, or anything else you want.

6. **Click OK.**

   Uh-oh — disaster! Your beautiful spreadsheet is full of number signs, as shown in Figure 8-15. Where are your numbers?

Figure 8-15:
A spread-sheet with number signs rather than numbers.

	A	B	C	D	E	F	G	H	I	J

(From boring to snappy)

	A	B	C	D
1	Expenses by Month			
2				
3		January	February	March
4	Gas	####	$56.14	####
5	Electric	####	$15.62	####
6	Rent	####	#####	####
7	Total	####	#####	####
8				
9				

Although the numbers are in the cells, with this new-and-improved format, Excel 98 doesn't have room to display them. It fills a cell with number signs to tell you that the real information doesn't fit. You can make the cells wider so that the information does fit, however.

7. **With the problem cells selected, choose Format⇨Column⇨ AutoFit Selection.**

   Congratulate yourself for not panicking. You're back on track for that raise. Figure 8-16 shows the spreadsheet so far.

Figure 8-16:
A good-
looking
spreadsheet!

	A	B	C	D	E	F	G	H	I	J
1	Expenses by Month									
2										
3		January	February	March						
4	Gas	$ 55.22	$ 56.14	$ 48.10						
5	Electric	$ 12.25	$ 15.62	$ 21.21						
6	Rent	$695.00	$695.00	$695.00						
7	Total	$762.47	$766.76	$764.31						
8										
9										

You can also format text — make it bold or italic or display text in 24-point type, for example. You can make the bottom row of a spreadsheet bold, for example. To format text, follow these steps:

1. **Select the cells you want to format.**

2. **Choose Format⇨Cells.**

   The Format Cells dialog box appears.

3. **Click the Font tab.**

4. **Choose an option from the scrolling Font Style list.**

5. **Click OK.**

If your changes mean that the text doesn't fit in the cells anymore, choose Format⇨Column⇨AutoFit Selection.

Although you can format text in other ways (gee, what a surprise!), the preceding method is the most powerful because it enables you to change everything in one swoop. In this case, though, you just made something bold. You can choose an easier way:

1. **Select the cells you want to format.**

2. **Click the Bold button (it looks like a capital *B*) on the Formatting toolbar.**

Figure 8-17 shows the Formatting toolbar and its plethora of Formatting options, which include font, size, alignment, and color.

Play around with the Formatting toolbar; it's time well spent.

Figure 8-17:
The
Formatting
toolbar has
more options
than you
can shake a
stick at!

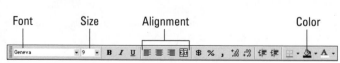

Font   Size   Alignment   Color

Chapter 9

Formulas Work — So That You Don't Have To!

In This Chapter

▶ Creating formulas

▶ Working with spreadsheet references

▶ Working with functions

*T*his chapter shows you how to make Excel 98 do the math for you. The program does this chore by manipulating the numbers in spreadsheet cells with formulas. A *formula* is just an instruction that tells Excel 98 what to do with the number in one or more cells. For example, a formula could tell Excel 98 to add the number in one cell to the number in another cell and put the result in a third cell. Because the use of formulas to do calculations is the biggest part of the point of using Excel 98, you may want to be especially careful as you work through some of the examples.

Introducing Formulas

Excel 98 can do all sorts of math for you, from the simplest addition to stuff you probably learned about and promptly forgot after the exam in high school or college. In this section, you start with the easy stuff and work your way up.

Starting with formulas

You begin with something interesting: figuring out how much money you have left after paying the bills. Here's how you do it with Excel 98:

1. **Create a new spreadsheet, and enter data to make it look like Figure 9-1.**

   Refer to Chapter 8 if you need to know how to create a spreadsheet.

Figure 9-1:
A spread-
sheet
showing
income and
expenses.

	A	B	C	D	E	F	G	H	I	J	
						net income					
1											
2											
3											
4		Income	800								
5		Expense	700								
6		Net									
7											
8											
9											

2. **Click the cell to the right of the word *Net*.**

   This cell is where you want to have Excel 98 put the difference between your income and your expenses.

3. **Press the equal (=) key.**

4. **Click the cell that contains your income (the number, not the word).**

5. **Press the minus (–) key on your keyboard.**

6. **Click the cell that contains your expenses (the number).**

   Notice that the cell contains the formula you've created so far. (So does the formula bar, but looking way up there for your formula right now isn't convenient.)

7. **If you like the formula, press the Enter key on the numeric keypad (or click the check mark next to your formula on the formula bar).**

   Note: Pressing Enter is not the same as pressing Return. If you press Enter, the formula is entered and computed, and the cell remains selected. If you press Return, the formula is entered and computed, and the *next cell down* is selected.

   Your answer appears. Hey, you're making money.

Every Excel 98 formula starts with an equal sign. Every one.

Look at the formula on the formula bar. This formula is almost understandable: *This* cell equals *that* cell minus some *other* cell. (If those cell references don't make sense to you, reviewing the beginning of Chapter 8 may do you good. Don't worry; I'll be here when you come back.)

Using names in formulas

Formulas would be easier to understand if you could type them the way you say them. In fact, you can. Follow these steps:

1. **Start by undoing the formula you just made in cell C6. Choose Edit⇨Undo Typing.**

   You're back where you started.

2. **Press the equal (=) key to begin the formula.**

3. **Type** Income - Expense **in the cell (or on the formula bar).**

4. **Press Enter.**

   You get the same answer as before, except that this formula is in English. Pretty nice.

You've made a simple formula. So far, no big deal. You could have created this formula faster on a calculator or on paper or even on your fingers. Ah, but Excel 98 does more than calculate the difference between the numbers as they are entered — it enables you to plug in *different* numbers, and the formula keeps on working!

Suppose that you get a raise, from $800 monthly to $900 monthly. To change the spreadsheet's values, follow these steps:

1. **Type** 900 **in the cell next to the word** *income.*

2. **Press Enter (or click the check mark on the formula bar).**

   Now you're doing even better. This step leaves more money to buy black-and-yellow how-to books for all that software you've acquired.

Try typing other numbers in both the monthly-income and monthly-expense cells. Remember to press the Enter key (or click the check mark on the formula bar) to tell Excel 98 that you're done typing.

You can improve this little spreadsheet by making it something you can use for a couple of months. To do so, you need more cells for future income and expense data. Follow these steps:

1. **Click the cell on top of the column of numbers (C3).**

2. **Type** January.

3. **Press the Enter key.**

4. **Click the fill handle in the bottom-right corner of the cell that contains the word *January*, and hold down the mouse button.**

   The mouse pointer looks like a thin, black cross when you're close enough to the fill handle to click it.

5. **Drag the fill handle to the right. As you drag, a yellow ScreenTip box shows the value of the cells you're filling. Drag until the ScreenTip shows that you've gone all the way to June.**

6. **Release the mouse button.**

   Your spreadsheet should look like the one shown in Figure 9-2.

Figure 9-2:
A spread-
sheet with
month
headings.

	A	B	C	D	E	F	G	H	I	J	
1											
2											
3			January	February	March	April	May	June			
4		Income	900								
5		Expense	700								
6		Net	200								
7											

net income

To add some data for those other months, click a cell and type. Leave the "Net" alone for now because you're going to calculate it for each month.

If you highlight, before you start typing, the cells in which you're going to enter data, you can get the entering done in a hurry. Try highlighting the Income and Expense cells (just drag through them). Then press the Enter key repeatedly, and notice how the selected cell moves around. When you type numbers and then press Enter, Excel 98 automatically selects the next cell for you. After you enter data this way a few times, you develop a rhythm: type numbers, press Enter, type numbers, press Enter.

If you've filled your spreadsheet with data for the months other than January, you're ready to figure out the amount of money left over for each month, all in one shot. Follow these steps:

1. **Select the one cell that already has the net figured out (the cell that contains a formula).**

2. **Click the fill handle.**

3. **Drag the fill handle to the right.**

   If all has gone well, the difference between income and expenses is displayed for every month. Figure 9-3 shows how your screen looks if you typed the same numbers I typed.

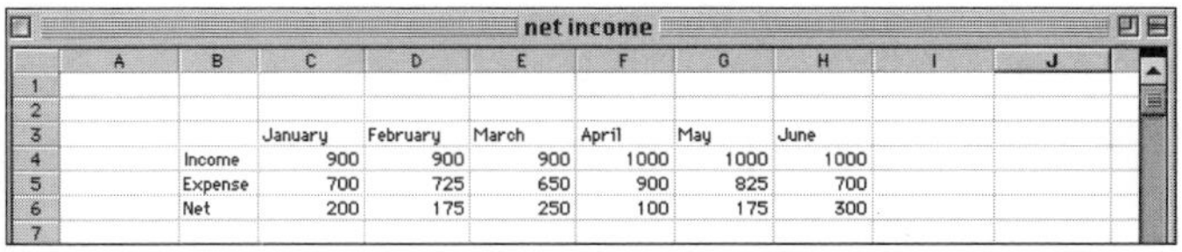

Figure 9-3:
A spread-
sheet with
net values
calculated
for every
month.

Formatting the spreadsheet with AutoFormat

If you're feeling cocky (and why wouldn't you, with a net income like yours?), try applying the AutoFormat feature to your work so that it looks a little nicer. You can see in Chapter 8 how to use AutoFormat, but here's a quick refresher:

1. **Select all the cells in the spreadsheet that have something in them.**

2. **Choose Format⇨AutoFormat.**

   The AutoFormat dialog box appears.

3. **Pick a formatting scheme from the list on the left.**

4. **Click OK.**

Figure 9-4 shows how the spreadsheet may look, depending on which AutoFormat scheme you choose.

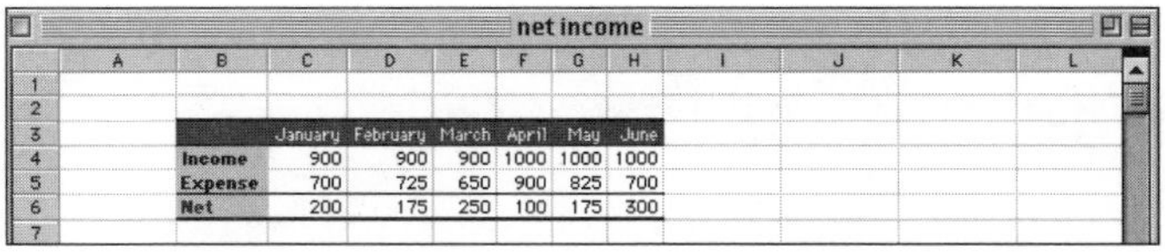

Figure 9-4:
A net-
income
spreadsheet
after
applying
Auto-
Formatting.

The hardest part about doing what you just did wasn't the formatting; it was the selecting. As usual, you have a choice of the ordinary way to do things and the unbelievably cool way to do things. Here's how to select cells the unbelievably cool way:

1. **Click _one_ of the cells you want to select.**

2. **Choose Edit⇨Go To.**

3. **Click Special.**

    The Go To Special dialog box appears.

4. **Click the Current Region radio button.**

5. **Click OK.**

    The active area of the spreadsheet gets selected.

Is this method exceptionally cool? You bet it is. Remember it, and dazzle your friends.

Want to _really_ impress people? Put the Select Current Region button on a toolbar so that it's literally a click away. Not sure how to add a button to a toolbar? Have no fear — the Microsoft Excel 98 Assistant is here. Follow these steps:

1. **Choose Help⇨Microsoft Excel Help.**

    The Office Assistant appears.

2. **Type the question** How do I add a button to a toolbar?

3. **Click the Search button.**

    The Assistant shows you the rest of what you need to know.

This method is even more cool than unbelievably cool. Cosmically cool, perhaps.

Adding another formula

Now you're ready to create another formula. You use the same spreadsheet to figure out how much you ought to be saving each month, based on the assumption that 25 percent of your net income is the amount you ought to save. Follow these steps:

1. **Click the cell below the word _Net_ and type** Savings.

2. **Move one cell to the right and type** = (an equal sign).

3. **Click the cell directly above the one that contains the Net amount.**

4. **Type * (an asterisk).**

   The asterisk tells Excel to multiply. The easiest way to enter an asterisk is to press the asterisk key on the numeric keypad.

5. **Type** 25%.

   Typing **0.25** also works.

6. **Press Enter on the keyboard or click the check mark next to the formula bar.**

   Your answer appears in the cell.

You can drag the cell's fill handle to the right to fill in the formula for the other months. If you change the income or expense data, your savings numbers change as well. The formula is live — not a one-time deal.

Editing a formula

You have to know how to edit formulas because people sometimes make mistakes or simply change their minds. Yes, it could even happen to you.

Suppose that you look at the spreadsheet you've been working on and think, "Gee, 25 percent seems like a lot to put away each month. I'll make it 10 percent." Okay, Mr. or Ms. Spendthrift — no problem. Just follow these steps:

1. **Click the cell that contains the savings calculation.**

   The formula bar should display something like C6*25%, as shown in Figure 9-5.

2. **Click the formula bar and change 25% to 10%.**

3. **Press Enter on the keyboard or click the check mark next to the formula bar.**

   Excel 98 computes a new savings target.

You can drag the cell's fill handle to the right, wiping out the old 25 percent formulas and replacing them with your new 10 percent ones. See how easy?

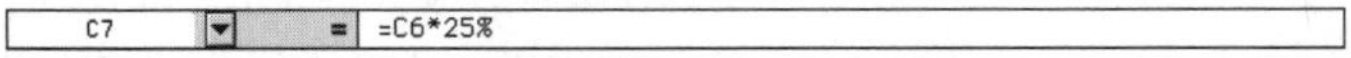

Figure 9-5:
A formula
on the
formula bar.

| C7 | ▼ | = | =C6*25% |

Deleting a formula

Think that editing a formula is easy? Wait until you try deleting one. This process is so easy that getting paid to write about it is embarrassing (but I'll get over it).

First, think about why you want to delete a formula. Maybe setting your savings goal as a percentage of net income is the wrong way to do things. Maybe simply having a dollar amount in mind each month — $50, for example — makes more sense. Follow these steps to make the change:

1. **Click the January savings cell.**

2. **Type** 50 **(assuming that you want to save $50 in January).**

3. **Press the Enter key on the keyboard or click the check mark to the left of the formula bar.**

   The number you typed replaces the formula.

If you want the formula to come back, you can choose Edit➪Undo Typing 50 in C7 (or whichever cell you typed in) — but only if you choose the command right away. Otherwise, you have to enter the formula the same way you did the first time.

Incidentally, you don't have to *replace* the formula with anything. You can just as easily (and just as properly) press the Delete key and type **50**. In that case, your cell would be blank — which, perhaps, is exactly what you're looking for.

May I See Your References?

Excel 98 uses *references* to describe cells and ranges. References are important because they keep Excel 98 from using the wrong numbers in your formulas. References come in two flavors — relative and absolute — as you see in this section.

Creating cell and range references

Excel 98 uses notations such as C1 to describe a cell in a spreadsheet. The first part of the notation — in this case, the C — specifies the column the cell is in. The second part of the notation — in this case, the 1 — specifies the row. You use the net income spreadsheet you've been working on in this chapter to illustrate the use of cell references in formulas.

Suppose that you want to see how much money you would save if you saved 15 percent of your net income each month. You could redo the formula easily enough. But what if you then want to see how much money you would save if you saved 16 percent? Or 17 percent? Or whatever? You would soon grow tired of redoing formulas. Wouldn't it be helpful if you could simply type the percentage number in a cell somewhere and have Excel 98 use it in the formula? Well, guess what — it's not only helpful but also easy to do, and you're going to do it now. Follow these steps:

1. **Click Cell C10.**

2. **Type** Savings Rate.

3. **Press Enter.**

4. **Select the cell below Savings Rate (C11).**

5. **Type** 15%.

6. **Press Enter.**

Did your savings numbers change? Of course not. You haven't worked the savings rate into the formula. All you've done so far is create a box in which to type a rate you want. Here's how you make Excel 98 use your number in the calculation:

1. **Select the cell containing the savings number for January.**

2. **Press the = (equal sign) key on the keyboard.**

3. **Click the cell containing the Savings Rate number (15%).**

4. **Press the * (asterisk) key.**

5. **Click the cell containing the net figure for January.**

6. **Press Enter.**

   Excel 98 figures out the target savings number, using your 15 percent rate.

If you type another rate (try it!), the number for January changes as soon as you press Enter.

Uh-oh — you forgot about the rest of the months. You haven't pulled the formula over from January to the rest of the months. Solving this problem is easy. Just click the savings figure for January, and grab the cell's fill handle; then drag the fill handle over to the column for June. Now you're done.

Or are you? Except for January, all the savings numbers are zero! What's going on here?

An examination of the formulas in the cells provides the answer. Start by clicking the savings cell for January. Look at the formula bar; the formula refers to the savings-rate number you typed earlier. If your spreadsheet looks just like mine at this point, the reference is to Cell C11.

Now click the savings cell for February. Notice that the formula doesn't refer to C11 anymore — it refers to *D*11 instead. Because Cell D11 is empty, the formula computes a big zero. The story is the same for the rest of the months. The formulas don't refer to C11; rather, the column references increase by 1 as you move across the months. For February, the reference is D11; for March, E11; for April, F11; and so on.

In many cases, this method of *relative referencing* is just what you needed. But not this time. You have to tell Excel 98 to use the value in Cell C11 all the time, no matter what, *absolutely.* Follow these steps:

1. **Click the savings cell for January and look at the formula bar.**

   You should see a formula like the one shown in Figure 9-6.

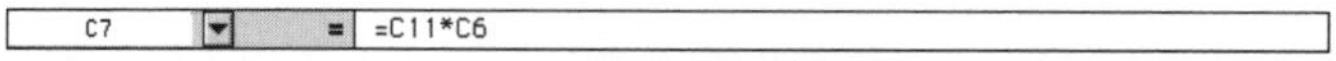

Figure 9-6:
A formula
with
relative
reference.

| C7 | ▼ | **=** | =C11*C6 |

2. **On the formula bar, change the formula to look like the one shown in Figure 9-7.**

   (Just click the formula bar and type the dollar signs in the appropriate places.)

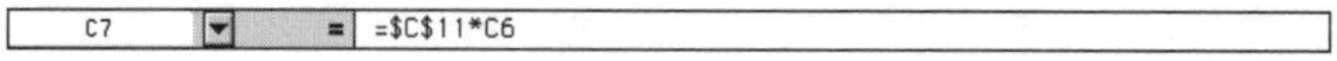

Figure 9-7:
A formula
with
absolute
reference.

| C7 | ▼ | **=** | =C11*C6 |

3. **Press Enter.**

No difference yet, right? But what happens when you drag the January cell's fill handle to the right? Ah — you get some savings numbers! If you click those numbers, you see that the formulas for each of them use the value in C11. This process is called using *absolute* references (as opposed to relative ones), and in cases like this one, it's exactly what is called for.

When you put a dollar sign before a column reference, you tell Excel 98 to refrain from changing the column. When you put a dollar sign before a row reference, you tell Excel 98 to refrain from changing the row. It is entirely possible, and in many cases entirely handy, to lock down only the row or only the column, rather than both.

That's about all there is where individual cell references are concerned. Sometimes, it's convenient to refer to a *group* of cells rather than to each one individually. Because Excel 98 uses range references often, you may as well find out how to do them yourself.

If you were to talk about the income numbers for all the months in your spreadsheet, you would talk about C4, D4, E4, F4, G4, and H4, using cell references. If you had a spreadsheet that covered several years, you would have to type a large number of cell references to describe the lot of them.

Range references are simply notations describing the starting and ending cells in question. Because your income numbers start at C4 and end at H4, the range reference becomes `C4:H4`.

Range references really just describe the beginning cell through the ending of a group of cells you have selected. Put a colon between the cell references, and there you are.

Grouping references with parentheses

I hate to do this to you, but I have to show you some math.

Suppose that you want to make a formula that subtracts one number from another and multiplies the answer by another number. (This is what you're doing in the savings row, except that you first figure out the net income in a separate formula.) Suppose that you want to do all these things in one shot. Here's one way the formula may look:

```
C7 = C4 - C5 * C11
```

If you plug in the numbers from your worksheet, you get this result:

```
C7 = 900 - 700 * 15%
```

And the answer is . . . $795. That can't be right, can it? No, it can't be. In this scenario, you save more than your net income for the month. Something must be wrong.

Something *is* wrong, and it's the formula. Because Excel 98 is not very good at figuring out what you mean, you have to be explicit. In this case, Excel 98 multiplied C5 and C11 and then subtracted their product from C4, which is not what you intended. You wanted *first* to figure out what C4 minus C5 is and then multiply the result by 15 percent. Here's how the formula has to look for Excel 98 to get the answer right:

```
C7 = (C4 - C5) * C11
```

And the answer is . . .$30, which makes more sense.

Technically, what you're doing is the same thing you did in high-school algebra class — namely, using the *distributive property*. In case you were sick that day, the distributive property states that for any real numbers A, B, and C:

```
(A + B) * C = A*C + B*C
```

(This question will not be on the final exam.)

The parentheses tell Excel 98 "do this first." All you have to do is get the parentheses into the formula, which is a snap. Just follow these steps:

1. **Click the January savings cell.**

2. **Press the = (equal-sign) key.**

3. **Click Cell C4.**

   Watch the formula bar as your formula takes shape.

4. **Press the minus (–) key.**

5. **Click Cell C5.**

   Again, notice how your formula is being recorded on the formula bar.

6. **Press the asterisk (multiply) key.**

7. **Click Cell C11.**

8. **Press Enter.**

   If all goes according to plan, your answer is $795.

I had to trick you into making a mistake to give you something to correct, and you've done the first part. Here's how to correct the mistake:

1. **Click the January savings cell.**

2. **Insert right and left parentheses into the appropriate places in the formula bar's formula.**

   You need an opening parenthesis before C4 and a closing one after C5.

3. **Press Enter.**

   Your answer should be $30.

Does this process seem to be complicated? It isn't, really. Just remember that Excel 98 evaluates the stuff inside parentheses before it performs any other calculations.

Excel 98 is smart enough to catch — and offer to fix — common mistakes and typos you may make in a formula. If you leave off a parenthesis and press the Enter key, for example, the Office Assistant complains and asks to fix the problem, as shown in Figure 9-8.

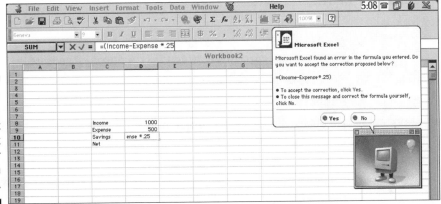

Figure 9-8: The Office Assistant tries to fix your formula typo.

Using Functions

Remember sines and cosines? How about square roots? No? Excel 98 does. In fact, Excel 98 remembers these and 326 other _functions_. With functions, you plug in the numbers, and Excel 98 computes the answer. In this section, you get your feet wet with functions by computing an average monthly income, using the same spreadsheet you've been using in this chapter.

Suppose that you want your average monthly income to show up in the cell just to the right of June's income figure. Follow these steps:

1. **Click the desired cell.**

2. **Press the equal key on the keyboard.**

3. **Choose Insert⇨Function.**

   The Paste Function dialog box appears, as shown in Figure 9-9. Notice that the Excel 98 functions are divided into categories.

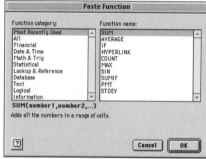

4. **If you want to see all the functions, click the All category; otherwise, choose a category to see only that category's functions.**

   Because Average is a statistical function, you should click Statistical.

5. **Choose Average from the list on the right side of the dialog box.**

   Excel 98 displays a description of the Average function at the bottom of the dialog box.

6. **Click OK.**

   Excel displays the formula palette to help you finish the formula. Excel's first guess — that you want to average all the cells in the income row — is correct.

7. **Click OK in the formula palette.**

Notice that Excel 98 uses a range reference (C4:H4) in the formula rather than list each cell in the computation individually.

This news probably won't come as a shock to you: you can use another method to put a function into a formula, and it's faster. Use this other method to compute the average for the expenses by following these steps:

1. **Click the cell at the end of the expenses row (just below where you figured out the average for income).**

2. **Press the equal key on the keyboard.**

3. **Open the pop-up menu that appears to the left of the formula bar (see Figure 9-10).**

   This list contains recently used functions, including AVERAGE.

4. **Choose AVERAGE.**

   You're back in a familiar place.

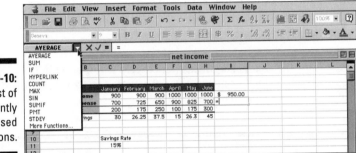

Figure 9-10:
The list of recently used functions.

Excel 98 should have displayed C5:H5 in the formula palette. If not, you need to show Excel 98 which numbers you're averaging. Follow these steps:

1. **Click the small button in the formula palette (see Figure 9-11).**

   The Formula Palette shrinks to enable you to select the cells you want to use in the function. Select Cells C5 through H5.

2. **Click the button you clicked to shrink the formula palette.**

   The palette expands, showing the range of cells you want to average.

3. **Click OK.**

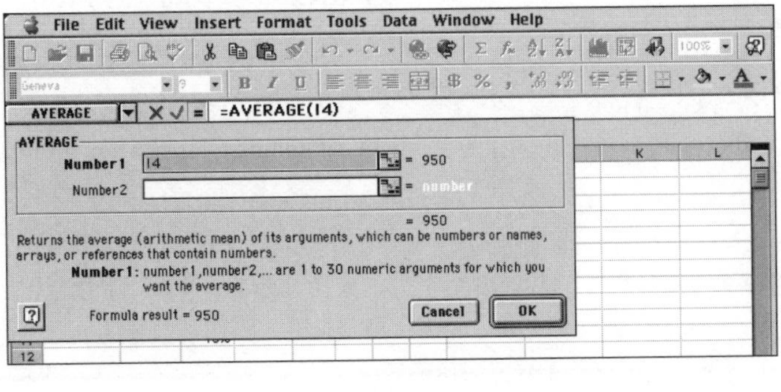

Figure 9-11:
Click to shrink the formula palette.

You can do one more thing: Figure out how much money you will save if you manage to meet your savings goal each month. To do it in the easiest way possible, follow these steps:

1. **Click the cell at the end of the savings row.**

2. **Click the AutoSum button on the toolbar.**

   The symbol on the button is a capital sigma — something that symbolizes summation to math majors.

   Excel 98 guesses that you want to add everything to the left of the current cell, which is why it put SUM(C7:H7) in the formula.

3. **Press Enter.**

Nine times out of ten, Excel 98 guesses correctly when you click the AutoSum button. If it doesn't guess correctly, you can fix things by editing the formula on the formula bar.

Everyday Excel 98 functions

Even though Excel 98 has hundreds of available functions, most of them are specialized functions for people who do statistics, hardcore financial forecasting, or scientific calculations. The following list gives you a rundown of what commonly used Excel 98 functions do, followed by an example of their format:

AVERAGE: Finds the average of a range of cells

AVERAGE(number1,number2)

CONCATENATE: Joins several text strings into one text string

CONCATENATE (text1,text2)

COUNT: Counts how many cells in a range contain numbers rather than text

COUNT(value1,value2)

IF: Applies a logical test in a formula, such as performing a calculation only if the value of a particular cell is zero

IF(logical_test,value_if_true,value_if_false)

MAX: Finds the largest number in a range of cells

MAX(number1,number2)

MIN: Finds the smallest number in a range of cells

MIN(number1,number2)

ROUND: Rounds a decimal number to a specified number of places

ROUND(number,num_digits)

SQRT: Finds the square root of a number

SQRT(number)

SUM: Adds the values in two or more cells

SUM(number1,number2)

Chapter 10

Working with Worksheets and Workbooks

- -

In This Chapter

▶ Naming worksheets

▶ Creating and deleting worksheets

▶ Linking worksheets with formulas

▶ Adding worksheets to workbooks

- -

*E*xcel 98 calls the documents you make *workbooks* and the pages in the workbooks *worksheets*. Pages, you say? Yessiree, Bob! Excel 98 workbooks can have as many pages as you want them to have, and this chapter tells you all about them.

Naming Worksheets

Before you start naming worksheets, you have to be clear about the worksheet concept. Here goes.

When you create a new Excel 98 document, it's an empty grid of cells. The cells go to the right for 256 columns, and they go down for 65,536 rows. Although it sounds like a great deal of room to work in, it isn't always enough. Sometimes, you need a second page.

Or you don't *need* a second page, but you want one anyway. Suppose that you're keeping track of the students in a small school and you want to keep the first grade, second grade, and third grades on separate spreadsheets. One way, of course, is to make separate Excel 98 documents for each grade. A better way, however, is to make separate pages — or *worksheets* — in a single Excel 98 document, called a *workbook*. This way, you have only one document to keep track of, one document to back up, and one document taking up room on your screen.

Figure 10-1 shows how you can set up the first grade's worksheet. (Granted, the class is small.)

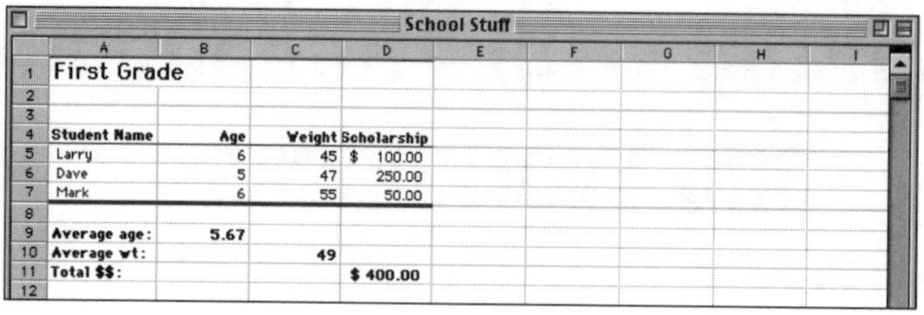

Figure 10-1:
A work-
sheet for
the first
grade.

		School Stuff							
	A	B	C	D	E	F	G	H	I
1	First Grade								
2									
3									
4	Student Name	Age	Weight	Scholarship					
5	Larry	6	45	$ 100.00					
6	Dave	5	47	250.00					
7	Mark	6	55	50.00					
8									
9	Average age:	5.67							
10	Average wt:		49						
11	Total $$:			$ 400.00					
12									

Naming the sheets makes it easier for you and for Excel 98 to keep track of which sheet you're working on. Name the sheet before you go any further:

1. **Double-click the tab that says Sheet1 at the bottom of the window.**

    The current title (the generic, default Sheet1) is highlighted.

2. **Type the title you want for the sheet.**

    For example, you could type **First Grade**.

3. **Press Enter.**

If you ever feel like changing the name again, just repeat these steps. Excel 98 enables you to change the name of a worksheet whenever you want.

You can use one of a couple of ways to make a second sheet just like the first — this time, with information for the second grade. Here's one of the easiest methods:

1. **Select all the cells that have something in them.**

    You can select all the cells (whether they contain something or not) if you want. The fastest way is to press ⌘+A, which is the shortcut for Select All.

2. **Choose Edit⇨Copy.**

    Although nothing seems to happen, a copy of the First Grade page has been placed on the Clipboard, ready for pasting.

3. **Double-click the Sheet2 tab.**

    This step has the dual effect of switching to the second worksheet in the workbook and of selecting the name of the sheet so that you can give it a new name.

4. **Rename the sheet by typing** Second Grade **and pressing Enter.**

    Now you're ready to paste.

5. Choose Edit⇨Paste.

Your new Second Grade worksheet looks just like the first!

You can change the data for the Second Grade sheet by just typing over it. One of the nice things about this copy-and-paste technique is that it brings along the formatting, so make sure that you like the formatting of the First Grade page before you start copying and pasting it all over the place. There's no sense in doing the formatting more than once.

At this point, creating a Third Grade worksheet should be a snap for you. Go ahead and do it, following the same steps you used to make the Second Grade sheet.

Now try moving between the worksheets. Just click the correct tab — the one with the correct name at the bottom of the window. Notice that the worksheet in the front has a white tab, whereas the other worksheets have gray tabs, as shown in Figure 10-2. That color difference is the only clue you have to which worksheet you're in, so watch for it!

Figure 10-2:
The white tab shows you the active, frontmost worksheet in the workbook.

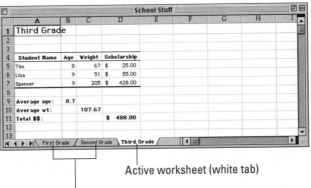

Active worksheet (white tab)

Inactive worksheets (gray tabs)

Creating and Deleting Worksheets

You're probably wondering what happens if you want another sheet — for the fourth grade, maybe? You don't have any more worksheet tabs to click, so it looks as though you're out of luck. As you may suspect, however, you aren't really out of luck because you aren't really out of sheets.

By default (which means "unless you explicitly take steps to make a change"), Excel 98 puts three worksheets in a workbook. You can change this default action by choosing Tools⇨Preferences. The rest you can figure out on your own.

No matter how many worksheets your workbook has, you can always add another. (Excel 98 places no limits on the number of sheets in a workbook, though your computer may poop out after a couple of hundred.) Adding a sheet is as easy as choosing Insert⇨Worksheet.

Excel 98 doesn't necessarily put the new sheet where you want it, however. Excel 98 doesn't even ask. Instead, the new sheet is placed *before* the sheet you're now using. What a drag.

Actually, "a drag" is exactly what's called for here. Want to move a sheet to a new location? All you do is drag it:

1. **Click the tab for the sheet you're trying to move, and hold down the mouse button.**

2. **Drag the tab to the location you want.**

   A small, black triangle points to the place where the sheet will land if you drop it.

3. **When the triangle points just after the Third Grade tab, release the mouse button.**

How about that!

Deleting worksheets is just as easy. Activate the sheet you want to delete and then choose Edit⇨Delete Sheet. Excel 98 gives you one chance to change your mind, although that's all you get. When that chance is gone, it's gone. Undo doesn't work.

The one way to get the sheet back is to close the document without saving it. Excel 98 asks whether you want to save an unsaved workbook, and if you've made a big mistake, the answer is No. The next time you open that workbook, it reverts to the way that it looked the last time you saved it. Saving your workbook just before you do something extreme, such as delete sheets, makes this technique more useful; otherwise, you lose too much work.

Linking Worksheets with Formulas

Although it's useful to have different worksheets within a workbook, one of the real strengths of Excel is its capability to make all the worksheets cooperate. In the grade example used in the preceding section, it would be a good idea to have a single summary page with results from each of the individual grade pages.

If you don't have four worksheets in your workbook, add one and name it Summary. Drag the Summary sheet to a place *in front of* the First Grade sheet. (The idea is to make this page an executive summary, with the supporting data behind it. This kind of thing makes the boss very happy.)

Listing just the total amount of scholarship money on the Summary page, by grade, may be interesting:

1. **On your summary page, create some labels for the data, as shown in Figure 10-3.**

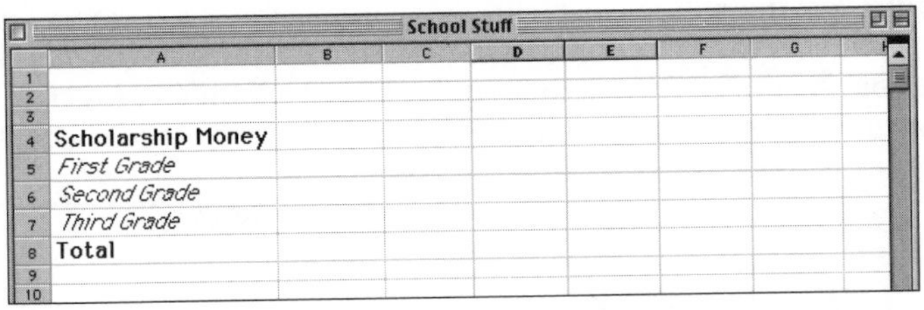

Figure 10-3: Labels on the Summary sheet.

2. **To get the numbers from the individual sheets to show up on the Summary sheet, start by clicking the cell next to the First Grade label.**

   For this example, click Cell B5.

3. **Type = (an equal sign), which is how every formula in Excel 98 begins.**

4. **Click the First Grade tab to switch to the First Grade worksheet.**

5. **Click the cell of the First Grade sheet that contains the Total Scholarship figure.**

6. **Press Enter.**

   Excel 98 takes you back to the Summary sheet, where the formula was created, and you see the total scholarship number from the First Grade sheet.

To see whether the Summary sheet is updated if you change something on the First Grade sheet, follow these steps:

1. **Switch to the First Grade sheet by clicking its tab.**

2. **Change the scholarship amount for Dave from 150 to 250.**

   Notice that the total scholarship money for First Grade changes, as it should, to $400.

3. **Switch back to the Summary sheet by clicking its tab.**

   Hey — the sheet has been updated! The Summary sheet's number really is linked to the corresponding number on the First Grade sheet.

Using AutoSum

Repeating this process with the Second Grade and Third Grade sheets is a snap, so go ahead and do it. That Total cell on the Summary sheet is just waiting for you to fill it in. If you click it and then click the AutoSum button on the toolbar, Excel 98 creates the formula for you.

If you click the AutoSum button, you get a chance to review what Excel 98 thinks you want to add. If Excel guesses right, all you have to do is press Enter. If Excel doesn't guess right, you can change the formula and *then* press Enter. On the other hand, when you have a hunch that Excel 98 will get it right on the first try, you can *double-click* the AutoSum button. When you do, Excel not only figures out the formula but also, in effect, presses the Enter key for you. Pretty swell.

Analyzing your data

After the data has been brought into the Summary sheet, you can do some analysis on it. You may want to know, percentagewise, how much of the total scholarship money is going to the first, second, and third grades, for example. To figure that out, follow these steps:

1. **Give Column C the heading** Percentages.

2. **Click Cell C5, which is next to the First Grade scholarship-money cell.**

3. **Press the = (equal) key to begin a formula.**

4. **Click the cell that contains the First Grade total.**

5. **Press the / (slash, or division) key.**

6. **Click the Total number (B8).**

7. **Press Enter.**

The number doesn't look like a percentage, but ignore that fact for now. Repeat Steps 2 through 7 for the second- and third-grade figures, and you end up with something that looks like Figure 10-4.

Figure 10-4:
A summary
sheet
showing
poorly
formatted
percentages.

	A	B	C	D	E	F	G
1							
2							
3							
4	Scholarship Money		Percentages				
5	*First Grade*	$ 400.00	0.3167063				
6	*Second Grade*	$ 375.00	0.2969121				
7	*Third Grade*	$ 488.00	0.3863816				
8	Total	$ 1,263.00					
9							
10							

School Stuff

To change the appearance of those percentage figures, follow these steps:

1. **Select the cells that contain the percentages (Cells C5 through C7).**

2. **Click the Percent button on the Formatting toolbar.**

Your numbers look a little more like percentages. The problem, however, is that the percentages don't add up to 100. (In this example, they add up to 101.)

The problem has to do with the way Excel 98 rounds numbers. The only way to really see what's going on is to *add precision* (more decimal places) to the percentage numbers:

1. **Select the percentage numbers again, if they aren't still selected.**

2. **Click the Increase Decimal button on the Formatting toolbar.**

Your numbers now show another decimal place, and now (because the numbers aren't being rounded off) they do indeed add up to 100.

Using worksheet references

You probably understand the concept of cell references, and you may even have a feeling for what range references are. Now you take another step in the same direction, a step that takes you to *worksheet references, which define relationships between two or more worksheets.*

Worksheet references are important because Excel 98 needs to know which sheet you're talking about when you say "Use Cell D11." The worksheet references are inserted automatically when you make your formulas the way you do in the preceding sections. If you wonder what the formulas look like, click the cell that contains the first-grade scholarship total (B5) on the Summary sheet; then look at the formula bar, which should look like this line:

```
='First Grade'!D11
```

The first part of the formula tells you the name of the worksheet. Excel requires that the name be enclosed in single quotes. You can't use double quotes because Excel uses double quotes to store text in formulas. The exclamation point just says, "The stuff up to now was a worksheet reference." D11 is just D11, but not any old D11 — it's the D11 on the First Grade sheet.

Although you can type this formula (don't forget the single quotes, and don't use double quotes), having Excel 98 do it for you is much easier.

Adding Worksheets to Workbooks

Combining individual spreadsheets into workbooks makes a great deal of sense, and it's easy to do if you're thinking about it at the beginning. The problem is that you're likely to have some old Excel 4 or 5 single-sheet documents lying around, in a one-sheet-per-document format, and you don't want to re-create them in a multiple-sheet format just because I say that that format is cool. What you might do, though, is *combine* the existing sheets into multiple-sheet workbooks, as long as it's easy enough to do. You can decide for yourself whether the steps are easy enough:

1. **Create a new Excel 98 document and save it.**

   (You bring the other documents into this one.)

2. **Open one of your old documents, and make sure that the page you want to move or copy is in front.**

   Click the tabs at the bottom of the window to switch to the proper sheet, if necessary.

3. **Choose Edit⇨Move or Copy Sheet.**

   A poorly designed dialog box appears, as shown in Figure 10-5. This dialog box is so unintuitive that it feels like the first time every time you see it, which shows that Excel 98 still has room for improvement.

   You use the Move or Copy dialog box to tell Excel 98 to which workbook you want to move or copy the current worksheet and where (in front of which current worksheet page) you want to put it.

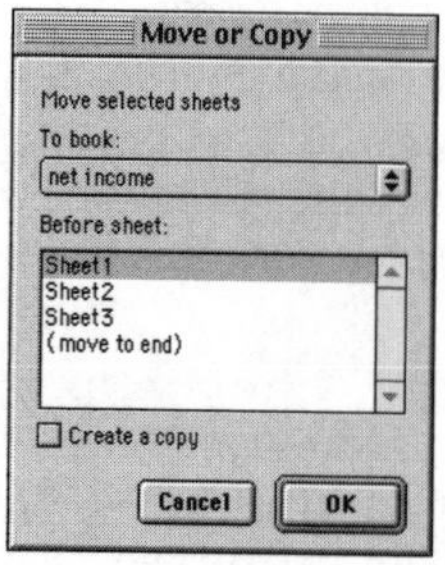

Figure 10-5:
The Move
or Copy
dialog box.

4. **Choose a target workbook from the To Book drop-down list (where the sheet will go).**

5. **In the Before Sheet scroll box, select the worksheet (page) that the moved or copied sheet will be placed in front of.**

6. **Decide whether to move or copy the sheet.**

   (Copying is safer and usually the better choice.)

7. **Click OK.**

Excel 98 does what you ask it to, and if you check, you see that you have indeed added a worksheet to your new Excel 98 document. Half the time, you will have the wrong sheet in the wrong place, but you get better with practice. Remember to save your documents just *before* making major moves such as this one, just to be safe.

Chapter 11

Turning Numbers into Pictures with Charts

● ●

● ●

*I*f a picture's worth a thousand words, then a chart is worth a million and twelve cells in a spreadsheet. Excel 98 lets you turn humdrum rows and columns of numbers into eye-grabbing, message-sending, wallop-packing charts — all without breaking a sweat.

The Right Kind of Chart

As far as Excel 98 is concerned, charts come in 12 basic types. Choosing the right chart type for the type of data you're representing is important because the wrong chart type may either mislead viewers or hopelessly confuse them. The figures in this section display each chart type and explain how each one is used.

A *column chart,* as shown in Figure 11-1, is perfect for showing how something changes over time, such as sales or expenses per quarter.

A *bar chart* is much like a column chart turned on its side, as shown in Figure 11-2. Most bar charts could have been column charts, but bar charts are useful when you are not trying to emphasize the passage of time.

A *line chart* displays the same kind of data as a column chart, with the addition of *trend lines,* which show you how the data is changing, as shown in Figure 11-3. With a line chart, you convey an idea of *how* something changed, not just what the changes were.

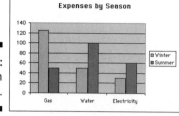

Figure 11-1:
A column chart.

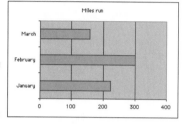

Figure 11-2:
A bar chart.

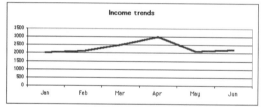

Figure 11-3:
A line chart.

Seemingly everybody's favorite, a *pie chart* is excellent for showing percentages of something, as shown in Figure 11-4. The pie wedges always add up to 100 percent.

Figure 11-5 shows an *XY chart* (or *scatter chart*), which plots data points against two axes (X and Y). This chart type is commonly used for scientific data.

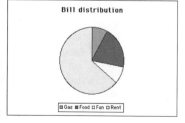

Figure 11-4:
A pie chart.

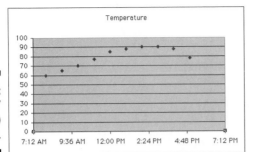

Figure 11-5:
An XY
(scatter)
chart.

An *area chart* is a cross between a column chart and a pie chart. As you can see in Figure 11-6, this type of chart displays, in essence, pie-chart data changing over time.

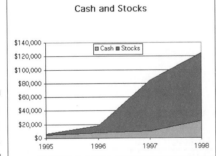

Figure 11-6:
An area
chart.

I'm tempted to tell you that doughnut charts are for charting doughnuts, but I'll refrain. A *doughnut chart* is much like a pie chart, in fact, with one pie placed atop another, as shown in Figure 11-7. Multiple pie charts can convey the same information, but not as neatly as a single doughnut chart.

A *radar chart* looks like a line chart with multiple-value axes. This chart type shows how the shape of the connected lines can show how two things are similar or different (see Figure 11-8).

Figure 11-7:
A doughnut
chart.

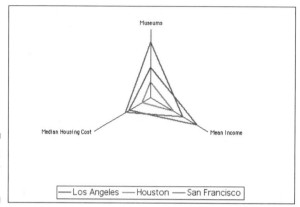

Figure 11-8:
A radar
chart.

A *surface chart* is similar to a topographic map, showing areas that fall into the same range of values, as shown in Figure 11-9. This type of chart is easy to make incorrectly!

A *bubble chart* is a variation of an XY chart. Figure 11-10 shows how the sizes of the bubbles represent the value of a third variable.

A *stock chart* can be used to display any changing data (including stock high–low–close prices). This type of chart, as shown in Figure 11-11, is similar to an XY chart with multiple Ys per X.

Cone, cylinder, and *pyramid charts* are nothing more than gussied-up column and bar charts, as shown in Figure 11-12.

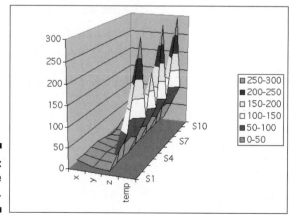

Figure 11-9:
A surface
chart.

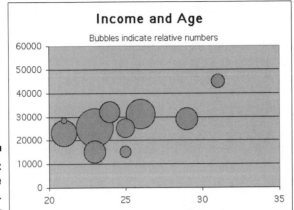

Figure 11-10:
A bubble
chart.

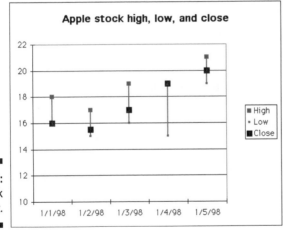

Figure 11-11:
A stock
chart.

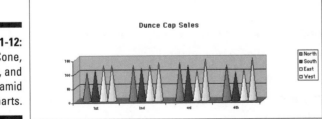

Figure 11-12:
Cone,
cylinder, and
pyramid
charts.

Enough about what charts are and when to use them! In the following section, you get on with the business of making them.

Creating a Chart with the Chart Wizard

You can use Excel 98 to make a chart in at least a couple of ways. The Chart Wizard is by far the easiest way, especially for beginners. In this section, you use the Chart Wizard to make a simple chart, and when you're done, you'll know enough to make almost any type of chart you want. To turn those boring numbers into a thrilling column chart, follow these steps:

1. **For starters, you need a spreadsheet with some data in it. Create a new Excel 98 document and put data in it, as shown in Figure 11-13.**

Figure 11-13:
A spread-
sheet with
data
in it for
charting.

	A	B	C	D	E	F	G	H	I
1									
2	Quarterly Sales by Region								
3									
4		1st Qtr	2nd Qtr	3rd Qtr	4th Qtr				
5	North	100	110	105	115				
6	South	60	75	70	80				
7	East	95	105	105	100				
8	West	125	115	135	140				
9									
10									

Charting Examples

2. **Select the portion of the spreadsheet that contains the data you want to chart.**

   Figure 11-14 shows you the right stuff to select.

Figure 11-14:
Selecting
the data you
want to
chart.

	A	B	C	D	E	F	G	H	I
1									
2	Quarterly Sales by Region								
3									
4		1st Qtr	2nd Qtr	3rd Qtr	4th Qtr				
5	North	100	110	105	115				
6	South	60	75	70	80				
7	East	95	105	105	100				
8	West	125	115	135	140				
9									
10									

Charting Examples

3. **Click the Chart Wizard button on the Standard toolbar.**

   The Chart Wizard dialog box appears.

4. **Choose Column as the chart type.**

5. **Choose the first chart subtype, as shown in Figure 11-15.**

6. **Click the Next button.**

   The next page in the Chart Wizard dialog box shows a miniature version of your chart-to-be.

Figure 11-15:
The Chart
Wizard
dialog box
with the
column
chart type
and first
subtype
selected.

7. **Assume that Excel 98 guessed correctly, and click Next.**

   Page 3 of the Chart Wizard gives you the opportunity to pretty things up.

8. **Enter a title for the chart in the Chart Title box.**

9. **Enter labels for the X (horizontal) and Y (vertical) axes.**

   You can click the tabs across the top of the dialog box to do a number of things to the chart (but don't do them now).

10. **Click Next.**

    The last page of the Chart Wizard gives you a choice between putting your chart in a new worksheet (in the same workbook) or in the same worksheet that contains your data.

11. **Choose As Object In to place the chart in the worksheet you're working on.**

12. **Click Finish.**

Wow! You have a chart, and it's much nicer to look at than the numbers. Notice that the chart itself is selected, and so are parts of the data. A special Chart toolbar has also appeared. Figure 11-16 shows the changes.

Excel 98 outlines with a thin, blue border the data (numbers) it plotted. The program outlines the *series labels* (the words in the legend) with a thin, green border and outlines the *category labels* (the words across the category axis) in purple.

The chart is *live,* which means that if you click one of the cells containing the information you charted and then change that data, the chart changes too. Because of this arrangement, you can make the chart once and forget about it because the chart is always connected to the data in the spreadsheet. This is known as A Very Good Feature.

Series labels   Category labels   Data

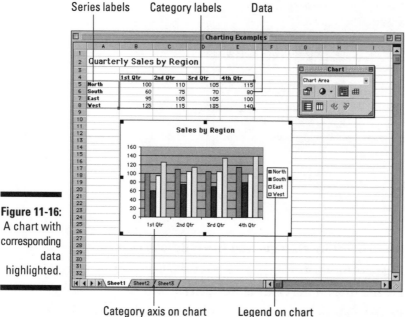

Figure 11-16:
A chart with
corresponding
data
highlighted.

Category axis on chart   Legend on chart

Modifying a Chart

Excel 98 does a good job of guessing what you want in a chart, but some-
times you have another chart in mind. Or maybe after seeing the chart
Excel 98 created, you come up with another idea. Or maybe you just want to
experiment with different options to see how things turn out. No problem —
Excel 98 charts are flexible, and you can easily change just about anything.
The Chart toolbar, as shown in Figure 11-17, comes in handy for this purpose.

Format Chart Area

Chart Type

Legend

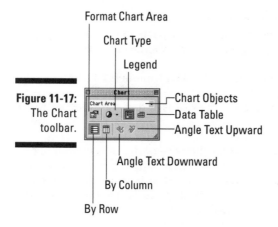

Figure 11-17:
The Chart
toolbar.

Chart Objects
Data Table
Angle Text Upward

Angle Text Downward

By Column

By Row

Changing the chart size

Start by changing the size of the chart. The Chart toolbar has a pop-up menu, which you use to select parts of the chart for later modification. Follow these steps:

1. **Open the Chart Objects pop-up menu.**

2. **Choose Chart Area, as shown in Figure 11-18.**

   The entire chart area (not just the chart but also the area around it, including the legend and the title) is selected.

3. **Click and drag a handle at the edge of the chart to resize the chart.**

4. **Release the mouse button.**

Figure 11-18:
Choosing
Chart Area.

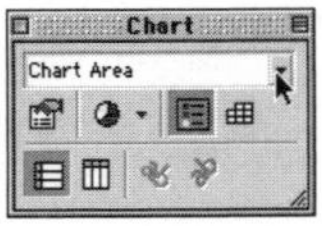

Changing the chart orientation

Now you can change the nature of the chart. Right now, you have a chart with different-colored columns for North, South, East, and West. Maybe it would be more interesting if the chart had North, South, East, and West across the bottom as category labels and 1st Qtr, 2nd Qtr, 3rd Qtr, and 4th Qtr in the legend.

To make these changes, click the By Column button on the Chart toolbar. The chart changes as you want it to. If you click the By Rows button, you change it back.

If you forget which toolbar button is which, just place the mouse pointer on a button and wait a moment. Excel 98 displays the button's name on a small, yellow label, called a *ScreenTip*.

When you click the By Column button, you're telling Excel 98 that you want to look at *columns* of data rather than rows. For the example in this section, the *columns* (1st Qtr, 2nd Qtr, 3rd Qtr, and 4th Qtr) are the data series — not the rows. When you click the By Row button, you're telling Excel 98 just the opposite. A *data series* is a group of numbers in a particular category. Data series are a big deal because Excel 98 creates entirely different charts for different data series. The most important thing is to remember that you can flip things around by clicking the By Column and By Row buttons.

Changing the chart type

You can change the chart type, if you want. (Choosing a chart type is the first step in the Chart Wizard process.) Naturally, you can wipe out what you have and run through the Chart Wizard again, but you don't have to do that. Instead, you can use the Chart toolbar and change the type instantly, without doing any other work:

1. **Open the Chart Type pop-up menu on the Chart toolbar.**

   A long list of chart types appears.

2. **Slide down to the button labeled Bar Chart.**

   If you don't see the label, wait a moment for it to appear.

   You can tear off the list of chart types and make them a separate toolbar. Your clue that this act is possible is the double dotted lines across the top of the Chart Type list. To tear off the list, just click the down arrow next to the Chart Type button, drag to the edge of the menu that appears, and then *keep going.* The menu sticks to your mouse pointer, and when you release the mouse button, you see a separate Chart Type toolbar, giving you a choice of places from which to choose a chart type.

3. **Release the mouse button.**

   The result is shown in Figure 11-19.

Figure 11-19:
A finished
bar chart.

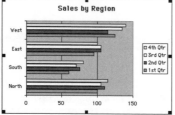

You can easily spin things around by clicking the By Column and By Row buttons. Give them a try! Notice that if you click By Row, the chart may appear to be upside down, as shown in Figure 11-20 (with 4th Qtr at the top and 1st Qtr at the bottom).

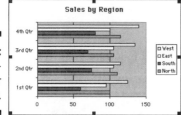

Sales by Region
4th Qtr
3rd Qtr
2nd Qtr
1st Qtr
□ West
□ East
■ South
■ North
0   50   100   150

Figure 11-20:
An upside-
down bar
chart.

Changing the axis of a bar chart

You shouldn't be surprised to know that you can change the axis of a bar chart. All you need are your friend the Chart toolbar and a little instruction. You want to change the category axis (the value axis is the one that displays numbers, and you do *not* want to change that one). Follow these steps:

1. **Choose Category Axis from the Chart Objects pop-up menu on the Chart toolbar.**

2. **Click the Format Axis button.**

   This button changes names, depending on what is selected in the Chart Objects list.

   The Format Axis dialog box appears, displaying a gaggle of options. Because you want to reverse the order of things in the category axis, and nothing in the Patterns section can help you in this regard, you're in the wrong place and should move on.

3. **Click the Scale tab at the top of the dialog box.**

   (Check out the other tabs in this dialog box on your own someday.)

4. **Click the Categories in Reverse Order check box.**

5. **Click OK.**

You now know the general routine for changing part of a chart: Choose a part from the Chart Objects drop-down list, click the Format button, and then choose some options. As usual, you can do these tasks in other ways, although they're harder and slower. What's the point?

Part IV
Getting Net Savvy with Internet Explorer and Outlook Express

The 5th Wave   By Rich Tennant

SOFTWARE APPLICATION
TESTING CENTER

EXIT

"WE TEST FOR COMPATIBILITY, PERFORMANCE, SERVICE, AND FORMATTING. IF IT FAILS THESE, THEN IT'S TESTED FOR THE DISTANCE IT CAN BE SAILED ACROSS THE PARKING LOT AND ONTO THE EXPRESSWAY."

In this part . . .

In just a few short years, the Internet has gone from a meek academic backwater to a bustling marketplace of information and ideas. The World Wide Web has begun to change the way people communicate, and the explosion in the use of electronic mail has accelerated the shrinking of our world.

This part of the book shows you how to use two Office 98 Internet programs, Internet Explorer and Outlook Express, to browse the Web, download files, send and receive e-mail, and participate in Usenet, the worldwide bulletin board.

Chapter 12

Web Surfing with Internet Explorer 4.0

• •

In This Chapter

▶ Finding out about the Internet

▶ Using the button bar

▶ Going places with the address bar

▶ Playing Favorites

▶ Subscribing to Web sites

▶ Channel surfing

▶ Downloading files

▶ Customizing Internet Explorer

• •

*E*very day, more and more people use the Internet to share information, learn, and play. Most of this action happens via electronic mail and a part of the Internet called the World Wide Web. Because the Internet has become such an important part of the way people work, Office 98 includes many ways to use the Internet to make your job easier. If you're interested in knowing how to use the Office 98 programs to share information over the Internet, check out Chapter 19.

Office 98 comes with two programs that help you work directly with the Internet. Microsoft Internet Explorer enables you to use the World Wide Web and download files, and Microsoft Outlook Express enables you to send and receive e-mail and access the Internet's worldwide bulletin board. Chapters 13 and 14 cover Outlook Express, and this chapter tells you what you need to know about Internet Explorer.

A Bite-Size Guide to the Internet

Unless you've been hiding in a cave since 1994, chances are that you've heard and read more about the Internet than you ever wanted to know. For you cave dwellers (and for anyone who hasn't really cared about the Internet until now), here's a thumbnail view of the Internet.

First, you can't point at anything and say "That's the Internet." The Internet is nothing more than thousands of computers connected by extremely fast phone lines and speaking a common (computer) language. These computers are owned by private citizens, universities, businesses, governments — any person or organization that can hook a computer to the worldwide network. People use the network to send a tremendous amount and variety of information around the world. Using the Internet, you have access to up-to-the-minute news, online encyclopedias, the latest research, entertainment features, and lots more.

Because no group owns the Internet, there tends to be no one to whom you can complain when things go wrong. Instead, organizations own and maintain their little pieces of the Internet, and voluntary groups work together to make sure that things run smoothly.

To access the Internet, you need a few things:

- ✔ **A Macintosh.** Almost any Mac will do; I've successfully used a 1987-vintage Macintosh SE/30 for such tasks as e-mail. If you want to use the World Wide Web, however, you should use a Macintosh that supports color, which includes every Mac made since about 1988.

- ✔ **Mac OS 7.5 or later.** If you're still using an earlier version of the system software, you should definitely upgrade.

- ✔ **A modem or other type of connection to the Internet.** Most businesses, for example, have their Macintoshes linked in a Local Area Network, and the network has the Internet connection.

- ✔ **An Internet Service Provider (ISP).** An *ISP* is a company that is in the business of connecting people and organizations to the Internet. If you're an individual Internet user, you should find a reliable ISP by asking your Net-savvy friends. If you're a corporate user, your employer should already have a relationship with an ISP for the company's network.

For a much more detailed account of the Internet, I recommend that you buy *The Internet For Macs For Dummies,* 3rd Edition, by Charles Seiter (published by IDG Books Worldwide, Inc.).

Rather than focus on what the Internet is, you should know what you can do with the Internet. Many types of services run on the Internet; the four most important are discussed in this section.

The World Wide Web

Until the invention of the World Wide Web, the Internet was used mainly to send e-mail and files among a relatively small group of researchers at universities, in the military, and in private business. The Web lets you easily access text and pictures from all over the world, and the experience is so interesting that the Web has become the focus of the Internet. In fact, many people think that the Web *is* the Internet. That isn't the case, however; the Web is just one of the many services that run over the Internet.

You access the Web with a program called a *Web browser,* two of which are included with Mac OS 8. One of them is Microsoft Internet Explorer (which also comes with Office 98), and the other is Netscape Navigator. Despite all you may have read about the so-called browser wars, it doesn't really matter whether you use Internet Explorer or Navigator to browse the Web; because both companies are in fierce competition, the two browsers are roughly equivalent in features and capabilities. Naturally, this chapter focuses on the browser that comes with Office 98.

Wondering how big the Web is? You're not alone. One recent study estimated that as of March 1998, at least 275 million pages were on the Web. The Web isn't standing still, either. The same study showed that the Web doubled in size in less than nine months and was growing at a rate of about 20 million pages per month!

File downloads

A terrific thing about the Internet is the easy availability of useful programs and other files you can copy from machines anywhere in the world over the phone lines to your Mac. This transfer process is called *downloading*. Sending a file from your machine to another is called *uploading*. Many places on the Web are repositories of these downloadable files. These places are called *FTP sites,* so named because of the method used to download files.

Because the Internet started as the computer network built by geeks for other geeks, tons of barely comprehensible terms, acronyms, and jargon are associated with it. Here's a perfect example: To get different computers to communicate, the Internet gurus came up with standard rules for tasks such as sending e-mail, transferring files, and viewing Web pages. The gurus could have called these rules standards — but no, these standards are called *protocols*. Every time you do something on the Internet, the programs you use understand one or more of these protocols. The standard used on the Internet to transfer files is called FTP, which stands for File Transfer Protocol. The Web standard is called HTTP, which is short for HyperText Transfer Protocol. Usenet news has NNTP, or Network News Transfer Protocol, and e-mail has two main protocols: Internet mail servers use SMTP (Simple Mail Transfer Protocol) to send mail and POP (Post Office Protocol) to receive mail.

Because Internet Explorer has a built-in FTP program, you can use it to download files from the Internet. To find out how, see the section "Downloading files," later in this chapter.

E-mail

Electronic mail, usually abbreviated as *e-mail,* is the most popular reason that people use the Internet. E-mail enables you to communicate with people all over the world and to keep in touch with business contacts, family members, and friends. Unlike recipients of regular mail, the people you write to can be reading your messages within minutes after you send them, whether the recipient is across the street or halfway around the world. That's one reason that regular mail is often facetiously called *snail mail.*

The free e-mail program that comes with Office 98 is called Outlook Express; Chapter 13 is all about using Outlook Express to manage your e-mail.

Newsgroups

The Internet also has a part called Usenet. You can think of *Usenet* as a worldwide bulletin-board system, enabling people from everywhere to post public messages and join discussions about subjects that interest them. Each subject is called a *newsgroup.* Usenet has more than 25,000 newsgroups, covering every subject under the sun.

Outlook Express not only handles e-mail but also is a good newsgroup-reading and posting program. Turn to Chapter 14 for more information about how to access Usenet with Outlook Express.

Using Internet Explorer

When you first start Internet Explorer, you see a window with lots of buttons and features, as shown in Figure 12-1.

Button bar   Address bar   Title bar   Favorites bar

Figure 12-1:
The Internet
Explorer
browser
window.

Status bar   Browser window

One big reason that the Web has become so popular in the past several years is that it is so easy to use. If you've never browsed the Web (often called *surfing* the Web), try it now:

1. **Launch Internet Explorer.**

2. **In the text box on the address bar, type** http://www.yahoo.com; **then press Return.**

   Yahoo!, which is a directory of Web sites, appears on your screen, as shown in Figure 12-2.

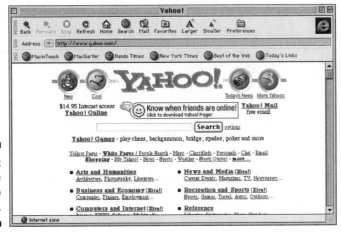

Figure 12-2:
Surfing the
Yahoo! Web
site.

3. **Click one of the subject links.**

   In the News and Media category, for example, you can click TV (or choose another subject link that interests you more; I don't mind). You go to another page that shows you subcategories of the main category you clicked.

4. **Click a subcategory that interests you.**

   If you chose the TV category, for example, you may click the Ratings (Nielsens) link.

   The subcategory page appears. These pages usually have links to other Web sites that match the category.

5. **Click one of these links to get to the information you're looking for.**

   You leave the Yahoo! Web site and go to an entirely different site, such as the TV Ratings page of the Mr. Showbiz site, as shown in Figure 12-3.

Figure 12-3: The latest TV ratings, courtesy of Mr. Showbiz.

The preceding steps are just enough to get you far on the World Wide Web. Most Web surfing is just that easy: Type the destination on the address bar, press the Return key, and then click links to go further.

Using the button bar

At the top of the Internet Explorer browser window is a row of buttons collectively called the *button bar,* made up of the buttons shown in Figure 12-4.

Figure 12-4:
The Internet
Explorer
button bar.

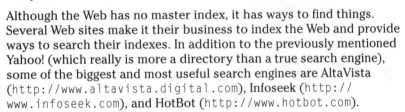

The buttons are

- ✔ **Back:** Takes you back to the most recently viewed Web page.

- ✔ **Forward:** Returns you to the page you were on if you clicked the Back button.

- ✔ **Stop:** Tells the browser to stop trying to load a Web page.

- ✔ **Refresh:** Downloads the current page from the Internet again.

- ✔ **Home:** Loads whatever page you told Internet Explorer you want to see when you start the program.

- ✔ **Search:** Tells Internet Explorer to go to the search engine you previously selected.

Although the Web has no master index, it has ways to find things. Several Web sites make it their business to index the Web and provide ways to search their indexes. In addition to the previously mentioned Yahoo! (which really is more a directory than a true search engine), some of the biggest and most useful search engines are AltaVista (http://www.altavista.digital.com), Infoseek (http://www.infoseek.com), and HotBot (http://www.hotbot.com).

- ✔ **Mail:** Starts your e-mail program.

- ✔ **Favorites:** Opens the Favorites editing window (see the section "Playing Favorites," later in this chapter).

- ✔ **Larger/Smaller:** Font buttons that increase or decrease the point size of the fonts used on the page you're viewing.

- ✔ **Preferences:** Opens the Internet Explorer Preferences dialog box.

Going places with the address bar

The *address bar,* which you normally find below the button bar, is simple to understand and to use. This bar contains a text box in which you type the URL (the Web address) of the Web site you want to reach. When you finish typing the URL, press Return to send the browser on its way.

Microsoft built some intelligence into the address bar. You don't have to type `http://`, for example, because Internet Explorer puts it in for you automatically. You usually don't have to type the `www.` or the `.com` portion of an address (although with some nonstandard Web servers, you'll see that they require you to add the prefix and suffix anyway). If you want to get to the Apple Computer Web site, for example, you can just type **apple** and press the Return key. The AutoComplete feature tries to fill in the rest of a URL after you type a few letters.

Next to the address box is a button with a down arrow. This button is active only when the insertion point is in the address box. Clicking the down-arrow button displays a menu of Web sites, culled from your Favorites and History lists, that contain the text before the address bar's selection, as shown in Figure 12-5.

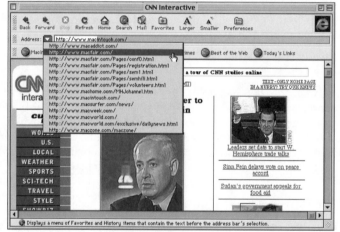

Figure 12-5: Using the Address pop-up menu.

Playing Favorites

When you've been to a Web site you like, chances are that you will want to find your way back again. Rather than require you to memorize the intimidating URL, Internet Explorer remembers the URL for you. All you have to do is add the Web site to the Internet Explorer Favorites list. To save a Web site as a Favorite, follow these steps:

1. **Go to the page you want to add to your Favorites list.**

2. **Choose Favorites⇨Add Page to Favorites or press ⌘+D.**

   The title of the page you saved is added to the Favorites menu. The next time you want to visit that particular Web site, just choose its name from the Favorites menu.

If you've ever used Netscape Navigator, you'll recognize Favorites as the Explorer equivalent of Navigator's bookmarks.

Organizing your Favorites

In a surprisingly short time, you'll have about a zillion Web sites added to your Favorites list. Although you can scroll wildly every time you want to visit a site, a better way exists: You can organize your Favorites in folders and move them around in any way that makes sense to you. When you put a bunch of Favorites in a folder, the folder shows up on the Favorites menu and you can get to the items in the folder through a hierarchical menu. To organize your Favorites, follow these steps:

1. **Choose Favorites⇨Open Favorites or press ⌘+J.**

   The Favorites window opens, as shown in Figure 12-6.

Folders   Favorites

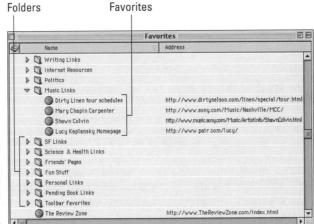

Figure 12-6:
The
Favorites
window.

2. **To create a new folder, choose Favorites⇨New Folder.**

   An untitled folder appears in the Favorites window. This folder acts like folders in the Finder; you can rename it or open it by double-clicking.

3. **Type the name you want to use for the folder; then press the Return key.**

4. **Drag to the new folder the Favorites you want to organize in that folder.**

5. **Repeat these steps until you're done organizing your Favorites.**

6. **Click the close box in the top-left corner of the Favorites window.**

You can move Favorites and folders around until they are in the order you want. Just drag the Favorite or folder up or down in the list. A black bar indicates where the item will appear when you release the mouse button.

To delete a folder or favorite, select it in the Favorites window and then press the Delete key. Be careful, though: Items deleted in this manner go away forever, and you can't use the Undo command to get them back.

Using the Favorites bar

The *Favorites bar* is a toolbar that holds your extra-special Favorites. Using this bar is a little more convenient than choosing things from the Favorites list. You can add Web sites to your Favorites bar in any of four ways:

- ✔ Hold down the ⌘ and Shift keys as you choose Favorites⇨Add Page to Favorites.
- ✔ Drag a link from a page to the Favorites bar.
- ✔ In the Favorites window, drag an item to the special Toolbar Favorites folder.
- ✔ Drag an item from the Favorites window directly to the Favorites bar.

Subscribing to Web sites

When you use the Internet Explorer Subscription feature, Internet Explorer automatically checks for new content at the sites to which you subscribe, according to any schedule you specify. You can choose to be notified that the Web site has changed, for example, or Internet Explorer can download the updated pages automatically. This automatic downloading can be quite useful. You can set things up so that a series of Web pages you read every day are downloaded just before you get to work so that they're ready for you to read. The speed of your Internet connection doesn't matter if you're not there to agonize when pages take a long time to load.

To subscribe to a Web site, follow these steps:

1. **Go to the site to which you want to subscribe.**

2. **Choose Favorites⇨Subscribe.**

   The Subscribe dialog box appears, as shown in Figure 12-7. This dialog box also adds the site to your Favorites list.

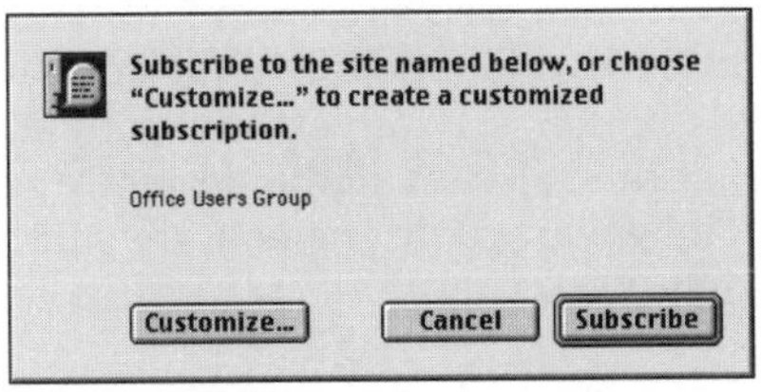

Figure 12-7:
The Subscribe
dialog box.

3. **By default, Internet Explorer updates a subscription once a day, so if that schedule is acceptable, click the Subscribe button; if you want to change the update interval, click the Customize button.**

   If you click Customize, the Favorites Info dialog box appears. Click the Schedule tab, as shown in Figure 12-8.

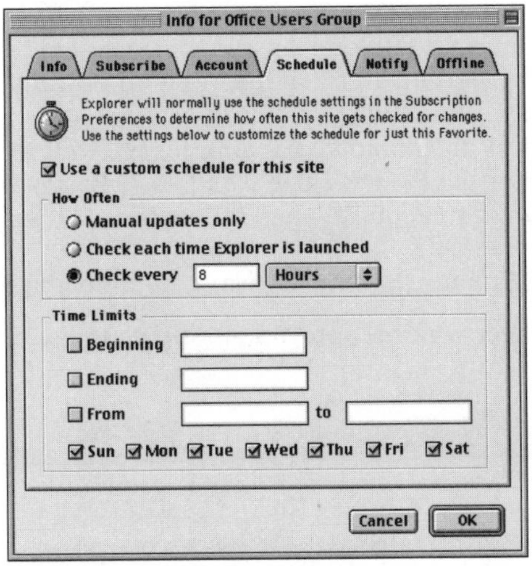

Figure 12-8:
Scheduling a
subscription.

4. **Click the Use a custom schedule for this site check box, and then make your changes in the schedule.**

5. **When you finish, click the OK button to close the dialog box.**

Channel surfing

A *channel* is a Web site designed to deliver information from the Internet to your computer, somewhat like subscribing to a favorite Web site. The difference is that instead of your machine's "pulling" information from the Internet whenever you want it, a channel "pushes" the information developed by the channel provider down to your computer, on a schedule set by the channel provider.

Channels, and the idea of so-called push Web sites, were a brief fad in 1997 and became yesterday's news by 1998, when people realized that the only folks who were really interested in push were advertisers, not users. Soon, even the advertisers realized that they already had a perfectly good push medium; it's called television. The general consensus in the industry is that Web channels do not have a bright future.

If you're interested in exploring channels, choose Go⇨Channel Guide. You go to the Microsoft Active Channel Guide, where you can sample some channels that offer Macintosh-specific content.

Downloading files

Internet Explorer knows how to download files via the FTP protocol, which means that you can use it to browse an FTP site and then download a file by simply clicking the link to the file. On FTP sites that use the Web as a convenient front end, using Internet Explorer means that you don't have to switch to a separate FTP program after you find a file to download.

To try the Internet Explorer downloading capabilities, go to the collection of downloadable Mac files at `http://www.download.com`. Browse the site until you find a file you want to acquire. Then follow these steps:

1. **Click the download link for the file you want, as shown in Figure 12-9.**

   The Download Manager window appears, as shown in Figure 12-10.

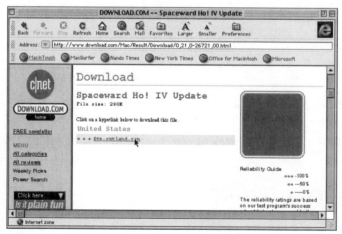

Figure 12-9: Downloading a file.

File	Status	Time	Transferred
Expo entrance	Complete	< 1 minute	34 KB
Power Zip line	Complete	< 1 minute	24 KB
Macintosh IA 2.0z.sea	Complete	< 1 minute	1.4 MB
51.day.jpg	Complete	< 1 minute	2,895 bytes
CARL17.AVI	Cancelled	< 1 minute	57 KB
sftvschd	Complete	< 1 minute	49 KB
Outlook Express 4.0 ...	Complete	16 Minutes	3.3 MB
3 main office icons	Complete	< 1 minute	10 KB
BBS Policies - test	Complete	< 1 minute	67 KB
IE 4.0 Recommended ...			3.5 MB of 9.2 MB, 41 KB/sec

Figure 12-10:
The Download Manager shows you the progress of the download.

If a file is taking too long to download, you can stop the process by choosing View➪Stop Loading. The file is marked as canceled in the Download Manager.

A check in the Download Manager shows that the file was transferred correctly.

2. **Click the close box of the Download Manager to close the window.**

Customizing Internet Explorer

You can change the appearance of Internet Explorer to suit your working style or to fit better on your screen.

Customizing toolbars

The easiest way to customize a toolbar is to show or hide any of the toolbars by checking or unchecking them on the View menu. You can also make several changes in the Browser Display pane of the Preferences dialog box. (To get there, choose Edit➪Preferences➪Browser Display.) You can choose to view the button bar, for example, with Icons and Text, Icons Only, or Text Only. If you're switching to Internet Explorer from Netscape Navigator, you can change the button bar to match the familiar Navigator buttons.

Moving toolbars

Drag handles are on the left edge of each of the toolbars. The handles enable you to rearrange the toolbars' order, move two toolbars to the same level, and resize the toolbars just as you would do with any Office 98 toolbar.

Changing the font size

You can fit more text on-screen by reducing the font size; to do so, click the Smaller button on the button bar. If you're especially eagle-eyed, you can shrink the text to a tiny size, as shown in Figure 12-11. Conversely, you can prevent eyestrain by increasing the font size, as shown in Figure 12-12.

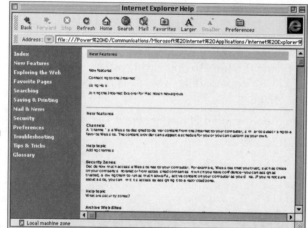

Figure 12-11:
You can shrink the text to fit more on your screen.

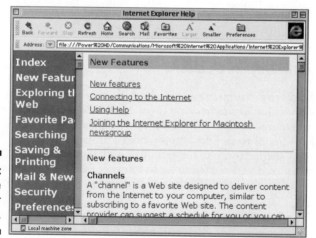

Figure 12-12:
You can make the text bigger than life.

Setting a Downloads folder

It's convenient to have downloaded files always go to the same spot on your hard disk so that you can open and examine them easily. To do that, you create a Downloads folder and then tell Internet Explorer to use it:

1. **In the Finder, Choose File⇨New Folder.**

   An untitled folder appears.

2. **Name the folder** Downloads.

3. **Switch to Internet Explorer.**

4. **Choose Edit⇨Preferences.**

   The Preferences window appears.

5. **Click the Download Options tab.**

6. **In the Download Folder section, click the Change Location button.**

   The Open dialog box appears.

7. **Navigate to your Downloads folder, select it, and then click the Select Downloads button.**

   The Open dialog box closes, and you return to the Download Options tab.

8. **In the Download Destination section, click the button next to Always Download Files to the Download Folder.**

   You can save yourself grief later if you make sure that the Automatically Decode MacBinary Files and Automatically Decode BinHex Files check boxes are checked. These two options have to do with the way files are encoded for easy transmission over the Internet, and decoding the files manually is a pain.

9. **Click the OK button.**

Chapter 13

Handling Your E-Mail with Outlook Express

• •

• •

*A*lthough the World Wide Web is the Internet service that gets all the attention, the true killer application of the Net is *electronic mail*, also known as *e-mail*. The almost instant communication e-mail provides has revolutionized the business world to an even greater extent than the adoption of fax machines in the 1980s. For many businesses, not having access to e-mail is now nearly unthinkable. Personal use of e-mail has lagged behind that of businesses, but not by much. In my family, for example, nearly everybody has access to e-mail at home or at work, and my son can exchange e-mail with two of his three grandparents.

The Office 98 e-mail program, Outlook Express, is free — you can download it from the Microsoft Web site, whether or not you own Office — and quite powerful. The program enables you to send and receive e-mail for multiple Internet accounts (but not America Online accounts), and you can also use it to read Usenet newsgroups. (See Chapter 14 for more information about using Outlook Express for reading newsgroups.) If you share your computer with a coworker or with another family member, each person can have her own setup in Outlook Express.

Setting Up Outlook Express

The main Outlook Express window makes reading and managing your e-mail easy, as you can see in Figure 13-1. Starting from the left side of the window and moving clockwise, you first see the *folder list,* which contains your Inbox, Outbox, and the folders you create to file your e-mail. At the top of the window is the *toolbar,* which has buttons that enable you to perform common tasks. The *message list,* below the toolbar, shows the messages in the Inbox or any other folder you're viewing. Below the message list is the *preview pane.* Clicking the title of a message in the message list displays the contents of the message in the preview pane.

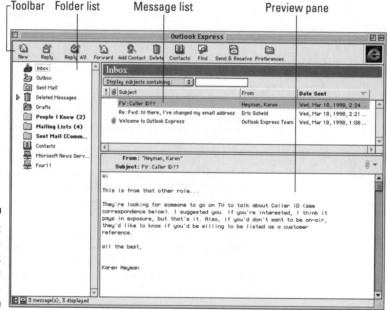

Figure 13-1:
The main Outlook Express window.

Before you can start getting your e-mail, you have to tell Outlook Express about your e-mail account. If you're accessing the Internet by using the company network, you can get this information from your network administrator. If you're logging on from home, your Internet Service Provider (ISP) should give you this information when you sign up for your account. Here's the information you need:

✔ **Your name.** You know what it is. If not, check your driver's license.

✔ **Your e-mail address.** People use this address to send e-mail to you — usually some form of your name, followed by @ and then followed by the domain name of your company or organization, which is something like `microsoft.com` or `pbs.org`.

✔ **The name of your organization or company.** (This information is optional.)

✔ **The SMTP server name.** The *SMTP server* is the computer that gets mail from you and sends it to other computers on the Internet.

✔ **Your account ID.** This information is the name of your e-mail mailbox. The ID is usually (but not always) the same as the first part of your e-mail address (the part before the @).

✔ **The POP server name.** The *POP server* is the computer that receives mail for you and holds it until you pick up the mail.

✔ **Your e-mail password.** Your password is the secret word that identifies you to the POP server.

Choose your password carefully because anyone who has your password can pick up your e-mail. Good passwords are at least six characters long, and they contain, ideally, both letters and numbers. Make sure that you don't choose easy-to-guess passwords — the names of your spouse or children, your address, or the like. And for goodness sake, don't use *secret* as your password; hackers in grade school know that one. Changing your password from time to time is also a good idea.

Follow these steps to set up your e-mail account:

1. **Launch Outlook Express by double-clicking its icon on the desktop.**

2. **Choose Edit⇨Preferences.**

   The Preferences dialog box appears, as shown in Figure 13-2.

   If necessary, click the E-mail line in the list on the left side of the dialog box to display the e-mail information area.

Figure 13-2:
The e-mail settings pane in the Outlook Express Preferences dialog box.

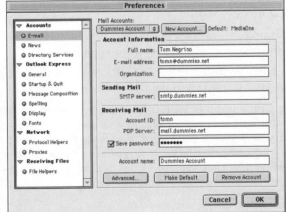

In the Account Information section, the first box is labeled Full Name. Your name may be in this box already because Outlook Express is smart enough to get the name from your Macintosh's Users and Groups control panel.

3. **If the Full Name box is blank, type your first and last name in it; if another name appears in the box, highlight that name and replace it with your name.**

4. **Type your e-mail address (with the @ sign in it) in the E-Mail Address box.**

   If you don't know your address, refer to the account information you got from your network administrator or Internet Service Provider.

5. **(Optional) If you want your company name to always show up along with your e-mail address, type it in the Organization box.**

6. **In the Sending Mail section, type the SMTP server information in the text box.**

   SMTP stands for *Simple Mail Transfer Protocol;* the SMTP server is the machine that takes mail from you and sends it to the rest of the Internet.

7. **In the Receiving Mail area, type your account name in the Account ID box.**

8. **Type the name of your POP server in the POP Server box.**

   POP stands for *Post Office Protocol.* The POP server is the machine that accepts mail from other people and holds it for you. Although it may seem strange that one machine sends mail and another machine receives mail, that arrangement is just part of the inexplicable weirdness of the Internet.

9. **If you want Outlook Express to remember your password, click the Save Password check box and then type your password in the adjacent text box.**

   To shield your password from potentially prying eyes, a line of bullets appears in the text box rather than what you type.

   If you don't enter your password in the Preferences dialog box, you'll be asked for your password every time you get your e-mail.

   If you share your computer with other people or work in a place where your computer isn't secure, *not* saving your password probably is a good idea. By saving your password, you're making it easy for anyone who sits at your computer to send and receive e-mail in your name. Imagine the mischief that someone could cause by sending a nastygram to your boss from your e-mail account.

10. **Type an account name, if you want one.**

    The Account Name box gives this mail setup a name so that you can easily switch between different accounts (if you have more than one).

11. Click the OK button to save the information.

Congratulations! You're done setting up your e-mail account. Your screen should look something like Figure 13-3.

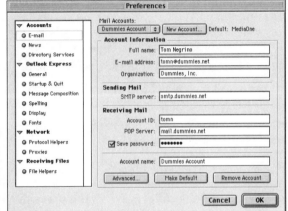

Figure 13-3:
Completed
e-mail
settings.

Working with E-Mail

Now that you've set up Outlook Express, it's time to get to work. To work with your e-mail, you don't have to be connected to the Internet (although, of course, you have to connect to receive your mail) — you can read incoming mail, create outgoing messages, and save those messages in your Outbox until you're ready to connect. Then Outlook Express connects to your Internet Service Provider (ISP) and fires off all the messages. If you work in an office and your Macintosh is on a network, you don't have to worry about dialing up the Internet, because your network is always connected.

Reading your e-mail

E-mail that other people send to you is stored on your mail server (the POP server) until you tell Outlook Express to retrieve it. Outlook Express dials up your ISP, retrieves your mail, and places it in your Inbox, ready for you to read.

To retrieve and read your e-mail, follow these steps:

1. Do one of the following things:

- Choose Tools⇨Send & Receive.

- Click the Send & Receive toolbar button.

If you connect to your ISP via a modem, you should hear the modem dial and connect. When you're connected, you should see a brief progress dialog box as Outlook Express retrieves your mail from the mail server. If you have mail, the name of your Inbox in the folder list appears in boldface, indicating that you have unread mail.

2. **Click the Inbox in the folder list.**

   In the message list, Outlook Express displays the subjects of the messages, the senders, and when the messages were sent.

3. **Click one of the messages to read it in the preview pane.**

   If the preview pane isn't big enough, you can resize the window or double-click a message title to display the message in its own window.

4. **To move to the next message, click that message's title or press the down-arrow key on the keyboard.**

When you read an e-mail message in the preview pane, a bar appears at the top of the pane, showing the sender's name, e-mail address (the From field), and the message subject (the Subject field). Below the bar is the body of the message, as shown in Figure 13-4. If you display the message in a separate window, you see similar address information.

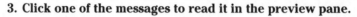

Sender's name and e-mail address   Subject field   Message body

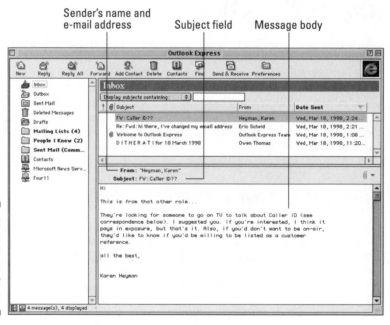

Figure 13-4:
Reading an e-mail message in the preview pane.

If the e-mail is from someone with whom you think you'll be corresponding in the future, now is a good time to add that person's name and e-mail address to your Contacts list, which is the Outlook Express address book. To add the sender's address of the opened e-mail message to your Contacts list, choose Tools⇨Add Sender to Contacts.

Replying to your e-mail

After reading an e-mail message, you will often want to reply. To reply to an e-mail message, follow these steps:

1. **In the folder list, click the folder that contains the message to which you want to reply.**

   Usually, this folder is your Inbox. The titles of the messages in the folder appear in the message list.

2. **In the message list, click the e-mail message to which you want to reply.**

3. **Click the Reply or Reply All toolbar button.**

   You should use Reply All when the original message was also sent to other people and you want everybody to get a copy of your reply. Clicking the Reply button sends your reply to only the person listed in the From field.

   The Message dialog box appears, displaying a copy of the original message in the message window, along with the recipient's e-mail address.

4. **Type your reply.**

5. **Click the Send button.**

Outlook Express doesn't send your mail when you click Send; it just stores the message in the Outbox. To send the mail on its way, you have to click the Send & Receive toolbar button or choose Tools⇨Send & Receive.

Forwarding e-mail

If you receive a message you want to send to someone else, Outlook Express enables you to forward it. To forward your e-mail, follow these steps:

1. **Select a message in the message list.**

   The text of the message appears in the preview pane.

2. **Click the Forward toolbar button, choose Message⇨Forward, or press ⌘+J.**

   A new message appears, with the contents of the message you are forwarding already entered in the message body.

3. **Enter the recipient's e-mail address in the Address box.**

4. **In the message body, add any text you want to send along with the forwarded message.**

5. **Click the Send button.**

   The next time you send and receive e-mail, the message is forwarded.

Creating and sending new e-mail

To write a new e-mail message, follow these steps:

1. **Choose File⇨New⇨Mail Message, click the New toolbar button, or press ⌘+N.**

   An untitled Message dialog box opens, as shown in Figure 13-5. The insertion point is in the To field, ready for you to begin addressing the message.

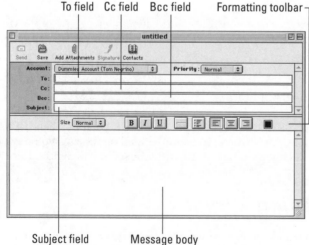

To field   Cc field   Bcc field   Formatting toolbar

Figure 13-5:
Creating a
new e-mail
message.

Subject field   Message body

2. **Begin typing the name of the person to whom you are sending the e-mail.**

   If that name is already in your Contacts list, Outlook Express finishes typing the name for you.

In any of the Outlook Express address fields, you can enter as many names as you want. Just separate the names with a comma or a semicolon.

3. If you want to send a copy of your message to someone other than the primary recipient, type that person's name in the Cc (carbon copy) field.

If you want to send a copy of a message to a person without that person's name or address appearing in the recipient list, you can make an entry in the Bcc (blind carbon copy) field. In other words, the people listed in the To and Cc fields won't know that you sent a copy of your message to anybody listed in the Bcc field.

4. Enter the names of your Bcc recipients (if any).

5. In the Subject field, type the subject of your e-mail message.

6. Type your message in the message body.

As you type, Outlook Express automatically checks your spelling. If you make a mistake, the incorrect word gets marked with a wavy red underline. To correct the error, hold down the Control key and click the incorrect word. A list of suggestions appears, as shown in Figure 13-6. Choose one of the suggestions, or choose Add to add a correct but unknown word to your custom user dictionary (which is shared by the other Office 98 applications, by the way).

Figure 13-6:
Correcting
a spelling
error.

7. Use the formatting toolbar to change the appearance of the text in your message, if you want.

The text is formatted as HTML, which has its good and bad points. The good part is that you can format your message in much the same way as you would in a word processor, in bold, italic, or even colored type.

The bad part is that your nicely formatted message looks horrible to any recipient whose mail program doesn't understand HTML-formatted text, because your words are surrounded by the HTML formatting tags. My advice: Unless you're sure that all your recipients can handle HTML-formatted e-mail, turn off the formatting by choosing Format⇨Rich Text (HTML).

8. **Send or save your mail.**

   To send your message immediately, click the Send button, choose Message⇨Send Message Now, or press ⌘+K. Outlook Express connects to the Internet and sends your mail on its way.

   If you prefer to save your message and send it later, click the Save button, choose File⇨Save, or press ⌘+S.

9. **When you finish writing all your messages, click the Send & Receive toolbar button to have Outlook Express send all the mail in your Outbox and receive any e-mail that's waiting for you.**

Attaching a file

You can send any sort of a Macintosh file along with an e-mail message by attaching the file to the message. If you're working on a report in Word 98 and want to share that report with a coworker, you can e-mail the Word document to your friend. To attach a file to an e-mail message, follow these steps:

1. **Create a new e-mail message.**

2. **Write and address a new message as you normally would.**

3. **Click the Add Attachments toolbar button.**

   The Open dialog box appears, as shown in Figure 13-7.

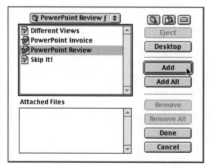

Figure 13-7:
Adding files
to be
attached.

4. **Select the file or files you want to attach, and then click the Add button.**

5. **Repeat Step 4 until you have added all the files you want to attach.**

6. **Click the Done button.**

   The icons of the files you attached appear at the bottom of the message form, as shown in Figure 13-8.

7. **Send the message.**

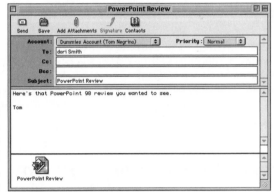

Figure 13-8:
A file
attached to
an e-mail
message.

Deleting e-mail

By default, Outlook Express saves (in the Sent Mail folder) a copy of every message you send. After awhile, that folder can accumulate a huge number of messages, and you may want to get rid of some of them. To delete messages you no longer want, follow these steps:

1. **In the folder list, click the folder that contains the messages you want to delete.**

   The messages in the folder appear in the message list.

2. **Select the messages you want to delete.**

   To select more than one message, Shift+click the messages. To deselect a message, ⌘+click the message.

3. **Click the Delete toolbar button.**

   Outlook Express moves the message to the Deleted Messages folder.

The message isn't irretrievably gone yet, however. If you made a mistake and want to get a message back, click the Deleted Messages folder, click the title of the message you want to retrieve, and then drag the message back to the folder it came from.

By default, Outlook Express empties the Deleted Messages folder when you quit the program. After that folder has been emptied, you have no way to get your mail back.

Filtering E-Mail

One of the most useful capabilities in Outlook Express is its facility for filtering incoming e-mail, called Inbox Rules. *Mail filters* enable you to automatically sort and prioritize mail as it comes in, add people to your Contacts list, and even trash unwanted mail. After you start using mail filters, you will wonder how you ever got along without them. This section shows you how to create three useful mail filters.

Adding people to your Contacts list

Suppose that you work regularly with people at a particular company. While writing this book, for example, I got a great deal of e-mail from some of the people at IDG Books Worldwide. Because I wanted to make sure that all those people are in my Contacts list, I set up an Inbox Rule to do the job.

To create an Inbox Rule to add people to your Contacts list, follow these steps:

1. **Choose Tools⇨Inbox Rules.**

   The Inbox Rules window appears, as shown in Figure 13-9.

Figure 13-9: The Inbox Rules window, with no rules defined (yet).

2. **Click the New Rule button.**

   The Define Inbox Rule dialog box appears, as shown in Figure 13-10.

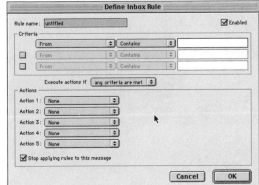

3. **In the first text box, type the name you want to use for the rule.**

4. **In the Criteria section, make sure that From and Contains are selected in the pop-up menu.**

5. **Type in the box to the right of the two pop-up menus the domain name used by the people you want to add to your Contacts list.**

   When I set up this rule, I used the domain name idgbooks.com, although you'll probably want to use something else. Notice that you put in everything to the right of the @ symbol in an e-mail address.

6. **Leave the Execute actions if pop-up menu set to any criteria are met.**

7. **In the Actions section, choose add sender to contacts from the Action 1 pop-up menu.**

8. **Leave the Stop applying rules to this message check box checked.**

   The completed rule should look something like the one shown in Figure 13-11.

9. **Click the OK button to save the new rule.**

Subsequently, whenever you get mail from someone at the domain you put in the rule, that person's address is automatically added to your Contacts list.

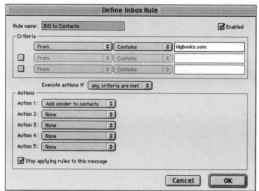

Figure 13-11:
The
completed
Contacts
rule.

Sorting your mail

Because the people in your Contacts list generally are people with whom you've already exchanged mail, it makes sense that mail from these folks is a higher priority than mail from people you don't know. You can create a mail filter that sorts mail from people in your Contacts list into a particular mail folder. To create this filter, follow these steps:

1. **Choose File⇨New⇨Folder to create a new folder, and name it.**

    I named my folder People I Know, but you can name yours whatever you want.

2. **Choose Tools⇨Inbox Rules.**

    The Inbox Rules window appears.

3. **Click the New Rule.**

    The Define Inbox Rule dialog box appears.

4. **In the first text box, type the name you want to use for the rule.**

5. **In the Criteria section, leave the pop-up menus set to From and Contains.**

6. **Leave the Execute actions if pop-up menu set to any criteria are met.**

7. **In the Actions section, choose Move message from the Action 1 pop-up menu.**

    A pop-up menu containing all the folder names appears next to Action 1.

8. **Choose from the folder pop-up menu the folder you created and named in Step 1.**

9. **Click the OK button to save the new rule.**

Getting rid of spam

Although e-mail is amazingly convenient, one of its real drawbacks is unsolicited commercial e-mail, sometimes known as *UCE* but more commonly referred to as *spam*. If you've ever had an America Online account, you're no doubt all too familiar with spam. Wouldn't it be nice if you could filter out that spam before you ever see it? Sure enough, you can get rid of most spam by using a fairly simple mail filter.

Because spammers are clever and forever figuring out new ways to annoy you, this filter doesn't catch all spam. Since I installed it, though, it has cut my spam load way back. The filter relies on the fact that most spam is sent with no entries in the To or Cc fields; your address is usually in the Bcc (blind carbon copy) field. Because you can't see the contents of the Bcc field, you can test to see whether your address is in the To or Cc fields — and if it isn't, the message is deleted.

To get rid of spam, follow these steps:

1. **Choose File⇨New⇨Folder to create a new folder, and name it.**

   Mine is called Suspected Spam; be creative.

2. **Choose Tools⇨Inbox Rules.**

   The Inbox Rules window appears.

3. **Click the New Rule button.**

   The Define Inbox Rule dialog box appears.

4. **In the first text box, type the name you want to use for the rule.**

   I call mine Spamkiller!

5. **In the Criteria section, choose To from the first pop-up menu and Does Not Contain from the second pop-up menu.**

6. **Type your e-mail address in the adjacent text box.**

7. **Click the check box in the second line of the Criteria section to make that line active.**

8. **In this line, choose Cc from the first pop-up menu, and choose Does Not Contain from the second pop-up menu.**

9. **Type your e-mail address in the adjacent text box.**

   So far, this rule is saying, "If the To field does not contain my e-mail address and the Cc field does not contain my e-mail address, take the following actions."

10. **Leave the Execute actions if pop-up menu set to any criteria are met.**

11. **In the Actions section, choose Move message from the Action 1 pop-up menu.**

    The pop-up menu with the folder list appears.

12. **Choose Suspected Spam (or whatever you named your folder in Step 1) from the pop-up menu.**

    If you like, you can move suspected spam directly to the Deleted Messages folder. I prefer, however, to move these messages to a folder I can check from time to time, just in case someone sends me a Bcc message I want to read. Usually, you can easily identify spam from the subject of the message.

13. **(Optional) Choose Set Color from the Action 2 pop-up menu; then choose some unpleasant color from the color list that appears.**

    This step shows how you can perform more than one action in one Inbox Rule.

14. **Click the OK button to save the new rule.**

If you created all three rules, your Inbox Rules window should look like the one shown in Figure 13-12.

Figure 13-12:
The Inbox Rules window displays the three new rules.

One problem with the way the rules are arranged is that the antispam rule doesn't catch as much spam as it could if it were at the top of the list, because a message starts at the top of the list and works its way down. If a rule catches a message, the message stops being processed. For that reason, you want the mail that is least important to you to be caught at the top of the stack, and you want your most important mail to appear toward the bottom.

To reorder the rules in the Inbox Rules window, select a rule and then click the Move Up or Move Down button. After a little rearranging, the list looks like the one shown in Figure 13-13, which is the optimum way to set up these rules. This way, the spam check comes first. If a message survives that test, it drops down in the list, and if it's from the right domain, it gets added to the Contacts list. Finally, if the sender is in the Contacts list, the message gets moved to the People I know folder.

Figure 13-13:
The best
arrangement
for the
three rules.

Chapter 14

Participating in Newsgroups with Outlook Express

• •

In This Chapter

▶ Understanding Usenet

▶ Setting up Outlook Express to read news

▶ Reading newsgroups

▶ Posting to newsgroups

• •

*T*he Internet has, in addition to the World Wide Web, which you surf with Internet Explorer, a part called *Usenet.* You can think of Usenet as being a worldwide bulletin-board system, in which people from everywhere can post messages and join discussions about subjects that interest them. Each subject within Usenet is called a *newsgroup,* and individual messages in a newsgroup are called *news articles.* Chapter 13 deals with using Outlook Express for e-mail; the other side of Outlook Express is its facility as a *newsreader,* which is a program that can read and post to newsgroups.

About Usenet

At last count, more than 25,000 commonly available newsgroups existed, covering virtually every subject you can imagine (and probably many you would rather not imagine!). You access newsgroups through computers called *news servers;* most Internet Service Providers (ISPs) have their own news servers.

To find a newsgroup that interests you, you have to know a little about the structure of newsgroup names. Usenet has a hierarchy of names. Table 14-1 shows the most common top-level newsgroup names.

Table 14-1	Common Top-Level Newsgroup Names
Identifier	*Subjects*
alt	Subjects that don't fit into any of the other, official categories
biz	Business
comp	Computers
news	News and other topical information
rec	Recreational hobbies and arts
sci	Scientific
soc	Social
talk	Debates
misc	Miscellaneous subjects

The top-level names in Table 14-1 are the ones agreed on by the loose affiliation of voluntary groups that administer Usenet (as much as any group can be said to administer it). The names are about as official as Usenet names get. Individuals and groups can create their own names, however, and they do it all the time. Just remember that you can find most newsgroups in one of these categories.

Until the past few years, most of the available newsgroups were located in one of the top-level newsgroup hierarchies. With the widespread use of the Internet, however, many colleges and universities, companies, and even private citizens have discovered the use of discussion forums, and they have created their own newsgroups outside the official hierarchy. Some of these newsgroups are available to anyone to use. Microsoft, for example, has a set of public newsgroups to support its products; the newsgroups have names such as microsoft.public.excel.mac and microsoft.public.internet.news.mac. Other privately run newsgroups are private and require you to use a password to subscribe to them.

To the right of the top-level identifiers can be any number of qualifying names that narrow down the subject, separated by periods. Table 14-2 shows examples of a few newsgroups.

Table 14-2	Sample Newsgroup Names
Newsgroup Example	*Subject*
alt.fan.pooh	Friends of a Bear of Little Brain
comp.sys.mac.games	Macintosh games

Newsgroup Example	Subject
`news.answers`	FAQ (Frequently Asked Questions) files for all the other newsgroups
`rec.arts.sf.movies`	Science-fiction movies
`soc.culture.japan`	Discussions of Japanese culture

Although Usenet can be a great source of information, it's similar to a stream that's always flowing by you: You see only the part of the discussion that is most recent. Some newsgroups have private archives, and those archives can be hard to find. The easiest way to search the Usenet archives is to go to Deja News, a Web site that maintains indexed, searchable archives of more than 50,000 Usenet groups, including many corporate, hard-to-find, and international newsgroups. Because Deja News also does a decent job of filtering out spam (intrusive, unsolicited advertising) from its archived messages (the site uses industrial-strength spam filters), your chance of finding useful information is increased. You can find Deja News at `http://www.dejanews.com`. For more information about spam, see the section in Chapter 13 about getting rid of spam.

For a more detailed account of Usenet and the rest of the Internet, I recommend that you buy *The Internet For Macs For Dummies,* 3rd Edition, by Charles Seiter (published by IDG Books Worldwide, Inc.).

Setting Up Outlook Express to Read News

Before you find the newsgroup of your dreams, you have to tell Outlook Express about your news server. To enter the necessary information about your news server, follow these steps:

1. **Choose Edit⇨Preferences.**

   The Preferences dialog box appears.

2. **In the list on the left side of the dialog box, click News to display the newsgroup settings, as shown in Figure 14-1.**

3. **Click the New Server button.**

   The New Account dialog box appears.

4. **Enter a name for your news server.**

   Almost any name will do; I suggest that you use the name of your Internet Service Provider (ISP).

5. **Click the OK button.**

   You return to the Preferences dialog box, where the name you gave the news server now appears in the Server Name box.

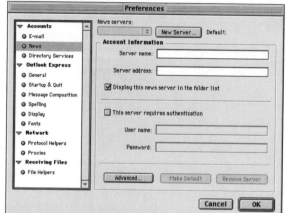

Figure 14-1:
News
preferences.

6. **In the Server Address box, type the address of the news server.**

   You can get this address (which is usually something like `news.jet.net` or `nntp.mediaone.com`) from your Internet Service Provider (ISP) or your company's network administrator.

   The acronym *NNTP* stands for *Network News Transfer Protocol,* which is the standard format for sending newsgroup messages on the Internet. Glad you asked, hmm?

7. **Make sure that the Display This News Server in the Folder List check box is checked.**

8. **(Optional) If your news server requires a username and password (and if yours does, your ISP or network administrator should have told you and assigned that information), click the check box labeled This Server Requires Authentication. Then type your assigned username and password in the appropriate text boxes.**

9. **If this server is your main news server (it's probably your only one, so it has to be your main one), click the Make Default button.**

10. **Click the OK button to save your settings.**

    The news server shows up in the Outlook Express folder list.

Connecting to Newsgroups

Now that Outlook Express knows how to get to your news server, you have to connect to your news server and download the list of newsgroups your news server supports. Because so many newsgroups exist, many news servers don't carry a complete selection. Some news servers in the United States don't carry newsgroups from other countries, and other news servers choose not to carry content that the people who own the server may find to be offensive or unsuitable. Many corporate and educational institutions, for example, refuse to carry newsgroups with sexually oriented content.

Downloading lists of newsgroups

To download the list of newsgroups your news server supports, follow these steps:

1. **In the Outlook Express folder list, click your news server's icon to select it.**

2. **Choose View⇨Get Complete Newsgroup List.**

   Outlook Express connects to your news server and downloads the list.

Don't be surprised if completing the download takes a couple of minutes, especially if you connect to the Internet via a modem. Because Outlook Express subsequently remembers the newsgroups, the process doesn't take as long the next time you connect.

If you don't see Get Complete Newsgroup List on the View menu, you didn't click the icon of your news server in the folder list. The View menu changes, depending on what's selected in the folder list. Just click your news server and try again.

When the newsgroup list finishes downloading, the newsgroups show up in the list on the right side of the Outlook Express window. Outlook Express also lists on the status bar the number of newsgroups in that list, as shown in Figure 14-2. Take a minute to scroll through the list and see the diversity of subjects.

Figure 14-2: The newsgroup list, with the total number of groups displayed on the status bar.

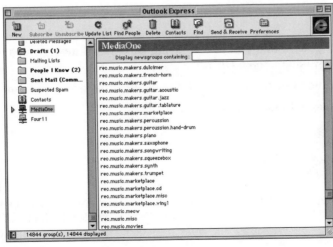

Subscribing to newsgroups

Before you can read newsgroups, you have to tell Outlook Express that you want to subscribe to a particular group or groups. Before you can subscribe, you have to find the right groups, by using either of these two methods:

✔ Scroll the newsgroup list until you find the group you want. As you may guess, this method works fine, but it's slow.

✔ In the Display Newsgroups Containing box at the top of the newsgroups window, type a keyword. If you're interested in the DVD videodisc format, for example, type **DVD** in this box. The list shrinks to show only the newsgroups that include *DVD* in their names.

When you find the newsgroups of your dreams, follow these steps to subscribe:

1. **Click a newsgroup name to select it.**

2. **Choose Tools⇨Subscribe.**

   The name of the newsgroup appears in boldface and also appears in the folder list below the news server.

3. **Repeat Steps 1 and 2 until you've subscribed to all the newsgroups that interest you.**

After you pick all your newsgroups, you no longer need to view the complete newsgroup list. To view only your subscribed newsgroups, choose View⇨Subscribed Only or press ⌘+Y.

Unsubscribing from newsgroups

If you get tired of a particular newsgroup and want to unsubscribe, follow these steps:

1. **Make sure that you're displaying subscribed newsgroups by choosing View⇨Subscribed Only.**

2. **In the newsgroup list, click the name of the group you want to delete.**

3. **Choose Tools⇨Unsubscribe.**

Reading the News

When you're sure that you're connected to your Internet Service Provider (ISP), you're finally ready to read some news articles. Pick one of your subscribed newsgroups, and open it by using one of these methods:

    ▸ Double-click the newsgroup's name.

    ▸ Click a newsgroup to select it and then choose File➪Open.

    ▸ Click a newsgroup to select it and then press ⌘+O.

Whichever method you use, Outlook Express downloads a group of messages and opens a split message window, as shown in Figure 14-3. The top half of the window displays the article headers; clicking an article puts the message in the bottom pane for you to read.

You can sort the messages in the article list by subject, by author, or by the date posted. Just click the appropriate column header. Clicking the column header again reverses the sort order. To move to the next message, click that message or press the down-arrow key on the keyboard.

In the article list, messages in boldface indicate that the message is unread. When you read a message, the boldface goes away.

You don't have to read every message; you can often tell just by the subject that a message or group of messages won't interest you. You should mark these messages as having been read so that Outlook Express doesn't show them to you the next time you look at the newsgroup. To do so, select the unwanted messages in the article list and then choose Message➪Mark As Read or press ⌘+T. You can make the read messages disappear from the article list by choosing View➪Unread Only or by pressing ⌘+Y.

Article list

Newsgroup name   Column headings

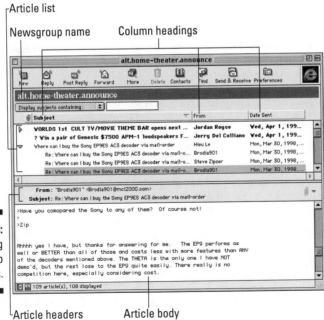

Figure 14-3:
Reading
newsgroup
messages.

Article headers   Article body

Message threads

If you refer to the article list shown in Figure 14-3, you see a message with the down arrow next to it. That down arrow marks the beginning of a *thread,* a series of responses to an original message. These messages are gathered together and stored with the original message. The replies to the original message are indented below the original. Outlook Express initially shows only the original message in a thread. Click the down arrow next to that message to display the rest of the thread.

Because of the huge volume of messages in many newsgroups, Outlook Express downloads from each newsgroup only a relatively small chunk of messages at a time. After you read (or mark as read) all the messages in the newsgroup, you can get the next chunk of unread messages by choosing View➪Get Next 500 News Subjects.

You can change the size of the chunk of messages that Outlook Express grabs from each newsgroup. Choose Edit➪Preferences➪General to display the General tab in the Preferences dialog box; then change the Get [Blank] News Subjects at a Time setting.

Posting Your Messages

Composing a message to be posted to a newsgroup is much like writing an e-mail message. As you do with e-mail, you open a new message window, address and write your message, and then send it off. To create and post a new message to a newsgroup, follow these steps:

1. **Open the newsgroup to which you want to post a message.**

2. **Choose File➪New➪News Message or press ⌘+N.**

   A new message window appears, already addressed to the newsgroup.

   If you want to send the message to another newsgroup as well (this act is called *cross-posting,* which is often considered to be somewhat rude), put the name of the other newsgroup after the first newsgroup and separate the names with a comma.

3. **Type the subject in the Subject box.**

4. **Type your message in the message body.**

   Your screen should look something like the one shown in Figure 14-4.

5. **Choose Message➪Post Message Now, press ⌘+K, or click the Post button.**

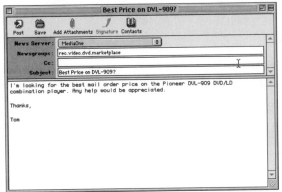

Figure 14-4:
This
message is
ready to be
posted to a
newsgroup.

Creating Replies

To post a reply to a newsgroup, follow these steps:

1. **In the article list, click the message to which you want to reply.**

   It's considered polite to quote a portion of the message to which you're replying so that other readers know the context of your message. On the other hand, it's rude to quote the entire message, so be selective in your quoting. To quote a portion of a message, select and copy it.

2. **Click the Post Reply toolbar button or choose Message⇨Reply to Newsgroup.**

   A new message form appears. If you want to reply by e-mail only to the sender of the news message rather than post the reply publicly, click the Reply toolbar button or choose Message⇨Reply.

3. **Fill out the message form.**

   If you chose to quote a portion of the message to which you are replying, you notice that the quoted portion appears at the bottom of the message, set off by an attribution line with the original poster's name and e-mail address, and with the actual message set off by greater-than and less-than signs (< and >), also called *chevrons*.

   Your finished reply should look something like the one shown in Figure 14-5.

4. **Click the Post toolbar button to send your message.**

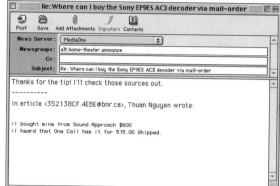

Figure 14-5:
A reply to a
newsgroup
posting,
ready to
be sent.

Netiquette: Making Nice on the Network

Most of Usenet is *unmoderated* — which means that nobody is really in charge. Although this arrangement means that you have the freedom to say virtually anything you want, it also means that you have nobody to complain to if someone else writes offensive posts. Over the years, people have developed standards for online courtesy, called *netiquette*. Netiquette is mostly common sense, combined with some simple ideas designed to keep network use down. This section discusses the most common netiquette guidelines.

Don't shout

In written communication in e-mail and newsgroups, capitalized words are used for emphasis. If you type your message in all uppercase letters, IT'S INTERPRETED AS SHOUTING. A related offense is Too! Much! Use! Of! Exclamation! Points!!!!!

A note about newsgroup spam

If you think that spam (unsolicited advertising) is a problem in e-mail, you haven't seen anything yet. Unfortunately, Usenet has been overrun by people who think that it's their sovereign right to spew out advertisements for multilevel marketing scams, pyramid schemes, solicitations for pornographic Web sites, and rip-off "business opportunities." Some estimates are that nearly 50 percent of all the messages within Usenet are spam.

What can you do to avoid newsgroup spam? Not that much, frankly. You can use the Outlook Express newsgroup rules (choose Tools⇨Newsgroup Rules) to try to filter spam based on the subject or address of the poster, but because spammers continually change their pitches and addresses, simple newsgroup filters aren't of much use.

Don't quote too much

Outlook Express makes it easy to quote an entire message when you reply to it. Try to avoid this practice whenever possible, however. Few things are more annoying than messages that quote an entire four-page post and then add nothing except a cheery "I agree!" Complete quotations are rude because you make people wade through a long message for no good reason. Get into the habit of selecting only the important part of a message before you click the Reply button.

Don't flame

Flames are personal attacks. You usually have no good reason not to be civil. You'll find, however, that legions of jerks are mighty brave when they're hiding behind their keyboards. The best thing to do is to ignore these folks.

Look before you jump in

Usenet can be a wild place, and old-timers can be merciless to new people *(newbies)* who ask what seem (to the old-timers) to be foolish questions. Be sure to spend some time reading the other messages before you post your first message to a newsgroup. Also read the newsgroup's FAQ (Frequently Asked Questions) file. You may save yourself a great deal of grief and avoid many nasty flames. You can find the FAQ files for many newsgroups at `http://www.faqs.org`.

Never forget

Your messages can be read by potentially millions of people worldwide.

Part V

Putting On a Show with PowerPoint 98

The 5th Wave   By Rich Tennant

"IT'S A SOFTWARE PROGRAM THAT MORE FULLY RE-FLECTS AN ACTUAL OFFICE ENVIRONMENT. IT MULTI-TASKS WITH OTHER USERS, INTEGRATES SHARED DATA, AND THEN USES THAT INFORMATION TO NETWORK VICIOUS RUMORS THROUGH AN INTER-OFFICE LINK-UP."

In this part . . .

Unfair as it may seem, people don't always immediately agree with every idea you have. Unless, of course, you're the Dictator for Life in your particular country. However, the crack IDG Books Worldwide Marketing Research Department has assured me that very few Dictators for Life have been known to read books in the *...For Dummies* series. They're probably reading *World Domination For Dummies,* anyway. It's a good bet that, like most people, sooner or later you have to persuade your coworkers with a presentation. That's where PowerPoint 98 comes in.

In this part, you discover the basics of creating slide shows and sprucing up a plain presentation with sizzling images, exciting video, and flashy effects. One section even helps you battle the dreaded specter of stage fright.

Chapter 15

Creating PowerPoint Slide Shows

● ●

● ●

*F*or many people, giving presentations is the part of their jobs they like the least. Standing up in front of coworkers and speaking makes their hearts pound, their palms sweat, and their knees knock.

Although Microsoft Office 98 can't do much about stage fright, it can help you be prepared and confident in the quality of your presentation. You create your presentation by using PowerPoint 98 to outline your thoughts, turn those thoughts into slides, and then add interesting visuals to amuse and distract your audience. You can use PowerPoint 98 to show presentations on your computer, print them as handouts, or even produce 35mm slides. (You remember slides, don't you? That old analog film technology? See, before computers . . . oh, never mind.)

Creating Your First Presentation

To create a presentation in PowerPoint 98, you have three choices:

 ✔ **Have the PowerPoint 98 AutoContent Wizard walk you through the steps of creating the presentation.** The Wizard helps you with what to say and with the appearance of the presentation. This method is the best choice when you're starting with PowerPoint.

 ✔ **Build your show based on one of the dozens of templates that come with PowerPoint 98.** The templates take care of the attractive graphics; you take care of the interesting text.

 ✔ **Start with a blank canvas and create your presentation from scratch.**

It may seem that building a presentation from scratch gives you the most creative flexibility, and it does — if you're a talented graphic artist. If that were the case, though, chances are that you wouldn't be reading this chapter. Creating a good-looking presentation takes a special kind of talent, and Microsoft has already paid for that talent and put the results on the Office 98 CD-ROM. Why not take advantage of this Microsoft largess? Use the AutoContent Wizard or one of the templates to get started on your presentation. There's nothing to stop you from modifying them later.

Using the AutoContent Wizard

The AutoContent Wizard steps you through the process of creating a presentation, based on any of 23 preset presentation types. The Wizard asks you some basic questions about your presentation and then drops you into the PowerPoint Outline mode to add the text to your presentation.

To use the AutoContent Wizard to create a presentation, follow these steps:

1. Launch PowerPoint 98.

The New Presentation dialog box appears, as shown in Figure 15-1.

Figure 15-1:
Starting a presentation with the New Presentation dialog box.

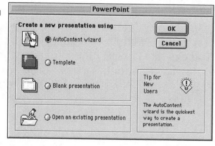

If the New Presentation dialog box doesn't show up, it may have been turned off in the PowerPoint Preferences dialog box. You can still get to the AutoContent Wizard by choosing File⇨New, clicking the General tab, selecting the AutoContent Wizard, and clicking the OK button.

2. Click the AutoContent Wizard radio button.

3. Click the OK button.

The informational screen for the AutoContent Wizard appears.

4. Click the Next button.

The Presentation Type window appears, as shown in Figure 15-2.

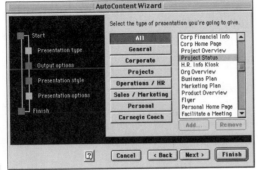

Figure 15-2:
Choosing a presentation type.

5. **Select a presentation type in the scroll box; then click the Next button.**

   The Output options window appears.

6. **Choose the output option you want to use — either Presentations, informal meetings, handouts or Internet, kiosk — and then click the Next button.**

   The Presentation style window appears, as shown in Figure 15-3.

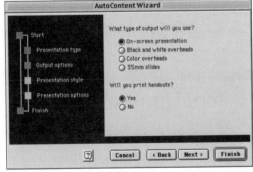

Figure 15-3:
Picking your presentation style.

7. **Pick the kind of output you need and specify whether you will be printing handouts. Then click the Next button.**

   The Presentation options window appears.

8. **Type the presentation title, your name, and any additional informa-tion you want to include on the first slide.**

9. **Click the Finish button.**

   PowerPoint 98 displays in Outline view the presentation you built, with the slide visible in a miniature preview window, as shown in Figure 15-4.

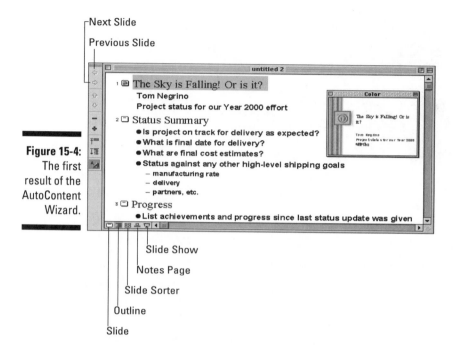

Next Slide

Previous Slide

Figure 15-4:
The first
result of the
AutoContent
Wizard.

Slide Show

Notes Page

Slide Sorter

Outline

Slide

10. **Replace the text provided by the AutoContent Wizard with your own text in the rest of the outline.**

11. **Click the Slide View button to get a full-size look at your slides.**

Stop me before I present again!

There's nothing quite like a brilliant presentation, one suffused with humor, wit, and solid information and presented with style and panache. Unfortunately, there's also nothing quite like a dull presentation. Okay, maybe a root canal (with apologies to our dentist friends).

Although PowerPoint 98 can add a great deal of visual flash to your presentation, there's no substitute for interesting content. All the clever slide transitions, animated text and charts, and whizzy graphics in the world can't punch up information that is dull, dull, dull.

Luckily, the solution is simple. When you create a slide show, spend most of your time working on your words in Outline mode. Share your outline with coworkers, and make changes based on their feedback. When the words are right, spice them up with visuals. Get the words right first, however.

Using a PowerPoint template

PowerPoint 98 comes with dozens of templates that contain predefined formats and graphics, just waiting for you to fill them with text. The difference between using the templates and using the AutoContent Wizard is that with a template, you have to add all the text from scratch. Microsoft has done the tough work for you, however, by creating the template. Follow these steps to use a PowerPoint template:

1. Choose File⇨New.

The New Presentation dialog box appears, as shown in Figure 15-5.

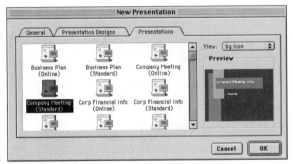

Figure 15-5:
The New
Presentation
dialog box.

2. Click the Presentations tab.

3. Click the icon for the template you want to use.

4. Click the OK button.

PowerPoint 98 shows you the first slide of the template.

5. Click a text box in the slide and edit the text.

6. Click the Next Slide button and edit the text in the new slide as necessary.

7. Repeat the editing process until you're done with the presentation.

Working with Your Slides

After you start a presentation with the AutoContent Wizard or a template, you'll want to change the presentation to your liking. PowerPoint gives you many tools to add features to your slides. In this chapter, I stick with the basics of adding text to slides; in Chapter 16, I show you how to add graphics, QuickTime movies, sounds, and animation to your presentation.

Creating a new slide

To create a new slide, follow these steps:

1. **Choose Insert⇨New Slide, press ⌘+M, or click the New Slide button in the Common Tasks window.**

   The New Slide dialog box appears, as shown in Figure 15-6.

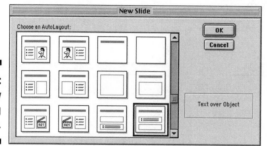

Figure 15-6: The New Slide dialog box.

2. **Choose one of the AutoLayouts.**

   An *AutoLayout* is a predefined arrangement of graphical elements and text boxes in a slide. PowerPoint suggests the AutoLayout it thinks is most appropriate for this point in your presentation.

3. **Click the OK button.**

4. **Edit the text boxes in the new slide.**

Deleting a slide

To delete a slide, click the Previous Slide or Next Slide buttons to display the slide you want to get rid of; then choose Edit⇨Delete Slide.

One annoying feature of PowerPoint 98 is that you don't see an "Are you sure?" dialog box when you delete a slide. *Be certain before you delete.* If you accidentally delete the wrong slide, you can choose Edit⇨Undo Delete Slide; you don't get an unlimited number of Undo chances, so be careful.

Working with text boxes

You can edit and add text to a text box you get from an AutoLayout. In addition to adding text, you can also modify the font, style, and size of the text in the text box. To edit a text box, follow these steps:

1. **Display the slide you want to change.**

2. **Click the text box you want to modify.**

   A patterned border and white handles appear at the edges of the text box.

3. **Make your changes.**

   You can select the text in the usual way and then choose the font, font size, or other options on the formatting toolbar.

   To resize a text box, drag one of the white handles.

   To delete a text box, click the border of the text box and then press the Delete key.

Most of the time, AutoLayout gives you a slide that has all the text boxes you need. If you want to add a text box to a slide, however, choose Insert⇨Text Box.

Reviewing Your Presentation

After you create a presentation, you should preview it to make sure that it looks right and that the content is the way you want it. PowerPoint 98 has five viewing modes; you switch among them by choosing them from the View menu or by clicking the View buttons at the bottom of the document window.

Using Slide view

Slide view, which displays one slide at a time, is the best view to work with when you're changing the appearance of a slide. Choose View⇨Slide to switch to Slide view.

Using Outline view

Outline view is the PowerPoint secret weapon for making better presentations (well, maybe it's not so secret anymore). The key to Outline mode is that it enables you to edit the content of your presentation without focusing on the presentation's appearance. Although you still see a miniature color preview window of the slide you're working on, the focus is on the text.

In Outline view, all you can do is edit text. Unlike Slide view, Outline view doesn't allow you to do any sort of editing of graphics.

Outline view is the best view to use if you want to move a bunch of text from one slide to another. You can do this task in Slide view, although it's not nearly as easy as it is in Outline view, which enables you to simply drag and drop text.

To switch to Outline view, choose View⇨Outline.

In Outline view, each heading represents a slide (and is also the title of the slide). A numbered slide icon appears to the left of each heading. Outline view works much like outlines in Microsoft Word: You can expand and collapse headings, move headings up and down in the outline, and promote and demote the levels of headings.

Creating a heading

When you create a heading in PowerPoint, you're creating a new slide. To make a new heading, move the insertion point to the beginning of an existing heading and then press the Return key. You can also create a new heading by choosing Insert⇨New Slide or pressing ⌘+M.

Deleting a heading

Sometimes, slides just fall out of favor — the honeymoon is over, and they need to go away. To delete a heading, click the slide icon for the heading you want to delete; then press the Delete key.

Moving a heading

To reorganize your presentation, you can drag headings in the outline, thereby rearranging the order of the slides. To move a heading to a different place in your presentation, click the slide icon of the heading you want to move and drag the heading to its new home.

Using Slide Sorter view

Slide Sorter view shrinks your slides so that as many slides as possible fit on your screen. This view gives you an overview of your presentation. You can change the number of slides that are visible at any time by choosing a different figure from the Zoom pop-up menu on the standard toolbar.

The selected slide has a thick, black border. To move a slide, drag it to a new position. PowerPoint 98 displays a vertical line where the slide will move when you release the mouse button.

Using Notes Page view

Notes Page view enables you to add speaker notes that go along with each slide. These notes can be printed as handouts. You can work with notes only in Notes Page view; the text doesn't show up on your slides.

To add notes to your presentation, follow these steps:

1. **Choose View⇨Notes Page.**

   Notes Page view appears, displaying the current slide with a text box below it, where you can enter your notes (see Figure 15-7).

2. **Click the text box and add your notes for this slide.**

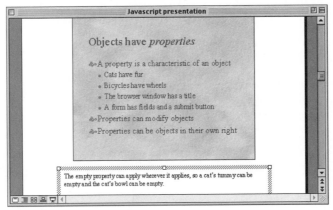

Figure 15-7:
Notes Page
view.

Playing a slide show

Now you're ready for the real preview. Slide Show view takes over your screen and shows you exactly how your presentation will look. You also use this view to check out slide transitions, examine slide timings, and ensure that you haven't made any mistakes.

To play a slide show, follow these steps:

1. **Choose View⇨Slide Show.**

   The first slide in the presentation appears full-screen.

   To start the slide show with the current slide rather than the first slide, click the Slide Show button at the bottom of the document window.

2. To get to the next slide, click the mouse or press the right-arrow key; to back up a slide, press the left-arrow key or ⌘+click the mouse.

3. To end the slide show, press ⌘+. (⌘+period) or press the Escape key.

Printing Your Presentation

When you're done with your presentation, you can print it as slides, hand-outs, or notes (which feature a slide and speaker notes), or you can print the outline. To print your presentation, follow these steps:

1. **Choose File⇨Print.**

   The Print dialog box appears.

2. **From the pop-up menu, choose Microsoft PowerPoint 98.**

3. **From the Print What pop-up menu, choose the kind of printout you want.**

4. **Click the Print button.**

Chapter 16

Spiffing Up Your Presentations

- -

In This Chapter

▶ Adding pictures and media to your slides

▶ Using the drawing tools

▶ Changing the appearance of your slides

▶ Adding slide transitions

▶ Adding interactivity to your show

- -

*I*n any good presentation, the text is the most important part. What you say will make or break your show. The good use of graphic elements will engage your audience's interest and help to highlight your key points. This chapter focuses on the numerous PowerPoint 98 tools that let you add visual flash to your presentations.

Adding Graphics and Media

Unless you're a skilled artist, you probably won't be drawing much in your slides other than basic shapes, such as lines, arrows, and boxes. (Later in this chapter, you find out how do that.) You have a practical alternative to drawing pictures that look like bad cave paintings — you can use some of the nearly 100MB worth of clip art that Microsoft thoughtfully included on the Office 98 CD-ROM. *Clip art* consists of graphics files, created by an artist, that you can reuse with the artist's permission. Office 98 has a shared Clip Gallery that includes clip art; you can also insert a picture that's on your hard disk. You can freely reuse in your documents any of the art in the Clip Gallery. If you find on the Internet some artwork you want to use, be sure to get permission from the person who owns the art before you use it, or else you could be the unfortunate target of a lawsuit. In addition, PowerPoint 98 can use *clip media,* which are QuickTime movies and sound files.

Putting in pictures

To add a picture from the PowerPoint 98 Clip Gallery, follow these steps:

1. **Choose View➪Slide to switch to Slide view.**

2. **Select the slide to which you want to add the picture.**

3. **Choose Insert➪Picture➪Clip Art.**

   After a short delay, the Microsoft Clip Gallery opens, as shown in Figure 16-1.

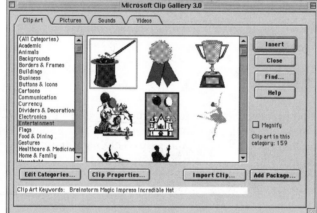

Figure 16-1: Selecting an image from the Clip Gallery.

4. **Click the image you want to use.**

   The scroll box of categories on the left side of the Clip Gallery window helps you narrow your choices and find your clip art faster.

5. **Click the Insert button.**

   PowerPoint 98 puts the image into the slide — where it almost certainly will be too large, in the wrong place, or both.

6. **To resize the graphic, click the graphic once to select it; then click one of the white handles and drag.**

   You can resize the graphic proportionally if you hold down the Shift key while you drag.

7. **If you need to move the graphic, click anywhere within the graphic and drag it to where you want it.**

If you created your own artwork (or picked up some good-looking art from an artist friend), you can add that art to your presentation without needing to add it to the Clip Gallery. Follow these steps:

1. **Choose Insert⇨Picture⇨From File.**

   The standard Open dialog box appears.

2. **Select the file that contains the artwork.**

3. **Click the Insert button.**

Again, you probably have to resize or move the image.

You can use two main types of graphics files in your presentations. *Bitmaps* are detailed pictures, such as photographs, that can't really be modified inside PowerPoint 98 except for simple changes, such as cropping and resizing. *Vector graphics,* like most of the clip art that comes with Office 98, can be ungrouped and then edited with the PowerPoint drawing tools.

Adding movies and sounds

Adding QuickTime movies and sound files is almost the same as adding pictures that don't move. Follow these steps:

1. **Choose View⇨Slide to switch to Slide view.**

2. **Select the slide to which you want to add the picture.**

3. **Choose Insert⇨Movies and Sounds⇨From File.**

   The standard Open dialog box appears.

4. **Select the movie or sound file you want to use.**

5. **Click the Insert button.**

If you inserted a QuickTime movie, the Movie toolbar also appears, as shown in Figure 16-2. You can use this toolbar to control playback.

Because movies are large files, they aren't saved inside PowerPoint presentation files. Instead, movie files are linked to the presentation files. If you show your presentation on another computer, you must remember to also copy the movie file when you copy the presentation file. If you don't, all you get is a single still frame of the movie.

PowerPoint 98 can handle video clips in these formats:

- ✔ QuickTime movies
- ✔ QuickTime VR movies (movies that enable you to tilt, pan, and zoom your viewpoint)
- ✔ MPEG videos
- ✔ Video for Windows (also known as AVI movies)

Movie toolbar

Figure 16-2:
Using a
QuickTime
movie in a
slide.

Boosting PowerPoint's Memory

Active media, such as video and sound, ask a great deal from your computer and from PowerPoint 98. To handle the load, you may have to increase the PowerPoint 98 memory allocation. To do that, follow these steps:

1. **Make sure that PowerPoint 98 is *not* open.**

2. **On the desktop, click the PowerPoint 98 icon *once* to select it.**

3. **Choose File⇨Get Info or press ⌘+I.**

   The PowerPoint 98 Info window appears, as shown in Figure 16-3.

4. **Click the Preferred Size box and increase the figure, taking into account the amount of RAM in your Mac.**

   If your Mac has tons of RAM, give PowerPoint a hefty increase. A good general rule is to try adding about 4,000K first and then adding more later if PowerPoint ever complains that it's running out of memory.

5. **Click the close box to dismiss the window.**

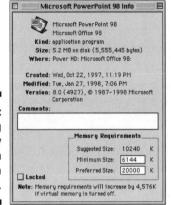

Figure 16-3:
Increasing
memory
allocation
in
PowerPoint.

Drawing in PowerPoint

You use the Drawing toolbar in PowerPoint 98 to create shapes, align objects, and add lines, connectors, and arrows. If you like, you can even draw free-form in your slides. Figure 16-4 gives you a close-up view of the Drawing toolbar.

To display the Drawing toolbar, choose View⇨Toolbars⇨Drawing. Alternatively, Control+click a toolbar to display the Toolbars pop-up menu. Then choose Drawing from the pop-up menu.

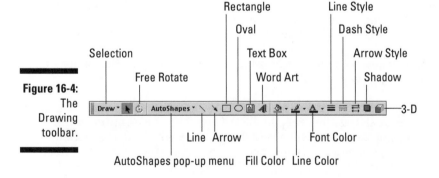

Figure 16-4:
The
Drawing
toolbar.

Drawing lines and arrows

Maybe you can't draw a straight line, but PowerPoint 98 certainly can. Lines are most often used in slides to set off one part of a slide from another; arrows are usually used to point out interesting information. To draw a line or an arrow in a slide, follow these steps:

1. **Choose View⇨Slide to switch to Slide view.**

2. **Select the slide to which you want to add the line or arrow.**

3. **Click either the Line or Arrow button on the Drawing toolbar.**

4. **Put the mouse pointer where you want your line or arrow to begin on the slide, hold down the mouse button, drag the mouse, and release the mouse button where you want the line or arrow to stop.**

   PowerPoint 98 draws the line or arrow.

Now you can format the line or arrow. To change the object's style, follow these steps:

1. **Click the object you want to modify.**

   PowerPoint 98 displays a handle at each end of the line or arrow.

2. **Click the Line Style, Dash Style, or Arrow Style button on the Drawing toolbar.**

   Each of these is a pop-up menu with various styles.

3. **Choose the style you want to use.**

4. **Repeat this process as necessary until the line or arrow is formatted as you like it.**

Using AutoShapes

AutoShapes are objects you can add to your slides. The shapes can be resized, rotated, colored, and modified in other ways. You can add text to AutoShapes, for example, and the text becomes part of the shape, so if you stretch, rotate, or flip the shape, the text follows suit.

The AutoShapes menu on the Drawing toolbar has 8 categories of objects, each offering from 6 to 24 items.

You can tear off any of the submenus of the AutoShapes menu, turning them into floating palettes. Just keep holding down the mouse button as you choose one of these submenus, and drag to the right. An outline follows your mouse pointer as you drag. Release the mouse button, and the floating palette appears, as shown in Figure 16-5.

To add an AutoShape to a slide, follow these steps:

1. **From the AutoShapes pop-up menu, choose a submenu and then, finally, an object.**

   The mouse pointer changes to a crosshair pointer.

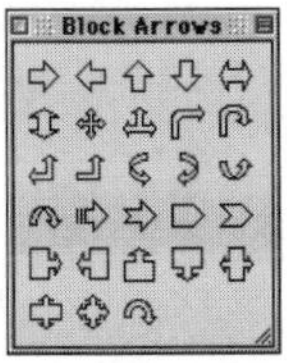

Figure 16-5:
A floating
palette
from the
AutoShapes
menu.

2. **Click and drag the mouse to draw the shape.**

3. **Release the mouse button.**

   The shape appears, with selection handles around it.

4. **Modify the shape by dragging its handles to resize it or by clicking any of the style buttons on the Drawing toolbar.**

For some cool effects, try using AutoShapes in conjunction with the Shadow or 3-D button. Depending on what you do, this experiment can also be the fast track to tastelessness.

Adding connectors

Connectors are smart lines. Each end of the line sticks to a different object, and moving that object causes the connector to follow along. Connectors are terrific for organizational charts, flowcharts, and any other chart you're using to denote a relationship between two things.

To add a connector, follow these steps:

1. **Using any of the drawing tools, draw a shape in a slide.**

   I suggest that you draw a rectangle or a box.

2. **Draw a second shape of the same type next to the first object.**

3. **From the Drawing toolbar, choose AutoShapes, and then choose one of the connectors from the Connectors box, as shown in Figure 16-6.**

   The mouse pointer turns into a combination of a crosshair and a small box.

Figure 16-6:
Choosing a
connector.

    4. Click the first shape you want to connect.

    5. Click the second shape.

Now, whenever you move either of the shapes to which the connector is connected, the ends of the connector's line are stuck to both objects. When you move one object, the connector moves along.

Taking notes with callouts

Another special type of AutoShape is the callout. Callouts are like cartoon thought balloons, and you add them the way you add any other AutoShape. Clicking inside a callout displays a blinking vertical text cursor and enables you to add text to the callout balloon.

Moving or deleting drawn objects

Easy come, easy go. If you want to move or get rid of an object you drew, follow these steps:

    1. Click the object you want to move or delete.

    PowerPoint 98 shows that the object is selected by displaying white handles around it.

    2. Move the object by dragging it, or bid it a fond farewell by pressing the Delete key.

Changing Slide Backgrounds and Styles

The longer you use PowerPoint 98, the better you become at judging which elements work in a presentation and which don't. If you've been using one of the templates or the AutoContent Wizard, you may get tired of the canned backgrounds and styles those features give you. No problem: You can freshen the appearance of your slides by switching backgrounds.

When you choose a slide background or style, remember that sooner or later you may print the presentation. To get an idea of what a slide will look like when you print it (on a noncolor printer, that is), choose View➪ Black and White.

Swapping backgrounds

To change the color of the background, follow these steps:

    1. Choose View➪Slide to switch to Slide view.

2. Select the slide you want to modify.

3. Choose Format⇨Background.

The Background dialog box appears, as shown in Figure 16-7.

Figure 16-7:
The
Background
dialog box.

4. Choose a new color from the Background Fill pop-up menu.

If you don't like any of the choices that PowerPoint 98 offers, click More Colors. The Colors dialog box appears, as shown in Figure 16-8. When you're done picking a color, click the OK button to return to the Background dialog box.

5. If you want your color changes to apply to all the slides in this presentation, click the Apply to All button; if you want to make changes only in the current slide, click the Apply button.

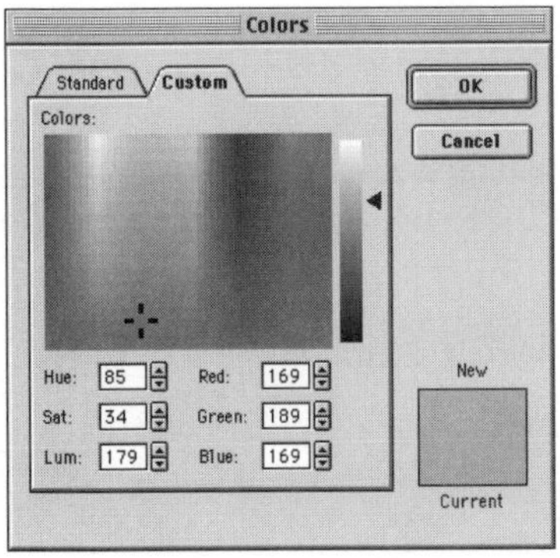

Figure 16-8:
Picking a
new color
from the
Colors
dialog box.

To change the style of the background, follow these steps:

1. Choose Format⇨Apply Design.

An Open dialog box appears, including a preview area that enables you to inspect the slide styles.

2. Select a style.

3. Click the Apply button.

Unlike background colors, which can vary from slide to slide, this new style is applied to all slides in your presentation. Be careful when you apply this style so that you don't inadvertently mess up all the slides.

Changing slide layouts

The *slide layout* specifies the location of text and pictures in a slide. Slide layouts should be taken as a starting point; you can always move things around. To pick a new slide layout for a particular slide, follow these steps:

1. **Choose View⬩Slide to switch to Slide view.**

2. **Select the slide you want to change.**

3. **Choose Format⬩Slide Layout.**

   The Slide Layout dialog box appears, as shown in Figure 16-9.

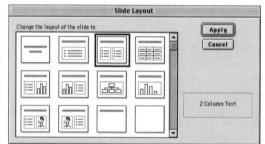

Figure 16-9:
Choosing a
new slide
layout.

4. **Select the new layout you want to use for the current slide.**

5. **Click the Apply button.**

   PowerPoint 98 changes the current slide's layout.

Creating Transitions

PowerPoint 98 enables you to create animated transitions between slides, and it can animate the way text or pictures appear in slides. You usually use animated transitions to reveal your bullet points one at a time, as you talk about each one, thereby keeping audience members interested (because they can't read ahead of you).

Slide transitions determine how your slide arrives on your screen. Think about the effects you see between scenes in a movie (the kind of movie you see in a theater, not the QuickTime sort). Slides can dissolve from one to another, wipe across the screen, reveal like an opening door, or zip up like a window shade to show the slide below. PowerPoint 98 also enables you to associate a sound with each of the 42 preset transitions (although if you do that, you may be cited by the Presentation Taste Police).

Text transitions affect how the bullet points on your slide reveal themselves. It's nice to have one bullet point appear and then have that point's text dim as the next point comes in. This type of transition keeps the attention of your audience on what you're saying now. PowerPoint 98 includes 56 types of text transitions.

Making slide transitions

To set the transition between slides in your presentation, follow these steps:

1. **Choose Slide Show⊏⟩Slide Transition.**

   The Slide Transition dialog box appears, as shown in Figure 16-10.

2. **Choose an effect from the Effect pop-up menu.**

   You see a preview of the effect in the preview box.

3. **Choose the transition speed by clicking one of the radio buttons below the Effect pop-up menu.**

   As you make changes, you again see a preview in the preview box.

4. **In the Advance section, choose how one slide will advance to the next.**

   Click the On Mouse Click button if you'll be advancing the slides manually by clicking the mouse (or using the keyboard). If your presentation will be running by itself (if it will run in an informational kiosk, for example), click the Automatically After check box and then, in the text box, enter the number of seconds' delay you want to occur between slides.

Preview box   Effect pop-up menu

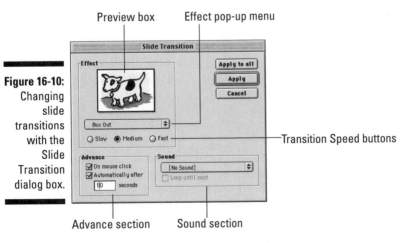

Figure 16-10:
Changing
slide
transitions
with the
Slide
Transition
dialog box.

Transition Speed buttons

Advance section   Sound section

Keeping your eye on the (nonbouncing) ball

When you're using flashy transitions and animated effects, you can easily slide right over the line between attracting attention and annoying your audience. The key to using effects is to use them sparingly. You want to persuade the members of your audience, not pummel them into submission via motion sickness. Here are a few points to keep in mind:

✔ Try to use the same transition effect for all the slides in your presentation. Audiences get disoriented if you change things after every slide.

✔ In the same fashion, be consistent with your text transitions within each slide. Having one line of text fly in and having the next one doing a rumba before it settles on the screen is a great way to get your audience running for the exits.

✔ The Preset Animation effects that use sounds (such as Typewriter and Laser Text) get old fast. If you use these effects at all, limit them to just the title of a slide.

✔ If you have any doubt about whether you should use an animated effect, don't use it.

Did you notice that both the check boxes in the Advance section can be checked? This arrangement means that you can have an automatically running presentation but override the time settings between slides by clicking the mouse.

5. **If you want PowerPoint 98 to play a sound file every time it changes slides, choose a sound from the Sound pop-up menu.**

6. **To apply the settings to only the current slide, click the Apply button; to apply them to all the slides in your presentation in one fell swoop, click the Apply to All button.**

7. **Repeat the preceding steps if you want to apply different transitions between some slides.**

Creating text transitions

One of the best ways to make a presentation is to use transitions from one slide to the next so that when the second slide appears, all the audience sees is the title of the slide. You introduce the slide's topic, and as you begin to talk about the slide's bullet points, they appear one by one.

To create a text transition, follow these steps:

1. **Click a text box in a slide.**

   PowerPoint 98 shows that the text box is selected by displaying a border and white handles around it.

2. **Choose Slide Show⇨Preset Animation, and then choose an effect from the hierarchical menu (as shown in Figure 16-11).**

3. **Choose Slide Show⇨Animation Preview to see what your text transition looks like in the small preview window; for a full-size view of the slide, choose View⇨Slide Show.**

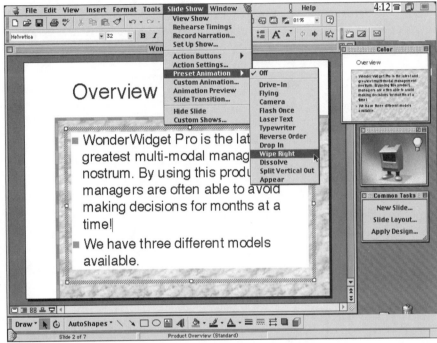

Figure 16-11:
The Preset Animation menu for text transitions.

Chapter 17

Doing the Presentation

· ·

In This Chapter

▶ Making your presentation interactive

▶ Creating Custom Shows

▶ Rehearsing the presentation

▶ Winning the stage-fright battle

· ·

I do not object to people looking at their watches when I am speaking. But I strongly object when they start shaking them to make certain they are still going.

— Lord Birkett (1883–1962), British lawyer and politician

This quote neatly pinpoints many people's fear of doing presentations. It's natural to be worried that you will make a mistake, bore your audience, be publicly humiliated, and be banished from society for the rest of your natural life. The ghost of Dale Carnegie will haunt you forever, tormenting you with a hollow laugh that only you can hear.

Relax — those things won't happen. In this chapter, you see how you can add interactivity to your presentations, customize your presentation for specific audiences, and rehearse your show so that it runs smoothly. By the time you're done, you'll have the tools you need to have your presentation go swimmingly.

Adding Interactivity to Your Show

You can have a presentation with a fixed order and format ready to go, and often, that's the best way to set up a presentation, especially if the presentation has to run automatically. Sometimes, however, you want to add more flexibility to your show so that you can either change it on the fly or allow other people to control it if they are running it for themselves.

Adding Action Buttons

Action Buttons are AutoShapes you can drop into your slides to enable a user to control the pace of your presentation. Action Buttons are just hyperlinks a user clicks to jump elsewhere — to another place in the same presentation, to another presentation on your hard disk, or to any Internet site.

To add an Action Button to a slide, follow these steps:

1. **On the Drawing toolbar, choose AutoShapes⇨Action Buttons.**

2. **Click the button that has the design you want to put in the slide.**

   The mouse pointer turns into a small cross.

   Another way to insert an Action Button is to choose Slide Show⇨ Action Buttons and then pick one of the 12 choices.

3. **Click the place in the slide where you want the button to appear.**

   You don't have to be too precise, because you can always move the button later.

   The Action Settings dialog box appears, as shown in Figure 17-1.

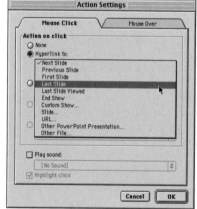

Figure 17-1:
The Action
Settings
dialog box.

4. **From the Hyperlink To pop-up menu, choose the value you want to use for this button.**

   You're not limited to the choices in the Hyperlink To list. You can choose any of the slides in your presentation by first choosing Slide from the pop-up menu. Pick a slide in the Hyperlink To Slide dialog box, as shown in Figure 17-2; then click the OK button.

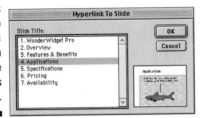

Figure 17-2:
Enable users
to jump to
a specific
slide with
appropriate
settings in this
dialog box.

5. Click the OK button.

The pop-up menu in the Action Settings dialog box also enables you to link to another PowerPoint presentation on your hard disk, to a URL on the World Wide Web, or to any other document on your hard disk. The latter feature enables you to create buttons that link to items such as Word 98 and Excel 98 documents.

Inserting hyperlinks to Web sites

Because all the Office 98 programs are Web-enabled, you can turn almost any text into a hyperlink. To turn text in a slide into a hyperlink, follow these steps:

1. **If you're not already in Slide View, choose View⇨Slide.**

2. **Select the slide into which you want to insert a hyperlink.**

3. **Select the text you want to turn into a hyperlink.**

4. **Choose Insert⇨Hyperlink or press ⌘+K.**

   The Insert Hyperlink dialog box appears, as shown in Figure 17-3.

5. **In the Link to File or URL box, type the URL that will be the destination of the hyperlink.**

6. **Click the OK button.**

   The text is underlined in blue, indicating that it is now a hyperlink.

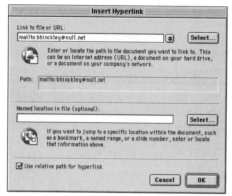

Creating Custom Shows

After you've been doing presentations for a while, you'll find that you're often asked to do a successful presentation more than once. Because the second (or subsequent) time around is for a slightly different audience, however, you change a few slides in your presentation. You can save the new version of your presentation as a new file (and indeed, previous versions of PowerPoint made you do just that). If you have many versions of the same presentation, however, remembering which specialized slides are in which version becomes a big pain.

PowerPoint 98 solves the problem with *Custom Shows,* which are like presentations inside presentations. Suppose that you're the product manager for the amazing new WonderWidget Pro. You're assigned to brief your company's manufacturing and sales departments about the product. Most of your presentation — the part that describes the product — is the same for both groups. The presentation to manufacturing, however, includes three slides detailing the special manufacturing processes required to produce the fabulous WonderWidget Pro. The salespeople don't need to see those slides; instead, they get a set of slides explaining their new commission structure for this product. Creating a Custom Show enables you to use one basic presentation for both audiences.

To create a Custom Show, follow these steps:

1. **Choose Slide Show⇨Custom Shows.**

   The Custom Shows dialog box appears, as shown in Figure 17-4.

2. **Click the New button.**

   The Define Custom Show dialog box appears, as shown in Figure 17-5.

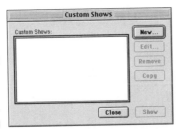

Figure 17-4:
Starting a
Custom Show.

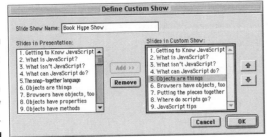

Figure 17-5:
Using
the Define
Custom Show
dialog box.

3. **In the Slide Show Name box, type the name for your Custom Show.**

4. **Double-click names of slides in the Slides in Presentation box to copy them to the Slides in Custom Show box.**

   You can change the order of items in the Slides in Custom Show box by selecting a slide and then clicking the up- or down-arrow button in the dialog box.

5. **Click the OK button to dismiss the Define Custom Show dialog box and return to the Custom Shows dialog box.**

6. **If you want to jump to Slide Show mode and view your Custom Show, click the Show button; otherwise, click the Close button.**

Practicing Your Presentation

Remember that old joke in which a man carrying a violin gets into a taxicab in New York City? He asks, "How do I get to Carnegie Hall?" The cabdriver eyes him and then says, "Practice, practice, practice."

That's how you get to be a good presenter, too — attention to detail and plenty of practice.

Running through your slide show

Testing your slide show before you subject it to the criticism of an audience is vitally important. A test run-through helps you find errors in slide transitions; typos in the slides themselves; and other mistakes, large and small.

To test your slide show, follow these steps:

1. **Choose Slide Show⇨View Show.**

   PowerPoint 98 displays the first slide in full-screen view.

2. **Advance through your presentation, noting any problems.**

   You can stop the slide show at any time by pressing ⌘+. (that's ⌘+period).

3. **Go back and fix the presentation's problems, or break out the champagne.**

Rehearsing your timing

Timing your presentation is a good idea, and PowerPoint 98 has some built-in tools to help with that task. You can rehearse the timings for each slide by choosing Slide Show⇨Rehearse Timings. The slide show starts, with a timer appearing in the bottom-right corner of the screen. Clicking the timer advances to the next slide and resets the timer. Rehearse your presentation, and when the presentation is done, PowerPoint 98 displays a dialog box, telling you how long the presentation is and asking whether you want to apply the amount of time you took for each slide to the slides in the presentation. That helps you if you decide to have the presentation run automatically while you speak instead of advancing slides manually.

In Slide Sorter view, you can manually add the number of seconds below each slide. Just click a slide to select it, and then click the Slide Transition button on the Slide Sorter toolbar, as shown in Figure 17-6.

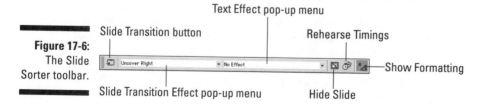

Figure 17-6: The Slide Sorter toolbar.

Text Effect pop-up menu

Slide Transition button

Rehearse Timings

Show Formatting

Slide Transition Effect pop-up menu

Hide Slide

Conquering Stage Fright and Doing the Show

All the preparation is done. Your PowerPoint 98 file is ready (not to mention brilliant), and suddenly, you're gripped with mind-numbing terror as you remember that you have to get up and give this speech. You're far from alone — the vast majority of people hate to speak in public. At least one study claims that people are more apprehensive about public speaking than they are about dying. Although that may be the case, personally, I'd rather die on stage than in real life. At least I can try to give that speech again and do a better job next time!

Here are some tips for conquering stage fright:

- ✓ **Unless you're speaking to a convention of your sworn enemies, realize that your audience wants you to succeed.** Think about the last time you saw someone else give a presentation. Were you thinking, "I sure hope this guy freezes up and makes a fool of himself"? Of course, you weren't. Your audience won't be thinking that about you, either.

- ✓ **Go early to the room where you'll be speaking, and get used to the place.** Stand at the podium, test the microphone, and make sure that you have a spot to place a cup of water. As the audience members come in, take a few minutes to chat with some of them. It's always easier to talk to people you know, even if you don't know them well.

- ✓ **Before you start to speak, take a moment to visualize yourself speaking — and doing a darned good job.** Picture yourself speaking well. Hear the audience's applause. This technique sounds weird, but it works.

- ✓ **Never apologize for being nervous.** Usually, you are the only one who knows that you're nervous, so if you don't say anything about it, nobody will notice.

- ✓ **Concentrate on your message.** By focusing on what you're saying, you don't let your nervousness gain a foothold.

- ✓ **Hone your message so that your most important information gets through to your audience.** Repeating your most important points is okay — it's common practice, in fact. Presenters have an old saw: "Tell them what you're going to tell them. Then tell them. Then tell them what you told them."

- ✓ **Be prepared.** The Boy Scouts truly got this one right. Audiences can usually tell when you're on top of a subject and when you're winging it.

✔ **Never read word for word from a script.** Only trained actors and professional speakers can read from a script without putting their audiences into a coma.

✔ **Don't run overtime.** (This rule is the one I struggle with the most.)

✔ **Do more presentations.** Every time you do a presentation, the next one gets easier.

The PowerPoint Viewer

To run a PowerPoint presentation, you normally need a copy of PowerPoint (gee, that makes sense). This requirement poses a problem, however, because it's not reasonable (unless you're Bill Gates) to assume that everyone will buy a copy of PowerPoint 98 just so that they can see your presentation. The solution is the free (and freely distributable) PowerPoint 97–98 Viewer, which you can download from the Microsoft Web site.

The Viewer is a program that can play PowerPoint presentation files but not edit them (for that task, you need the full copy of PowerPoint 98). The PowerPoint Viewer is also much smaller (in terms of disk space requirements) than PowerPoint 98 — although, sadly, it doesn't fit on a floppy disk, as the PowerPoint Viewer from Microsoft Office 4.2 does.

When I wrote this chapter in the spring of 1998, the Viewer wasn't done yet. A Microsoft representative told me that the PowerPoint Viewer should have been released by the time this book was published, in early summer 1998. If you go to the Web site and the Viewer isn't there, complain to Microsoft, not to me. The PowerPoint 97–98 Viewer will eventually be included on the Office 98 CD-ROM. Until then, check `http://www.microsoft.com/macoffice/`.

Part VI
Working Well with Others

"I TOLD HIM WE WERE LOOKING FOR SOFTWARE THAT WOULD GIVE US GREATER PRODUCTIVITY, SO HE SOLD ME A SPREADSHEET THAT CAME WITH THESE SIGNS."

In this part . . .

When you were a kid, did you get a check on your report card in the box that said "Works well with others"? No? That's probably because you didn't have Microsoft Office 98 to help you out. Using any of the Office programs, you can share information with colleagues around the corner or halfway around the world. In this part, you discover how to turn your documents into Web pages and how to turn your Macintosh into a powerful Web server.

You also see how you can mix and match information from any of the Office programs; how you can enlist your coworkers' help with your documents; and how new features in Office 98 make it easy to trade information with other Macintosh programs.

Chapter 18

Using the Office 98 Collaboration Features

*E*ach Office 98 program is an individual powerhouse, and you can use them together for even more power. You can bring an Excel chart into a report you create with Word, or you can include a Word table inside a PowerPoint presentation. Microsoft has made sharing information among the three programs easy, and orchestrating your effort among the Office programs can save you time and help you produce better work.

Office 98 also includes excellent capabilities to share and collaborate with your coworkers. Other people in your workgroup can review your documents, make revisions, and add comments. As you go through the revision process, you can save each revision as a version so that you can see the evolution of your document.

Share and Share Alike

The Office 98 programs offer a multitude of ways to share information between the programs. Because some of these ways are vestigial remnants of previously hot but now out-of-favor Microsoft or Apple technologies, I mention them here, although I don't fully explain them.

You can share information among programs in the following ways that I cover in detail in this chapter:

- ✔ **Copying:** Use the Clipboard to copy data between two programs.
- ✔ **Moving:** Use the Clipboard to cut data between two programs.
- ✔ **Dragging and dropping:** Select information in one document, and drag it into an open window in another program.
- ✔ **Linking:** Insert part of one document into another document. For example, you can insert part of an Excel spreadsheet into a report you create in Word.

You can also share information with these other, obsolete techniques, which I don't cover in this book:

- ✔ **Embedding:** A technique similar to linking (described previously) that includes an entire document from another application in your current document. It wasn't a beloved approach because it resulted in huge file sizes (and frequent crashes, in my experience).
- ✔ **Publish and Subscribe:** An Apple technology feature that was widely hyped but never widely used.

Of course, you can also share information between two programs by using one program to open a document created by another program — if the first program knows how to read the files created by the second. For example, you can use Word 98 to open files created in SimpleText, although SimpleText can't understand Word 98 documents.

In all the techniques I show you in this section, I make the assumption that you have at least two different programs open: Word and Excel, Word and PowerPoint, Excel and PowerPoint, or whatever. In this section, I discuss how to move information between two programs, so I refer to the program from which the data comes as the *source program* and the program where the data is going as the *destination program.* You always start in the source program, and you use one of the techniques described in the following set of steps to end with information in the destination program. Similarly, I refer to a document that contains the information to begin with as a *source document* and the document that receives the data as the *destination document.*

I refer to several of the buttons on the Standard toolbar throughout this chapter, as shown in Figure 18-1.

Copy

Cut   Paste   Insert Microsoft Excel Worksheet

Figure 18-1:
The buttons
used to
share
information.

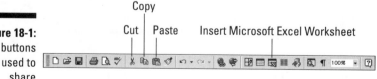

Copying and moving information

Copying and moving information between Office 98 programs is done in much the same way that you copy and moving information within a single program, except that in the middle of the process, you switch to a second program. To copy or move information between two programs, follow these steps:

1. **Select in the source program the information you want to copy or move.**

   The source program (remember that it could be any of the Office 98 applications) highlights the information.

2. **Do one of the following:**

   To copy the information:

   - Choose File⇨Copy.
   - Click the Copy button on the Standard toolbar (refer to Figure 18-1).
   - Press ⌘+C.

   To move the information:

   - Choose File⇨Cut.
   - Click the Cut button on the Standard toolbar (refer to Figure 18-1).
   - Press ⌘+X.

   The source program copies or moves the highlighted information to the Clipboard, although you don't see any changes if you're copying something.

3. **Switch to the destination program.**

4. **Click the insertion point in the destination document where you want the copied data to appear.**

5. **Do one of the following:**

   - Choose File⇨Paste.
   - Click the Paste button on the Standard toolbar.
   - Press ⌘+V.

   The information appears in the destination document.

Using Paste Special

After you cut or copy data, you usually choose to paste the data into the destination document. The data flows into the destination document and retains the formatting it had in the source document. Sometimes the original formatting is not what you want, however. For example, if you copy or cut a group of cells in an Excel spreadsheet and then paste them into Word, they show up in the Word document as a table. If you want the contents of the cells to flow in as regular text, choose Paste Special. Follow these steps:

1. **Select in the source program the information you want to cut or copy.**

   The source program highlights the information.

2. **Cut or copy the information.**

3. **Switch to the destination program.**

4. **Choose Edit⇨Paste Special.**

   The Paste Special dialog box appears, as shown in Figure 18-2.

5. **Select from the As box the format for the pasted data.**

   If you want the data to flow in as regular text, select Unformatted Text.

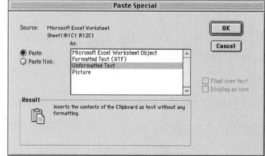

Figure 18-2:
The Paste
Special
dialog box.

Dragging and dropping information

Just as you can drag and drop information within the same document (for more about drag-and-drop editing, see the section in Chapter 5 about dragging and dropping), you can move information between Office programs by dragging and dropping. The support for Macintosh Drag-and-Drop is a new feature of Office 98; you can now trade information by dragging and dropping it with any other Macintosh program that is drag-enabled.

If you're not sure whether any particular Macintosh program is drag-enabled, you can easily find out. Just select some text or another object within the program, and try to drag and drop it on your desktop. The Finder is drag-enabled and can accept data from any other drag-enabled program. When you drop an object on the desktop, it becomes a *clipping file.* Clipping files can reside on your desktop or anywhere else on your hard disk, and you can drag them into any program that supports Macintosh Drag-and-Drop. When you drag a clipping file on a document, a copy of the clipping file's contents appears in the document. For example, I belong to a Macintosh users' group, and I often get questions about the group. On my desktop, I keep the clipping file that describes the group, its benefits, and information about how to join. Whenever I receive e-mail with a question about the group, I drag the clipping file from my desktop into a new e-mail message. The text I have previously written appears in the new message, and all I have to do is click Send. This clipping file saves me a tremendous amount of time.

Dragging information between Office programs

You may expect that because Office 98 is an integrated suite of programs, you can drag and drop information between any two of the programs in the same way, regardless of which programs you are using. If that was your expectation, then you have forgotten that these programs were written by Microsoft, which loves to throw the user a curve ball. Dragging and dropping between Word and PowerPoint, and dragging and dropping from either of these two programs to Excel, works in a simple, obvious fashion. You select, you drag, you drop, and you're done. Dragging and dropping from Excel to the other programs requires a slightly different technique, as you see in the following sections.

Dragging between Word and PowerPoint

To drag between a Word document and a PowerPoint document, arrange the two document windows on your screen so that you can see the point from which you want to drag and also the place to which you want to drop. Then follow these steps:

1. **Select in the source document the object you want to drag to the destination document.**

2. **Drag the object to the destination document's window.**

   As you move the cursor into the destination window, you see a dashed outline of the object you're moving, which gives you feedback about where you're going to drop the object (see Figure 18-3).

3. **Release the mouse button.**

   The object you dragged appears in the destination document.

Dragging from Excel to Word or PowerPoint

Dragging information from Excel to Word or PowerPoint doesn't simply copy the data. Instead, the spreadsheet data appears in your destination document with a *link* to the original spreadsheet. If you double-click the linked spreadsheet data in Word, Excel starts up and enables you to edit the data in Excel. Changes you make in the Excel document are reflected in the Word document. (Keep in mind that the changes flow only one way; changes you make in the Word copy of the data are not reflected in the Excel document.)

Word document (destination)   PowerPoint document (source)

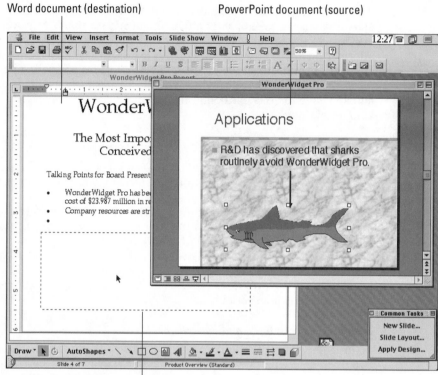

Figure 18-3:
Dragging a
picture from
PowerPoint
to a Word
document.

Outline of object being dragged

To drag cells from Excel to Word or PowerPoint, follow these steps:

1. **Select in the Excel document the cells you want to copy.**

2. **Move the cursor to one edge of the selection until the mouse pointer turns into an arrow.**

3. **Click and drag the selection to the destination document.**

   The selection appears in Word or PowerPoint as a linked spreadsheet object.

Working with text clippings from the Finder

It's convenient to keep boilerplate text in a clipping file on the desktop (see Figure 18-4) and then drag the clipping file into your Office document to insert the text in one step. Although you can do so in Word by using the AutoText feature (see the section in Chapter 5 about inserting text automatically with AutoText), I can tell you two advantages to using clipping files instead. One advantage is that the clipping file works in all the Office programs, not just in Word. The other is that you can drag that same clipping file into any other drag-enabled program, such as an e-mail program.

To create a text clipping, select some text in one of the office programs, and then drag the text from the document window and drop it on the desktop. The icon for the new clipping file appears.

To use the text clipping in one of your documents, drag the icon of the clipping file into your document window, and then release the mouse button. The text in the clipping file appears in your document.

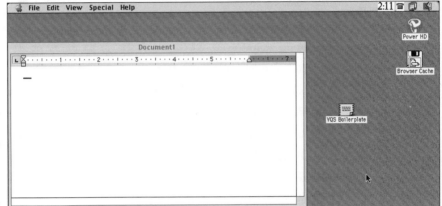

Figure 18-4:
A text
clipping file
on the
desktop.

Dragging graphics from the Scrapbook into Office programs

Because the Scrapbook is also drag-enabled, you can drag graphics from the Scrapbook directly into any Office document. Follow these steps:

1. **From the Apple menu, choose Scrapbook.**

   The Scrapbook appears.

2. **Scroll through the Scrapbook until you find the graphic you want.**

3. **Click and drag the graphic from the Scrapbook into the document window of the Office program you're working with.**

   The graphic appears in your document, as shown in Figure 18-5.

Linking information

Linking is useful when you want to make sure that the data in your document is always up-to-date. Suppose that you have a quarterly financial report in Word. You crunch the numbers for the report in Excel, and you know that you'll be making changes to the spreadsheet up to the last minute before you have to submit your report. Because you have a linked Excel spreadsheet inside your Word document, whenever you make a change in the Excel spreadsheet, the copy of the spreadsheet in your report is automatically updated. Because all the Office 98 programs have excellent support for linking, you can put almost any information from any Office program into any other Office document.

To link information, follow these steps:

1. **Switch to the program containing the information you want to link.**

   For example, if you are linking an Excel chart into a Word document, switch to Excel.

2. **Select the information you want to link.**

3. **Copy the information by choosing Edit⇨Copy or by pressing ⌘+C.**

4. **Switch to the destination program.**

5. **Put the cursor where you want the linked information to appear.**

6. **Choose Edit⇨Paste Special.**

   The Paste Special dialog box appears (refer to Figure 18-2).

7. **Click the Paste Link radio button.**

8. **In the As box, select the type of link you want, such as Formatted Text.**

9. **Click OK.**

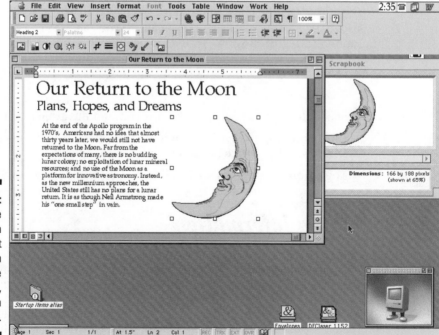

Figure 18-5:
The picture of the moon was just dragged in from the Scrapbook, which is on the right.

Sharing Information with Word

A few lucky writers have the ability to write completely clean first drafts, with little or no revisions needed. Most of us aren't that fortunate, and we need to hone and polish our work in multiple drafts until it shines. Word 98 has several tools to help with the revisions process. If your coworkers help with revisions, commenting and suggesting revisions for your work, Word 98 makes tracking and incorporating changes from many people easy.

Making comments

Comments let coworkers and other editors, which I call *reviewers,* add notes to your work without changing your text. When a reviewer adds a comment, Word inserts an invisible *comment reference mark* and uses yellow shading to highlight the word closest to the insertion point. If you selected text before you added the comment, Word highlights all the selected text.

To add a comment to a document, follow these steps:

1. **Select the text you want to comment on.**

2. **Choose Insert⇨Comment.**

   The *comment pane* opens at the bottom of the document window.

3. **Type your comment into the comment pane.**

You can view comments other people have made in your document in one of two ways. The easiest way is to simply put your mouse cursor over some highlighted text. In a couple of seconds, the comment pops up in a ScreenTip above the text, as shown in Figure 18-6. The other way is to view the comments in the comment pane of the document.

In previous versions of Microsoft Word, the Comments feature was called Annotations. The main improvement in the feature (besides a slightly friendlier name) is that you can now see at a glance where comments are in the document because of the highlighting that Word adds. Earlier versions of Word forced you to find all annotations in a separate pane of the document window.

Comment in ScreenTip

Figure 18-6:
Viewing
comments.

Comment in comment pane

Tracking changes

Besides simply commenting on your document, Word 98 enables reviewers to edit the document, and Word keeps track of all the changes that were made. Word uses revision marks to show you the modifications in your document. *Revision marks* show where text is deleted, inserted, or otherwise changed. If a reviewer deletes some of your text, for example, that text shows up on-screen formatted as ~~strikethrough.~~ Text inserted by reviewers is formatted as <u>underlined</u>. Word 98 assigns a different color to each reviewer. All changes made by one reviewer might show up in red, and all changes made by another reviewer could appear in green.

Word 98 doesn't show you the revision marks unless you ask it to. To see the revision marks in your document, follow these steps:

1. **Choose Tools➪Track Changes➪Highlight Changes.**

   The Highlight Changes dialog box appears, as shown in Figure 18-7.

2. **Click Highlight Changes on Screen.**

3. **Click OK.**

   The revision marks appear in your document.

If you want to know who made a particular change to your document, rest the mouse pointer over a change. A ScreenTip appears, identifying the reviewer who made that change and identifying the kind of change, as shown in Figure 18-8.

Figure 18-7:
Displaying
revision
marks
on-screen.

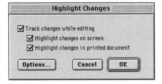

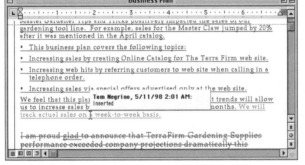

Figure 18-8:
Reviewing
changes
made by
others.

After you have received all the changes from your coworkers, you can
review the changes and accept or reject any suggested change. To review
changes, follow these steps:

1. **Choose View⇨Toolbars⇨Reviewing.**

   The Reviewing toolbar appears, as shown in Figure 18-9.

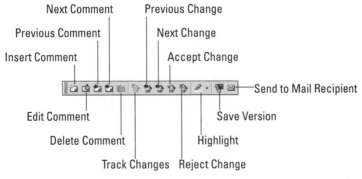

Figure 18-9:
The
Reviewing
toolbar.

2. **Click the insertion point before the revision you want to accept or
   reject.**

3. **On the Reviewing toolbar, click Next Change.**

   Word 98 selects the changed text.

4. **If you want to keep the changed text, click Accept Change on the Reviewing toolbar. If you don't like the change that was made, click Reject Change.**

   Word 98 automatically advances to the next change. If you accepted the change, the revision mark disappears from your screen. If you rejected the change, Word 98 deletes the rejected text.

5. **Repeat Steps 3 and 4 until you have worked through all the changes in your document.**

Keeping track of versions

A new feature in Word 98 is its capability to store multiple *versions* of a document in one file. You can record snapshots of the changes made to a document by saving multiple versions. After you've saved versions of a document, you can go back and open, review, print, or delete earlier versions.

To save a version of your document, follow these steps:

1. **Choose File➪Versions.**

   The Versions dialog box appears, as shown in Figure 18-10.

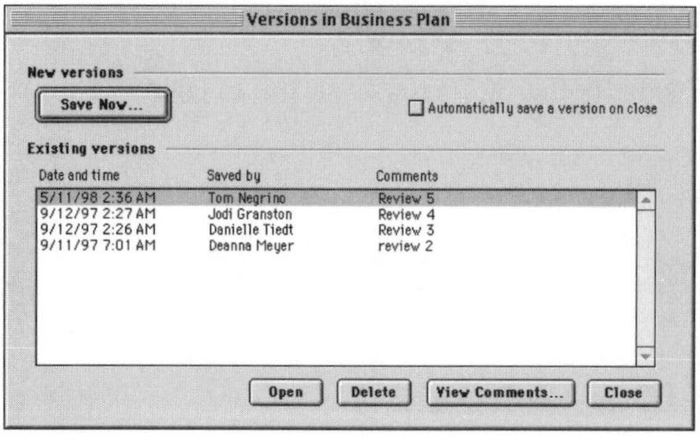

Figure 18-10:
Saving a snapshot of your document with the Versions feature.

2. **Click the Save Now button.**

   The Save Version dialog box appears.

3. **If you want, type a comment in the Comments or Version box to identify the version.**

4. **Click OK.**

   Word 98 saves the version.

Creating Excel worksheets in Word

Word enables you to create Excel spreadsheets from within Word. When you do so, you get all the power of Excel 98. When you save your Word document, the Excel 98 spreadsheet is also saved within your Word file.

To create an Excel worksheet in Word 98, follow these steps:

1. **In a Word document, click the insertion point where you want to create an Excel spreadsheet.**

2. **Click the Insert Microsoft Excel Worksheet button on the Standard toolbar.**

   A spreadsheet grid appears, as shown in Figure 18-11.

Figure 18-11: Setting the size of an Excel worksheet within Word.

3. **Click and drag in the grid to set the size of the spreadsheet in your Word document.**

   You're only setting the size of the spreadsheet's appearance in your Word document. You still have the full power of Excel, including the ability to use a bazillion cells.

4. **Office 98 switches to Excel, where you can type numbers, functions, or formulas in the usual manner. (To see how to use Excel, refer to Part III.)**

Sharing Information with Excel

Excel enables you to share spreadsheet and workbook information with other users. You can send workbooks to coworkers for review, much as you can with Word documents. You can also have a *shared workbook,* which is a workbook that has been set up to enable multiple users on a network to view and make changes at the same time. Because changes made to a shared workbook are live, each user sees the changes made by others.

Sharing workbooks

To set up a shared workbook on your company network, follow these steps:

1. **Choose Tools⇨Share Workbook.**

   The Share Workbook dialog box appears.

2. **Click the Editing tab.**

3. **Click the Allow Changes by More Than One User at the Same Time button.**

4. **Click OK.**

   Excel prompts you to save the workbook by displaying the Save dialog box.

5. **Give the shared workbook a name, and click Save.**

6. **Choose File⇨Save As, and then save the new shared workbook on a network server so that other users can access it.**

Using Word text in an Excel spreadsheet

Sometimes you want to use Word data inside an Excel spreadsheet. It could be that you have a fair amount of text you want to prepare in Word and then move into Excel, or you could copy a Word table and paste it into multiple spreadsheet cells.

When you link Word text to an Excel spreadsheet, any changes made to the Word document are reflected automatically in the Excel document. This automatic updating can save you a considerable amount of time and effort.

To link Word text into Excel, follow these steps:

1. **In a Word 98 document, select the text you want to link.**

2. **Choose Edit⇨Copy or press ⌘+C.**

3. **Switch to Excel 98.**

4. **Click the cell where you want the text to appear.**

5. **Choose Edit⇨Paste Special.**

   The Paste Special dialog box appears (refer to Figure 18-2).

6. **Click the Paste Link button.**

7. **In the As box, click Microsoft Word Document Object.**

8. **Click OK.**

Sharing Information with PowerPoint

PowerPoint shares information with Word and Excel in much the same way that those two programs share information with each other. You can copy, move, or link information among any of the three programs.

Building tables and charts from Excel information

To create an Excel worksheet inside your PowerPoint presentation, follow these steps:

1. **Choose Insert⇨New Slide.**

   The New Slide dialog box appears.

2. **In the Choose an AutoLayout box, find and select the layout named Object.**

3. **Click OK.**

   PowerPoint creates a new slide.

4. **On the Standard toolbar, click the Insert Microsoft Excel Worksheet button.**

   A grid that lets you size your spreadsheet appears.

5. **Choose the size of your spreadsheet by clicking and dragging with the mouse in the grid.**

   Excel launches (if it isn't already open) and gives you a blank worksheet.

6. **Type numbers and formulas as usual.**

7. **When you're done entering the spreadsheet data, choose File⇨ Close & Return to [the name of your presentation].**

   The worksheet closes, and you automatically switch back to PowerPoint 98, where the worksheet you created in Excel is inserted into your slide.

Linking Word text to your PowerPoint presentation

To copy Word text into PowerPoint, follow these steps:

1. **In a Word 98 document, select the text you want to copy.**

2. **Choose Edit➪Copy or press ⌘+C.**

3. **Switch to PowerPoint 98.**

4. **Click the text box of the slide where you want the text to appear.**

5. **Choose Edit➪Paste.**

Chapter 19

Sharing Information Over the Internet

● ●

In This Chapter

▶ Hyped on hyperlinks

▶ Using the Web toolbar

▶ Creating Web pages from Office 98 programs

▶ Using the Microsoft Personal Web Server

● ●

*W*hat a difference a few years make. When the preceding version of Microsoft Office was released, the Internet was used mainly by a relatively small group of people, mostly in universities. Since then, the World Wide Web has been invented; practically everyone and his or her grand-mother has an e-mail address; and the Internet has become the subject of a seemingly endless torrent of complaints, praise, and hype. In the real world, the Internet is neither the savior of humanity nor the destroyer of Western civilization; it's just a bunch of computers hooked up to one another over really fast phone lines.

Microsoft responded to the rise of the Internet by building Internet integra-tion features into all the Office 98 programs — Word, Excel, and PowerPoint can now save their documents as Web pages. In addition, you can put hyperlinks in any Office document. A *hyperlink* connects one part of your document to a Web page, to a different location in the same document, or to a different Office document on your hard disk. You can have a table of contents at the beginning of a long document, with each heading hyper-linked to the appropriate part of the document, for example. Clicking a heading in the table of contents takes you to that part of the document.

Using Hyperlinks

Hyperlinks enhance the usability of your documents by enabling readers to get to related or supporting information easily. To insert a hyperlink, you have to tell whichever Office application you're working in where the link starts and what its destination is. By convention, hyperlinks are formatted in blue and are underlined, although Office 98 enables you to change that formatting, if you want.

Linking to Web pages or Office documents

To insert a hyperlink that points to a Web page or to another Office 98 document, follow these steps:

1. **In your current document, select any text or picture you want to turn into a hyperlink.**

    2. **Choose Insert⏐Hyperlink, click the Insert Hyperlink button on the Standard toolbar, or press Ô+K.**

   The Insert Hyperlink dialog box appears, as shown in Figure 19-1.

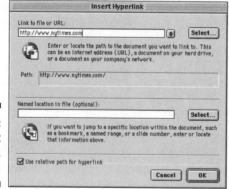

Figure 19-1:
The Insert
Hyperlink
dialog box.

3. **Do one of the following things:**

   • If you are hyperlinking to a Web site, type the URL of the Web page in the Link to File or URL box; then click the OK button.

   • If you're linking to another Office document, click the Select button next to the Link to File or URL box, find and double-click a file, and then click the OK button.

When you're typing a URL, it's important to type it exactly as it appears on the Web page. You can't change the capitalization or punctuation, add spaces, or change anything else. URLs aren't forgiving; if you mistype them, the hyperlinks just don't work.

The Office 98 program you're working in creates the hyperlink, formatting it blue and underlined. This formatting makes it easy to tell where the links in your document are.

Office 98 is smart enough to recognize all the standard forms of URLs (Universal Resource Locators, or Internet addresses) and can format them automatically as hyperlinks as you type them. To turn on automatic hyperlink formatting, follow these steps:

1. **Choose Tools⇨AutoCorrect.**

   The AutoCorrect dialog box appears.

2. **Click the AutoFormat As You Type tab.**

3. **In the Replace As You Type section, click the Internet Paths with Hyperlinks check box (see Figure 19-2).**

4. **Click the OK button.**

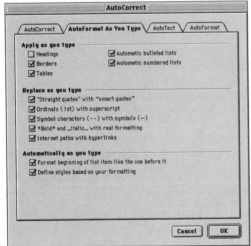

Figure 19-2:
Turning on
automatic
hyperlinking.

Hereafter, whenever you type a URL in your document, Word 98 turns it into a hyperlink. If the URL is for a Web page, when you're reading the document, clicking the hyperlink launches your Web browser (Internet Explorer or Netscape Navigator, for example), connects to the Internet, and loads the Web page. If the URL is an e-mail address, your e-mail program starts up, and a new e-mail message is created and addressed.

Creating internal links

An *internal hyperlink* jumps the reader from one part of your document to another part of the same document. The procedure differs slightly in each of the Office programs: In Word, you link to a part of your document that you have defined as a bookmark; in Excel, you link to a range of cells to which you've given a name; in PowerPoint, you link to a particular slide. I've shown you how to create the internal link in Word, which is the most common example. Follow these steps to create an internal hyperlink in Word:

1. **Select the text or picture you want to make the destination of the hyperlink (the point in the document the reader sees after clicking the hyperlink).**

2. **Choose Insert⇨Bookmark.**

   The Bookmark dialog box appears, as shown in Figure 19-3.

Figure 19-3: The Bookmark dialog box.

3. **In the text box, enter the name for your bookmark.**

4. **Click the Add button.**

5. **Select in your document the text or graphics you want to define as a hyperlink.**

6. **Choose Insert⇨Hyperlink, click the Insert Hyperlink button on the Standard toolbar, or press ⌘+K.**

   The Insert Hyperlink dialog box appears.

7. **Click the Select button next to the Named Location in File (Optional) text box.**

8. **The Bookmark dialog box reappears.**

9. **Click the bookmark you want to make the hyperlink's destination.**

10. **Click the OK button to return to the Insert Hyperlink dialog box.**

11. **Click the OK button in the Insert Hyperlink dialog box.**

Removing hyperlinks

After working with a document for a while, you may want to eliminate a hyperlink. To remove a hyperlink, follow these steps:

1. **Select the offending hyperlink.**

2. **Choose Insert⇨Hyperlink or press ⌘+K.**

   The Insert Hyperlink dialog box appears.

3. **Click the Remove Link button.**

Using the Web Toolbar

The Web toolbar (see Figure 19-4) is available in all the Office 98 applications, and it enables you to integrate Web browsing into your work. You use the Web toolbar when you're working on a document and want to look up something on a Web site.

Back button   Favorites menu

Forward button

Refresh button   Go menu   Address box

Figure 19-4:
The Web
toolbar.

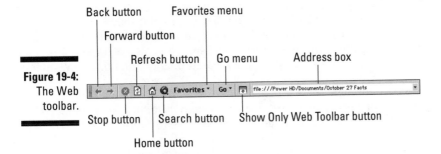

Stop button   Search button   Show Only Web Toolbar button

Home button

Displaying the Web toolbar

To display the Web toolbar, do one of the following things:

- ✔ Choose View⇨Toolbars⇨Web.
- ✔ Control+click any toolbar, and then choose Web from the resulting shortcut menu.
- ✔ Choose Tools⇨Customize to display the Customize dialog box, click the Toolbars tab, click the Web check box, and then click the Close button.

Browsing with the Web toolbar

When you make a choice from the Web toolbar, the Web page isn't displayed inside the Office program you're using. Rather, Office sends a message to whatever Web browser you set up as your default browser; that browser then launches and loads the Web page.

The Web toolbar has most of the same navigation buttons as Internet Explorer. Because Office uses the various settings you made when you set up Internet Explorer and Outlook Express, it inherits your home page and the search engine you prefer when you click the Search button. The toolbar also contains the Favorites menu, which contains all your Internet Explorer bookmarks.

To browse the Web with the Web toolbar, use the toolbar the same way you do in Internet Explorer (to get the details, refer to Chapter 12).

Creating Web Pages with Office 98

All the Office programs can save their documents in HTML format, which is Web format, but Word 98 does a much better job of it than Excel or PowerPoint do. Word 98 has many features that help you create Web pages, and considering that Word is a word processor, you can use it to create surprisingly credible Web pages. Although you probably won't turn to Word 98 as your main Web-page-creation tool, it's definitely worth using to convert your Word documents to Web pages. After converting, you may want to touch up the pages a little by using a true Web page editor, such as Claris Home Page, Symantec Visual Page, or GoLive CyberStudio.

Excel and PowerPoint lack the editing capabilities needed to create Web pages. Your best bet is to use the HTML export capabilities of these programs as a starting point, knowing that you'll be editing the resulting pages with Word 98 or another program for building Web sites.

Building Web pages in Word 98

You can use Word 98 to create Web pages in two ways. One way is to use Word from scratch to build the page, perhaps using the Word templates or Wizards for assistance. The other way is to save an existing Word document as HTML.

What's this HTML stuff?

HTML is an acronym for *Hypertext Markup Language,* which is the format used to create Web pages. There's nothing special about an HTML file; it's just plain text surrounded by *markup tags,* which tells the Web browser how to interpret the text inside the tags.

Suppose that I want to display the phrase *Office 98* in boldface on a Web page. The HTML code to do that looks like

`<B>Office 98</B>`

The first tag, `<B>`, starts the boldface formatting; the end tag, `</B>`, ends the boldface.

The nice thing about using Word 98 to build Web pages is that you generally don't have to mess with HTML. Nothing stops you, however, from editing the HTML pages Word creates. If you want to learn more about HTML, pick up any of the three billion books about the subject. You may want to start with either of two books: *HTML and Web Publishing Secrets,* by Jim Heid; or *HTML For Dummies,* 3rd Edition, by Ed Tittel and Stephen Nelson James. Both books are published by IDG Books Worldwide, Inc.

Using the Web Page Wizard

The Web Page Wizard produces a variety of pages that may be all you need for a simple Web site. The Web Page Wizard walks you through a series of steps to build a page. You just need to add your text and (sometimes) graphics to the page to finish it.

To use the Web Page Wizard to create a Web page, follow these steps:

1. Choose File⇨New.

The New dialog box opens, as shown in Figure 19-5.

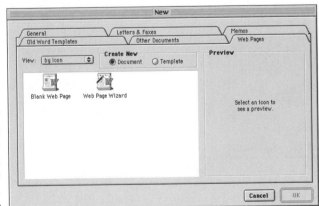

Figure 19-5:
The Web Pages tab in the New dialog box.

2. **Click the Web Pages tab.**

3. **Click the Web Page Wizard icon.**

4. **Click the OK button.**

   The Web Wizard dialog box appears, as shown in Figure 19-6. A new document also appears, behind the dialog box.

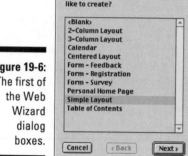

Figure 19-6:
The first of the Web Wizard dialog boxes.

5. **Select the kind of Web page you want to create; then click the Next button.**

   Notice that as you make choices, the page behind the dialog box changes to reflect your choice.

6. **In the next screen of the Wizard, choose the visual style of the page (see Figure 19-7).**

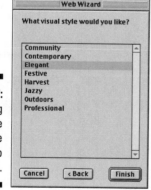

Figure 19-7:
Choosing the appearance of your Web page.

7. Click the Finish button.

The Web Wizard dialog box closes, and you're left with a document template ready for customization, as shown in Figure 19-8.

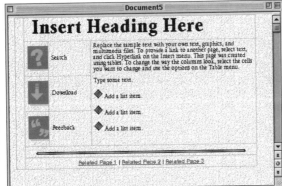

Figure 19-8:
The Web-
page
template.

8. Replace the sample text in the template with your own information.

The result should look something like Figure 19-9.

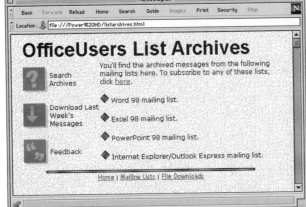

Figure 19-9:
The
complete
page,
viewed in
Netscape
Navigator.

The page template appears in Online Layout mode so that you can see how the page will look in a browser. You have no substitute, however, for looking at the page in a real Web browser; no exact correspondence exists between the way Word 98 displays a page and the way the page looks in a browser. Always preview your pages in a browser before you publish them to the Web.

Saving a document as HTML

To save an existing document as a Web page, follow these steps:

1. **Open the document you want to convert.**

2. **Choose File➪Save as HTML.**

   The Save As dialog box appears.

3. **In the text box, type the name of the new file.**

   For most Web servers to recognize the file, you have to add the
   .html extension to the filename. If you're writing about a bill that's
   moving through Congress, for example, you may name your file
   porkbarrel.html.

   It's vital to name HTML files without spaces or slashes, which confuse
   the heck out of Web servers. Using all lowercase letters is also a good
   idea (but not mandatory).

4. **Click the Save button.**

   The Office Assistant displays a message, warning you that some formatting may be lost in the conversion to HTML because you can't do all
   the things on a Web page that you can within Word.

5. **To complete the conversion, roll your eyes, mutter "Yeah, yeah," and
   click the Yes button.**

Adding flashy pictures to your Web pages

Most Word documents look fairly dull when you convert them into Web
pages, and one good way to liven them up is to add pictures to the page.
The Office 98 CD-ROM comes with tons of clip art and photographs you can
use on your Web pages.

To add pictures to a Web page, follow these steps:

1. **Put the insertion point where you want the picture to appear.**

2. **Do one of the following things:**

   • Choose Insert➪Picture➪ClipArt to pick a picture from the
     Office 98 clip art library.

   • Choose Insert➪Picture➪From File to choose another picture on
     your hard disk.

   • Choose Insert➪Picture➪Browse Web Art Page to connect to the
     Internet and check out the Web art at the Microsoft Web site.

3. **Select the picture you want to put on your page.**

4. **Click the Insert button.**

Turning Excel spreadsheets into Web pages

When Excel 98 saves a spreadsheet as HTML, it turns the file into a big, plain HTML table. You can then "pretty up" this table in a Web page editor or in Word 98. Excel uses a Wizard to step you through the process.

To save a spreadsheet as an HTML document, follow these steps:

1. **Open an existing Excel 98 spreadsheet, or create and save a new spreadsheet.**

2. **Select the part of the spreadsheet you want to convert to a Web page.**

3. **Choose File⇨Save As HTML.**

   The Internet Assistant Wizard appears, as shown in Figure 19-10.

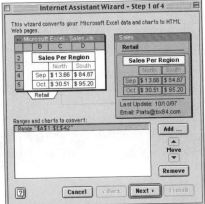

Figure 19-10: The first Internet Assistant Wizard window.

4. **Click the Next button.**

   Using the second Wizard screen, you create a new Web page or insert the converted data into an existing HTML file, as shown in Figure 19-11. If you create a new page, remember that you can always cut and paste the data into an existing page later.

5. **Click the radio button labeled Create an Independent, Ready-to-View HTML Document; then click the Next button.**

   The next screen enables you to add information to the HTML page, as shown in Figure 19-12.

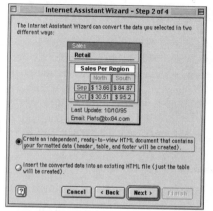

Internet Assistant Wizard – Step 2 of 4

The Internet Assistant Wizard can convert the data you selected in two different ways:

Sales
Retail

Sales Per Region
	North	South
Sep	$13.66	$84.87
Oct	$30.51	$95.2

Last Update: 10/10/95
Email: Piafs@bx84.com

◉ Create an independent, ready-to-view HTML document that contains your formatted data (header, table, and footer will be created).

○ Insert the converted data into an existing HTML file (just the table will be created).

[?] [Cancel] [< Back] [Next >] [Finish]

Figure 19-11:
Choosing to create a new HTML page.

Internet Assistant Wizard – Step 3 of 4

Enter header and footer information if you want:
Title: Royalty Workbook

Header: Summary

Description below header:

☐ Insert a horizontal line before the converted data.

Your converted data (tables and charts) appears here.

☐ Insert a horizontal line after the converted data.

Last update on: 4/12/98

By: Tom Negrino

Email:

[?] [Cancel] [< Back] [Next >] [Finish]

Figure 19-12:
Adding a title and other information to the Web page.

6. **Enter the information you want to use on the Web page; then click the Next button.**

   The final Wizard screen tells Excel 98 where you want to save the converted file, as shown in Figure 19-13.

7. **Click the Select button to choose where you want to save the HTML file; then click the Finish button.**

Internet Assistant Wizard – Step 4 of 4

Type or browse the pathname of the file you want to save.

File path:
Power HD:Excel.html   [Select...]

[?] [Cancel] [< Back] [Next >] [Finish]

Figure 19-13:
Saving the HTML page.

Converting PowerPoint presentations to Web pages

You can turn a PowerPoint presentation into a series of Web pages, and the process isn't terribly difficult. The trouble is that the results aren't great. PowerPoint exports each of the slides as a GIF or JPEG graphic, and the text on the slides tends to look jagged and unpleasant. Also, because each slide is one big graphic, you can't edit the result.

A better alternative to the built-in PowerPoint HTML export capability is Terry Morse Myrmidon (http://www.terrymorse.com), a $69 utility that gives HTML export capabilities to any program. Myrmidon does a superior job, and the pages it creates are completely editable.

To convert an existing PowerPoint 98 presentation to Web pages, follow these steps:

1. **Open an existing PowerPoint 98 presentation, or create and save a new presentation.**

2. **Choose File⇨Save As HTML.**

   The Save As HTML Wizard appears, as shown in Figure 19-14.

Figure 19-14:
The Save As HTML Wizard starts the conversion of your PowerPoint presentation to Web pages.

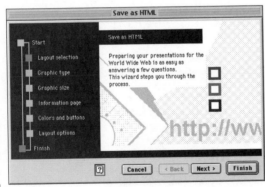

3. **Click the Next button.**

   The Wizard gives you a choice of standard or framed page layouts, as shown in Figure 19-15.

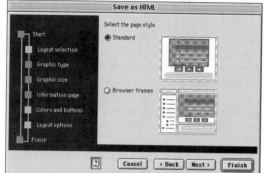

Figure 19-15:
Choosing
whether to
use frames.

4. **Click the Standard or Browser Frames button; then click the Next button.**

   You're asked whether you want to save graphics in GIF or JPEG format, as shown in Figure 19-16. Using the JPEG option is best because it more faithfully reproduces the colors in your slides. You can use the Compression pop-up menu to choose among four quality levels for the saved graphics. Best Quality produces better images but creates larger files. At the other end of the scale, Best Compression produces smaller files of lower quality.

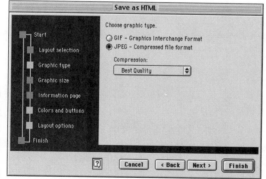

Figure 19-16:
Deciding on
a graphics
format.

5. **Click the GIF or JPEG button; then click the Next button.**

   The next screen enables you to choose the resolution for the saved graphics. Because you're saving files for the Web, the best thing to do is go for the lowest common denominator, which is 640 × 480 resolution, as shown in Figure 19-17.

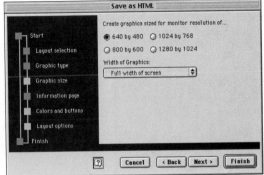

Figure 19-17:
Choosing
the graphics
size.

6. **Click the monitor resolution you want to use; then click the Next button.**

   On the next screen, as shown in Figure 19-18, the Wizard asks you for information you can put on the Web pages, such as your e-mail address or the URL of your home page.

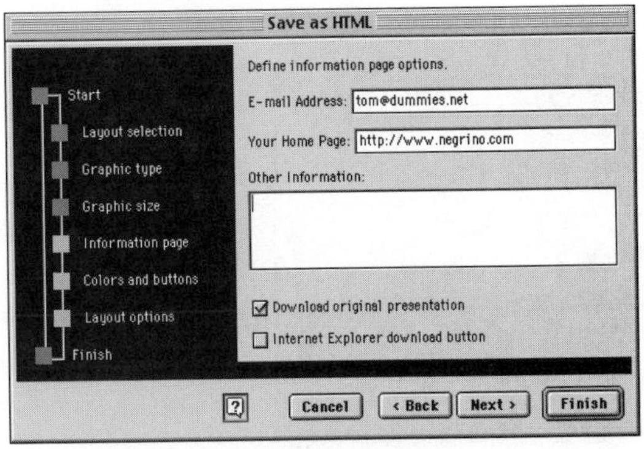

Figure 19-18:
Adding your
personal
information.

7. **Fill in the information you want to include on the Web page; then click the Next button.**

   The next part of the Wizard enables you to customize the colors used on the pages, including the colors of the background, text, links, and visited links (see Figure 19-19).

Figure 19-19:
Choosing
page colors.

8. **If you want to go with the standard browser colors, leave Use Browser Colors checked and then click the Next button; if you prefer to customize the colors, click the Custom Colors button and fiddle away with the color choices before you click Next.**

On the next screen, as shown in Figure 19-20, you get to pick the style of the navigation buttons the user clicks to move through your presentation.

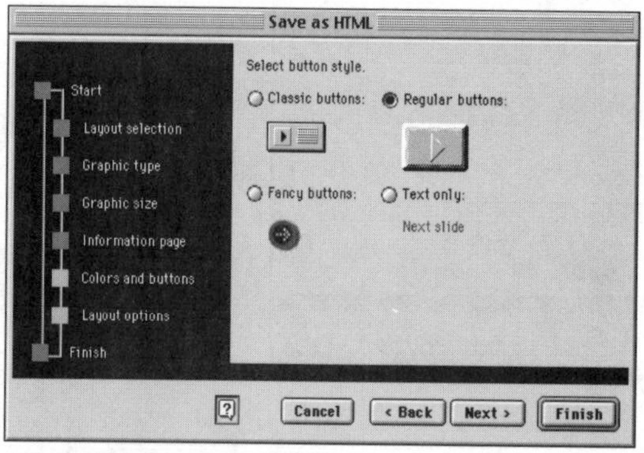

Figure 19-20:
Selecting a
button style.

9. **Pick a button style; then click the Next button.**

Yes, this process is almost at an end. In this next screen, you decide where the buttons you picked in the preceding screen appear: at the top, bottom, left, or right of the slides (see Figure 19-21).

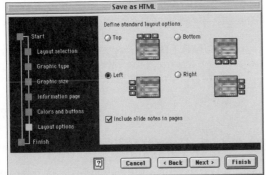

Figure 19-21:
Deciding on
the button
layout.

10. **Click the button that has the layout you want to use; then click the Next button.**

    Figure 19-22 shows the last choice you have to make.

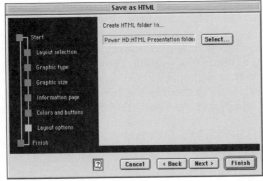

Figure 19-22:
Telling
PowerPoint
where to
save the
presentation
files.

11. **Pick the location where you want to save the files from the PowerPoint conversion.**

12. **Click the Finish button.**

A Web Server of Your Own

Most of the time you create documents for the Web, you upload them to your company's or organization's Web server so that the documents can be viewed by anyone on the Internet. You can share documents in another way, however: Fire up your very own Web server on your Macintosh. Sound complicated? Not at all! In fact, the software you need is probably already installed on your hard disk. The excellent Microsoft Personal Web Server (PWS) is installed along with the rest of the Easy Install of Internet Explorer 4.0.

Look inside the Microsoft Internet Applications folder on your hard disk; you should see a Personal Web Server folder. If not, insert the Office 98 CD-ROM, run the Internet Explorer Installer, and perform a Custom Install of the Personal Web Server.

Web serving with a personal touch

A personal Web server is designed for relatively light use — usually, within a company's network. The Microsoft Personal Web Server is easy to install and use, and it's surprisingly powerful. Because the program runs in the background, it doesn't slow your Mac; it needs only about 1.5MB of RAM; and it can serve thousands of Web pages per day without breaking a sweat.

You can be up and running in just a few minutes with the PWS, and the personal site you end up with will already have a home page, FTP upload capability, a visitor counter, a guestbook, and a way for your site visitors to leave you private messages. The site can even enable you to browse your hard disk over the Internet (don't worry — the feature is password-protected). This feature enables you to transfer files from your office machine when you're at home or traveling. People anywhere in the world can read Web pages that are running on your machine, and you can easily publish your travel schedule to the other people in your workgroup just by saving a file in Word 98 and putting it in your Personal Web Server folder.

An *intranet* is a private network that is running Internet-standard programs, such as e-mail, FTP, and Web servers. This arrangement means that people who are working on the company's intranet can use the same programs (Outlook Express, Claris Emailer, or Eudora for e-mail, for example, or Internet Explorer or Netscape Navigator for Web browsing) as they do to access other information from out on the Internet.

To use the Personal Web Server effectively, your Mac needs a full-time Internet connection. You can use the PWS with a dial-up connection, but then people will be able to get to your Web pages only while you're connected. Most companies' Net connection is full-time; if you're not sure, ask your network administrator. If you connect to the Internet over a Local Area Network rather than over a modem, you almost certainly have a full-time Internet connection.

Setting up the Personal Web Server

Setting up the Personal Web Server takes only a few minutes. Follow these steps:

1. **Choose Apple➪Control Panels➪Personal Web Manager.**

   The Main window appears, as shown in Figure 19-23.

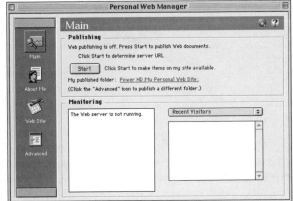

Figure 19-23: The Main window of the Personal Web Server.

2. **Click the About Me icon.**

   The About Me screen appears.

3. **Make a choice from the pop-up menu in the middle of the window to specify whether your Web site is for your company, home, school, organization, or community.**

   The bottom half of the window changes to reflect the choice you make.

4. **Fill in the About Me information, pressing the Tab key to move from box to box.**

   You don't have to fill in all the information. If you don't want to put your phone number on your Web site, for example, leave that box blank.

5. **(Optional) To put a picture on your home page, drag or paste a PICT, GIF, or JPEG file into either (or both) of the two picture boxes.**

   When you're done, the About Me information should look something like Figure 19-24.

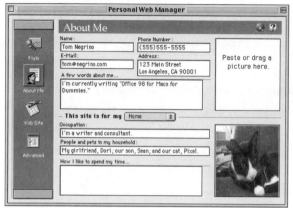

Figure 19-24:
The
completed
About Me
information.

6. **Click the Web Site icon.**

   The Web Site screen appears.

7. **In the Title box, type the title of your page.**

8. **(Optional) To put links to other sites on your home page, fill in the Link Description and URL boxes; then click the Add button.**

   Repeat this step as necessary until you have listed all links you want to list.

9. **Click the Main icon.**

   The Main screen reappears.

10. **Click the Start button.**

    The Personal Web Server starts, determines the URL for your server, and displays that URL in the Publishing section.

11. **To view your Web page, click the server URL in the Publishing section.**

    Internet Explorer starts (if it hasn't already) and displays your new page, which should look something like Figure 19-25.

Adding to your personal Web site

One of the automatic links generated on your home page is Access Shared Documents. This link is the key to making documents easily accessible through the Personal Web Server. Clicking this link takes you to a list of folders and files, as shown in Figure 19-26.

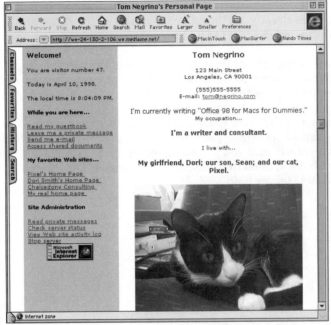

Figure 19-25:
Your new
Web page
should look
something
like this
figure.

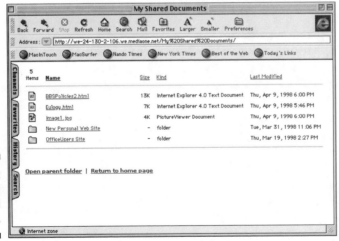

Figure 19-26:
Viewing
your shared
documents.

You can add files and folders to your site. The PWS puts a folder called
My Personal Web Site on the top level of your hard disk. Inside that folder
is a folder called My Shared Documents. To publish a text, HTML, or picture
file on the Web, drag it to the My Shared Documents folder. The PWS

automatically indexes the files and creates the document list. If you have a bunch of files already organized in a folder as a Web site, just drag the folder to the My Shared Documents folder.

If you have text-only documents, the Personal Web Server can publish them without your needing to convert them to HTML first. The server converts text files to HTML on the fly.

The Personal Web Server has many more features, including some that are usually available on industrial-strength Web servers. The program is amazingly robust, and you just can't beat the price. To learn more about PWS capabilities, open the Personal Web Manager and choose Help⇨ Personal Web Server Help.

Part VII
The Part of Tens

The 5th Wave By Rich Tennant

@RICHTENNANT

"FOR ADDITIONAL SOFTWARE SUPPORT, DIAL "9", "POUND," THE EXTENSION NUMBER DIVIDED BY YOUR ACCOUNT NUMBER, HIT "STAR", YOUR DOG, BLOW INTO THE RECEIVER TWICE, PUNCH IN YOUR HAT SIZE, PUNCH OUT YOUR LANDLORD,..."

In this part . . .

This part of the book is the one you should turn to when you want to hone and polish your skills with Microsoft Office 98. In the three chapters in this part, you find 30 ways to make working with Office faster, easier, and maybe even more enjoyable.

Chapter 20

Ten Tips to Tune Up Your Toolbars

- -

In This Chapter

▶ Showing and hiding toolbars

▶ Adding buttons to toolbars

▶ Removing buttons from toolbars

▶ Adding menus and macros to toolbars

▶ Creating a toolbar for AutoText

▶ Creating a button for text formatting in Excel

▶ Moving and copying buttons

▶ Creating separators in toolbars

▶ Turning a toolbar into a floating palette

▶ Moving your toolbars where you want them

- -

*T*oolbars in the Office 98 applications are amazingly useful; because of toolbars, access to virtually all the power of Office 98 is literally just a click away. Can you make those toolbars work harder to help you? Sure, you can! You can customize toolbars to a fare-thee-well, and this book is just the thing to show you how.

Here are ten useful ways to get your toolbars working both smarter and harder. By the time you're done with this chapter, you'll have your toolbars begging for mercy.

Toolbars: Now You See Them, Now You Don't

Not all the toolbars show up on-screen at the same time, and that's a good thing. Figure 20-1 shows what happened to Floyd Robbins, of West Alpaca, New York. It seems that all of Floyd's toolbars decided to party on his screen at the same time. Because Floyd didn't have this book, he didn't know how to break up the gathering.

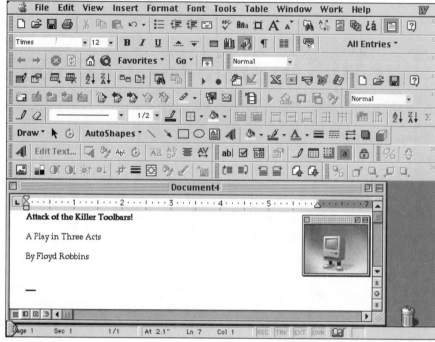

Figure 20-1:
All the
Word 98
toolbars
have come
to dinner.
It's not a
pretty sight.

Scary, no? This situation won't happen to you, though. To hide (or show) any toolbar, follow these steps:

1. **Control+click any toolbar.**

   A pop-up menu appears, with the active toolbars checked.

2. **Check (to show) or uncheck (to hide) the toolbar name on the pop-up menu.**

Adding a Button to a Toolbar

Adding a button to a toolbar is easy. Suppose that you often need to get a document's word count because you're paid by the word (I wish!). Follow these steps:

1. **Display the toolbar to which you want to add a button.**

2. **Choose Tools⇨Customize.**

   The Customize dialog box appears.

3. **Click the Commands tab.**

4. **In the Categories box, click the category for the command for which you want to create a button.**

   For Word Count, for example, click the Tools category.

5. **Scroll through the Commands box until you find the command you want, and drag it to the toolbar you displayed in Step 1.**

If you can't seem to find a command in a particular category, click All Commands in the Categories box.

Removing a Button from a Toolbar

To remove a button from a toolbar, follow these steps:

1. **Display the toolbar you want to modify.**

2. **While holding down the ⌘ key, drag the button off the toolbar.**

3. **Release the mouse button.**

   The toolbar button disappears.

You can't Undo the deletion of a toolbar button. If you make a mistake, add the button back to the toolbar, as described in the section "Adding a Button to a Toolbar," earlier in this chapter.

Adding Menus and Macros to a Toolbar

If you want to get ambitious about customizing toolbars, you can add any menu or macro to any toolbar. You're not limited to the menus that come with the Office programs; you can create your own custom menus and add them to toolbars too.

Putting one of the built-in menus on a toolbar

Follow these steps to add one of the built-in menus to a toolbar:

1. **Display the toolbar to which you want to add a menu.**

2. **Choose Tools➪Customize.**

   The Customize dialog box appears.

3. **Click the Commands tab.**

4. **In the Categories box, click Built-in Menus.**

5. **Drag the menu you want to use from the Commands box to the toolbar.**

Creating a custom menu on a toolbar

If you created any custom menus, you can add them to toolbars. Follow these steps:

1. **Display the toolbar to which you want to add a menu.**

2. **Choose Tools⇨Customize.**

   The Customize dialog box appears.

3. **Click the Commands tab.**

4. **In the Categories box, click New Menu.**

5. **Drag the New Menu item from the Commands box to the toolbar.**

   Next, you have to rename the New Menu item that's on the toolbar.

6. **Control+click the custom menu on the toolbar.**

   A pop-up menu appears, as shown in Figure 20-2.

7. **In the Name box, type the new menu's title; then press the Return key.**

   Now you can add commands to your new custom menu.

8. **Click the custom menu's name on the toolbar.**

   An empty box appears below the menu name.

Figure 20-2:
Naming a
custom
menu on a
toolbar.

9. **Drag a command from the Categories box of the Customize dialog box to the empty box on the custom menu.**

10. **Repeat Steps 8 and 9 until you've added all the commands you want to use on the custom menu.**

11. **Press the Return key.**

12. **Click the Close button.**

Adding a macro to a toolbar

To add a macro to a toolbar, follow these steps:

1. **Display the toolbar to which you want to add a macro.**

2. **Choose Tools⇨Customize.**

   The Customize dialog box appears.

3. **Click the Commands tab.**

4. **Click Macros in the Categories box.**

5. **Drag the macro from the Commands box to the toolbar.**

   Because macros have long, geeky names, you may want to rename the new macro on the toolbar.

6. **Control+click the custom menu on the toolbar.**

   A pop-up menu appears (refer to Figure 20-2).

7. **In the Name box on the pop-up menu, type the new menu's title; then press the Return key.**

Making an AutoText Toolbar

AutoText stores text or graphics you want to use again, whether those elements are boilerplate language, your signature, or your letterhead. You can save time and effort by creating a new toolbar for your AutoText entries. Follow these steps:

1. **Choose Tools⇨Customize to display the Customize dialog box.**

2. **Click the Toolbars tab.**

3. **Click the New button.**

   The New Toolbar dialog box appears, as shown in Figure 20-3.

Figure 20-3:
The New
Toolbar
dialog box.

4. **Type a name for the new toolbar.**

5. **Click the OK button to close the New Toolbar dialog box and return to the Customize dialog box.**

   You can't name the new toolbar AutoText because a built-in toolbar already has that name. Choose another name.

6. **Click the Commands tab.**

7. **Click AutoText in the Categories box.**

8. **Drag the AutoText items you want to use from the Commands box to the toolbar.**

Adding the Style Menu in Excel 98

Excel 98 enables you to create text styles, but because the Style menu isn't part of the standard Formatting toolbar, you have to make a trip to the Format menu and the Style dialog box whenever you want to format your text. To fix this hideous oversight, follow these steps:

1. **Choose Tools⇨Customize to display the Customize dialog box.**

2. **Click the Commands tab.**

3. **Click Format in the Categories box.**

4. **Drag the Style Menu command from the Commands box to the Formatting toolbar.**

   This command, the one that reads Style, has a blank box to the right of it — not the one that simply reads Style.

I suggest that you put the new Style menu to the left of the Font menu that's already on the Formatting toolbar, just the way it is in Word 98.

Moving and Copying Toolbar Buttons

You can rearrange toolbar buttons to your heart's content. If you want to move a button from one toolbar to another, first make sure that both toolbars are displayed. Then, to move the button, hold down the ⌘ key and drag the button to its new home — on the same toolbar or on a different toolbar. To copy the button, hold down the Option key while you drag.

Separating Those Toolbar Buttons

If you create your own toolbars, you may notice that the buttons all seem to run together. To create a separator bar between buttons, ⌘+click a button and drag it just a little to the right or left. When you release the mouse button, the separator bar appears.

If you drag the button too far, you end up moving the button to another toolbar or to a different place on the same toolbar. Just drag the button back to where you started and try again.

Letting Those Toolbars Float

Some people prefer toolbars; others prefer floating palettes. Office 98 can accommodate both sorts in perfect harmony. At the left edge of any toolbar is the move handle. Click the move handle and drag downward to turn the toolbar into a palette. You can also use the move handles to rearrange the toolbars. Just drag the toolbars where you want them.

Putting Your Toolbars Where You Want Them

Toolbars don't have to stay at the top of the screen. You can turn a toolbar into a floating palette and then drag the floating palette to any edge of the screen to dock it as a toolbar.

Chapter 21
Ten Quick Time-Saving Tips

In This Chapter

- ▶ Use the Format Painter
- ▶ Show formulas in Excel 98
- ▶ Save or close all windows
- ▶ Replace formatting and dingbats automatically
- ▶ Select a portion of text in Word
- ▶ Add blank lines in auto-numbered or auto-bulleted lists
- ▶ Shrink a document to fit
- ▶ Use the Spike
- ▶ Make a contextual move
- ▶ Quick-move a paragraph

Microsoft Office 98 is so chock-full of features and capabilities that I had a problem trimming the number of cool tips to only ten. Luckily, I was able to sprinkle throughout the rest of the book most of the tips I couldn't fit into this chapter.

Here are ten interesting tips, each one of which is guaranteed to save you time and effort. As a bonus, you can use these tips to amaze your friends and leave your office rivals in the dust.

Paint Your Formats

 In all the Office 98 programs, it's a snap to copy character and paragraph formatting from one place in your document to another. Just click the Format Painter button on the Standard toolbar.

To use the Format Painter, follow these steps:

1. **Format some text the way you like it.**
2. **Select the text you just formatted.**
3. **Click the Format Painter button.**
4. **Select the text to which you want to apply the formatting.**

You can quickly apply the same formatting to several locations in your document by double-clicking the Format Painter button; this action locks the formatting on. Click the button again when you're done formatting.

Flash Your Formulas

When you work in Excel 98, you often want to check out formulas in different cells. You can click each cell in turn and look at the formula on the formula bar. Alternatively, you can choose Tools⇨Preferences to display the Preferences dialog box, click the View tab, click the Formulas check box, and then click the OK button.

That procedure is way too much work, though, if you ask me. Instead, press Control+˜ (tilde) to display formulas in the cells, as shown in Figure 21-1.

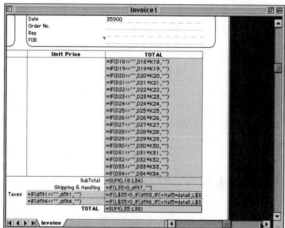

Figure 21-1:
When you toggle Display Fomulas on by pressing Control+˜, your spreadsheet's cells expand to display the formulas.

Save 'Em All, Close 'Em All

If you've used a computer for more than about a day, you've learned an unpleasant fact: Computers crash, and when they do, you lose all the work you did since the last time you saved. If you regularly work with more than one document open, the problem can be even worse because you have to keep switching among documents to save them all. Here's a better solution. Holding down the Shift key in Word 98 changes File⇨Save to File⇨Save All. (You have to use the mouse to choose Save All.)

A similar trick works in both Word 98 and Excel 98 to close all open windows. Holding down the Shift key changes File⇨Close to File⇨Close All.

Have AutoCorrect Do It for You

The Word 98 AutoCorrect feature is terrific for fixing misspelled words on the fly, but did you know that it can automatically insert symbols (called *dingbats*) for you? Suppose that you can never remember the right key combination for the copyright symbol (©). Just type **(c),** and Word 98 automatically replaces it with ©. Table 21-1 shows you the other symbol shortcuts.

Table 21-1	Automatic Symbol Replacements
What You Type	*Word 98 Replacement*
(c)	©
(r)	®
(tm)	™
...	... (true ellipsis)
:(	☹
:-(	☹
:)	☺
:-)	☺
:|	☺
:-|	☺

(continued)

Table 21-1 *(continued)*

What You Type	Word 98 Replacement
<- -	←
<==	⬅
- ->	→
==>	➔
<=>	⇔

You can also use AutoCorrect for bold and italic formatting on the fly. If you type * bold* and _ italic_, Word changes them to the real formatting, (**bold** and *italic*). You can use this technique with entire phrases as well as with individual words.

Select Just One Part

Although this trick has been around since Word 5.1, it's still a good one: You can draw a selection box in Word, just like you can in a graphics program. This capability is great when you want to copy a column of numbers that is in a tabbed list rather than in a table. Normally, you would have to copy the entire list and then laboriously edit each line. Not with this trick. Just click at the beginning of the text you want to select, hold down the Option key, and drag a selection box around the text, as shown in Figure 21-2. Then copy, cut, format, or do whatever else you want.

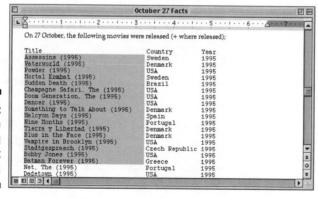

Figure 21-2:
The amazing Option+select trick.

Give an Automatic List a Break

When you use automatic numbering (or automatic bullets) in a Word document, a new number or bullet appears whenever you press the Return key. You've probably wanted to put a blank line between groups of numbered or bulleted lines. You can stop the auto-numbering or auto-bulleting by pressing Return twice and then restart the process by choosing Format⇨ Bullets and Numbering. No need, however; Office 98 has an easier way: Just press Shift+Return to insert the blank line; then press Return again to continue with the numbers or bullets, as shown in Figure 21-3.

Figure 21-3:
Inserting blank lines into automatic lists.

Shrink a Document to Fit

How many times have you tried to print a document and discovered that it's just a few lines too long to fit on one page? Word 98 provides a quick fix. In the Print Preview window, a Shrink to Fit button tries to make your document fit on one page by reducing the font size. This feature works best with short documents.

I use Shrink to Fit most when I'm printing drafts of documents for other people to see; when a document is in the draft stage. Because I don't care as much about its appearance as I do about its content, it's no big deal if the fonts look scrunched.

When you save and close the document, the new font size gets saved with it, so you should use Shrink to Fit just for printing and then choose Edit⇨ Undo Shrink to Fit before you leave Print Preview.

Use the Spike

Chances are that you've never heard of the Word 98 Spike. I hadn't either, until I started researching this book. The Spike is a way to move a group of text or graphics between nonadjacent locations. This feature is kind of like a Clipboard you can keep adding stuff to, except that you always cut items to the Spike; you can't copy them. The Spike (which was in Word 6 also) is definitely a carryover from the Windows version of Word, but it's a useful one (I guess that Microsoft got some things right!).

To use the Spike, follow these steps:

1. **Select text or a graphic.**

2. **Press ⌘+F3.**

   The selected item disappears from the document and goes to the Spike.

3. **Repeat Steps 1 and 2 for other items you want to move.**

4. **Click where you want to insert the Spike's contents.**

5. **Press ⌘+Shift+F3.**

   The Spike's contents spew out to the new location, in the order in which you put them on the Spike. The Spike is now empty; items don't stay on the Spike, as they do on the Clipboard. Weird, huh? — but still useful.

 You can insert the contents of the Spike without emptying it: Cut items to the Spike, choose Insert➪AutoText➪AutoText, and then click the AutoText tab. Click Spike in the Enter AutoText Entries Here box, and then click the Insert button.

Move Contextually

The contextual menu in the Office programs (and in Mac OS 8 and later) gives you lots of convenient features, although the capability to move contexually is one of the best. You can use the contextual menu to move, copy, or paste text and to do a few other things. Follow these steps:

1. **Select the text or graphics you want to copy.**

2. **Holding down both the ⌘ and Option keys, drag the selected item where you want it to go.**

   Make sure that you don't release those two keys!

3. **Release the mouse button.**

   A contextual menu pops up, as shown in Figure 21-4.

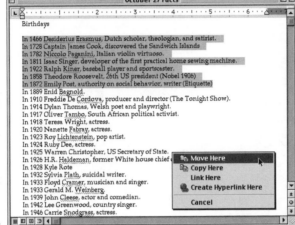

Figure 21-4:
The
contextual
menu for
moving text
and
graphics.

4. **Choose one of the menu options:**

   • **Move Here:** Moves the selected item to the indicated location

   • **Copy Here:** Puts a copy of the selected item in the indicated location

   • **Link Here:** Inserts a Link field that automatically updates the copy of the item you dragged whenever the original is changed

   • **Create Hyperlink Here:** Makes the indicated location a hyperlink, with the originally selected item as the hyperlink's destination

   • **Cancel:** Stops the operation

Move It, Mr. Paragraph!

You can rearrange paragraphs quickly by selecting the paragraph you want to move and then pressing Option+Shift+↑ to move it above the preceding paragraph or Option+Shift+↓ to move it below the next paragraph. You can also hold down the Option and Shift keys and repeatedly press an arrow key until the paragraph moves to the position you want.

Chapter 22

Ten (Or So) Ways to Customize Office 98

. . . .

In This Chapter

▶ Adding commands to menus

▶ Renaming commands

▶ Assigning custom shortcut keys

▶ Creating custom menus

▶ Recording macros

▶ Zooming in for a better view

▶ Using large toolbar icons

▶ Customizing the Recently Used lists

▶ Using Word 5.1's appearance in Word 98

▶ Turning off grammar checking

. . . .

*M*icrosoft Office 98 is an extremely powerful set of programs, enabling you to do practically anything you can imagine doing with a word processor, spreadsheet, and presentation program. All that power comes with the price of complexity, however. Sometimes, figuring out just how to do what you want to do can be difficult. You may disagree with the wizards at Microsoft about how to accomplish a particular task. No problem — the Office 98 programs are customizable. If you don't like the Microsoft way of doing things, you can change the programs so that they make sense to you.

Add Custom Menu Commands

One of the best ways to customize the Office programs is to add commands to any of the menus. If your work requires a great deal of revising documents, for example, you may want to put a strikethrough command on the Format menu.

To add a command to a menu, follow these steps:

1. **Choose Tools⇨Customize.**

   The Customize dialog box appears.

2. **Click the Toolbars tab.**

3. **Click the Menu Bar check box.**

   A customizable copy of the menu bar appears, as shown in Figure 22-1.

   The menu bar is just another customizable toolbar, as far as the Office programs are concerned.

4. **Click the Commands tab.**

5. **In the Categories box, click the category that contains the command you want to add to the menu.**

   If you can't find the command in a category, click the All Commands category.

6. **In the Commands box, click the command you want to add to the menu.**

7. **Drag the command to the name of the menu to which you want to add the command.**

   A horizontal line indicates where on the menu your command will appear.

8. **When the command is where you want it to be, release the mouse button.**

   The command appears on the menu.

9. **Press the Return key.**

   The Customize dialog box closes.

Figure 22-1:
A cus-
tomizable
copy of the
menu bar.

Copy of the menu bar

Rename Menu Commands

If you don't like the name of a particular menu command, change it! Follow these steps:

1. **Choose Tools⇨Customize.**

   The Customize dialog box appears.

2. **Click the Toolbars tab.**

3. **Click the Menu Bar check box.**

   A customizable copy of the menu bar appears (refer to Figure 22-1).

4. **On the copy of the menu bar, Control+click the command you want to change.**

   A pop-up menu appears.

5. **In the Name box in the pop-up menu, type the new name for the command.**

6. **Press the Return key.**

Add Your Own Shortcut Keys

Sometimes the shortcut keys that Microsoft thinks are logical make about zero sense to you. Again, you can change 'em if you don't like 'em. I've been used to toggling the Show/Hide Paragraph Marks command in Word 5.1 for six years by pressing ⌘+J, for example. Word 98 thinks that ⌘+J should mean Justify Text (it has a point — that does make more sense). But, heck, I'm used to doing it the old way, so I changed the shortcut key.

Follow these steps to assign shortcut keys any way you want:

1. **Choose Tools⇨Customize.**

   The Customize dialog box appears.

2. **Click the Keyboard button.**

   The Customize Keyboard dialog box appears, as shown in Figure 22-2.

3. **In the Categories and Commands boxes, select the command for which you want to add or change the shortcut key.**

4. **Click the Press New Shortcut Key box.**

   If a shortcut key is already assigned for this command, it appears in the Current Keys box.

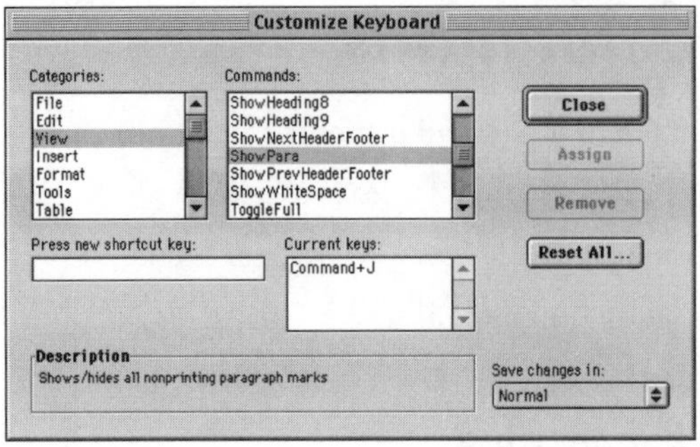

Figure 22-2:
Changing
shortcut
keys with
the
Customize
Keyboard
dialog box.

5. **Press on your keyboard the shortcut key combination you want to use.**

   If the combination is already in use, a message tells you which command now has it.

6. **Click the Assign button.**

7. **Click the Close button to close the Customize Keyboard dialog box and return to the Customize dialog box.**

8. **Click Close.**

Make a Custom Menu

You can create your own custom menus for particular projects and then hide or display them as needed. To create a custom menu and add it to the menu bar, follow these steps:

1. **Choose Tools⇨Customize.**

   The Customize dialog box appears.

2. **Click the Toolbars tab.**

3. **Click the Menu Bar check box.**

   A customizable copy of the menu bar appears (refer to Figure 22-1).

4. **Click the Commands tab.**

5. **In the Categories box, click New Menu.**

6. **Drag the selected New Menu item from the Commands box to where you want it to appear in the copy of the menu bar.**

   Next, you have to rename the new menu that's on the copy of the menu bar.

7. **Control+click the new menu on the copy of the menu bar.**

   A pop-up menu appears.

8. **In the Name box of the pop-up menu, type the new menu's title; then press the Return key.**

   Now you want to add commands to your new menu.

9. **Click the new menu name on the copy of the menu bar.**

   An empty box appears below the menu name.

10. **Click the Categories box of the Customize dialog box; then drag the command to the empty box on the new menu.**

11. **Repeat Steps 9 and 10 until you have added to the new menu all the commands you want to use.**

12. **Press the Return key.**

13. **Click the Close button.**

Record a Macro

All too often, people use their computers as barely smarter versions of objects they used before they had computers. Terrific programs such as Word 98 are available, and most people use it as though it were a typewriter. Excel is used to add columns of numbers — the least of its capabilities. Computers should be saving people from doing repetitive dogwork, thereby making it easier to do their jobs. That's the idea behind the Office 98 AutoText, AutoFormat, and AutoCorrect features: trying to relieve people of some of the tasks that come up again and again.

Macros take this idea one step further. You can record a series of actions and commands as a macro and then play the macro to repeat the actions automatically.

Suppose that you write a report every week. Although the beginning of the report has different text every week, it always has the same format. You can record a macro that assigns styles to the first several lines of your document and does the repetitive formatting for you.

Any set of actions you perform more than once, you can record (and play back) as a macro. After you try macros a few times, you'll wonder how you got along without them.

After you record a macro, assign a toolbar button to it, assign a shortcut key to it, or add it to a menu.

Macros in Word 98

To record a macro in Word 98, follow these steps:

1. **Choose Tools➪Macro➪Record New Macro.**

   The Record Macro dialog box appears, as shown in Figure 22-3.

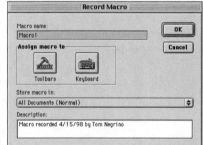

Figure 22-3:
The Record
Macro
dialog box.

2. **Type a name for your macro in the Macro name box.**

3. **(Optional) Assign the macro you're creating to a toolbar button or a shortcut key.**

   • To assign the macro to a toolbar button, click Toolbars. The Customize dialog box appears. In the Commands box, click the macro you're recording and drag it to a toolbar. Then click the Close button to begin recording the macro.

   • To assign the macro to a shortcut key, click Keyboard. The Customize Keyboard dialog box appears. Click the Press New Shortcut Key box; then press the shortcut key you want to assign to the macro. Click the Assign button; then click the Close button to begin recording the macro.

   The Stop Recording toolbar appears, as shown in Figure 22-4.

Stop button

Figure 22-4:
The Stop
Recording
toolbar.

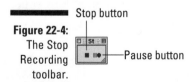

Pause button

4. **Perform the actions you want to record in the macro.**

5. **Click the Stop Recording button when you are done.**

To play back your macro, use the toolbar button or shortcut key you assigned in Step 3 or choose Tools⇨Macros. The Macros dialog box appears, as shown in Figure 22-5. Click the macro you want to run, and then click the Run button.

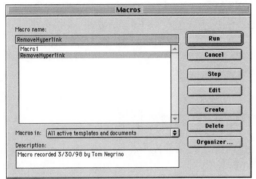

Figure 22-5:
Running a
macro from
the Macros
dialog box.

Macros in Excel 98

Recording macros in Excel 98 is somewhat different from recording them in Word 98, although the basic idea is the same. Again, you use a macro to record a series of actions you want to repeat.

To record a macro in Excel 98, follow these steps:

1. **Choose Tools⇨Macro⇨Record New Macro.**

   The Excel Record Macro dialog box appears, as shown in Figure 22-6.

2. **Type a name for your macro in the Macro name box.**

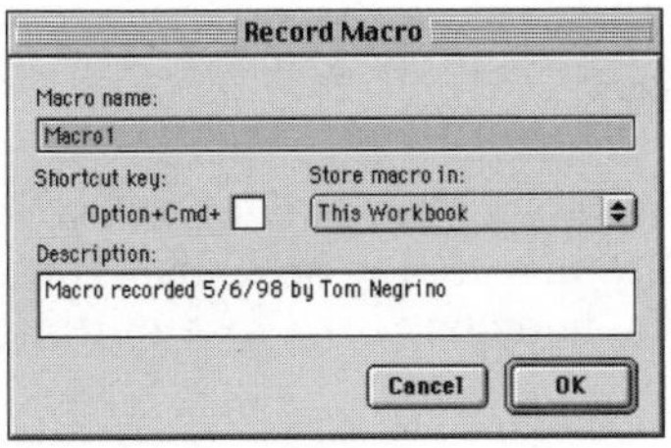

Figure 22-6:
The Excel 98
Record
Macro
dialog box.

3. **(Optional) If you want to run the macro with a shortcut key, type the letter of the key in the Shortcut Key box.**

Excel 98 isn't as flexible as Word 98 when it comes to assigning shortcut keys. The only acceptable key combination is ⌘+Option+*letter,* in which *letter* is any lowercase letter on the keyboard.

4. **Click the OK button.**

A Stop Recording toolbar appears (refer to Figure 22-4).

5. **Perform the actions you want to record in the macro.**

6. **Click the Stop Recording button when you are done.**

To play back your macro, use the shortcut key that you assigned in Step 3 or choose Tools⇨Macros.

Macros in PowerPoint 98

This topic is a bit of a sore point. Microsoft generally did a good job of updating the programs in Office 98 so that they're equivalent to their Windows 95 counterparts in Office 97. Unfortunately, PowerPoint 98 for the Mac got shortchanged: Significant capabilities are lacking on the Mac side, and one of those is the capability to record macros. If you want to use macros in PowerPoint 98, you must program them yourself by using the Microsoft programming language, Visual Basic for Applications. Programming, however, is way outside the scope of this book.

Helping the Visually Impaired

With so many icons, toolbars, and other interface widgets in the Office 98 programs, your screen often seems to be cluttered. If you happen to be visually impaired, the problem is even worse. This section describes two ways to take the strain off your eyes.

Blow up those buttons

You can make the buttons in the toolbars big — really big. First, choose Tools⇨Customize to display the Customize dialog box. Click the Options tab. Click the Large Icons check box. Then click the Close button. You see the result shown in Figure 22-7.

Figure 22-7:
Large toolbar
buttons are
easier to
see.

Zoom in for a better view

All the Office programs enable you to magnify (or shrink) the document window. This capability is especially useful if you're using small-point-size fonts in your document. You can zoom in while you're working on the document without messing up page breaks and margins. To zoom in, follow these steps:

1. **Choose View⇨Zoom.**

   The Zoom dialog box appears.

2. **Click the radio button for the magnification you want to use or enter a custom magnification in the text box.**

   If you want to zoom in on one small portion of the document window, select it first and then click the Fit Selection button in the Zoom dialog box. Just that portion of your document zooms to be as large as necessary to fit on your screen.

3. **Click the OK button.**

The Standard toolbar also has a Zoom menu. Some people find using this menu to be faster than using the Zoom dialog box.

Customize the Recently Used File List

If you tend to work with and switch among many documents, you'll appreciate the capability to expand the Recently Used File List on the File menu. To do so, follow these steps:

1. **Choose Tools⇨Preferences.**

   The Preferences dialog box appears, as shown in Figure 22-8.

2. **Click the General tab.**

3. **Adjust the number in the Recently Used File List box.**

   Acceptable numbers are 0 through 9.

4. **Click the OK button.**

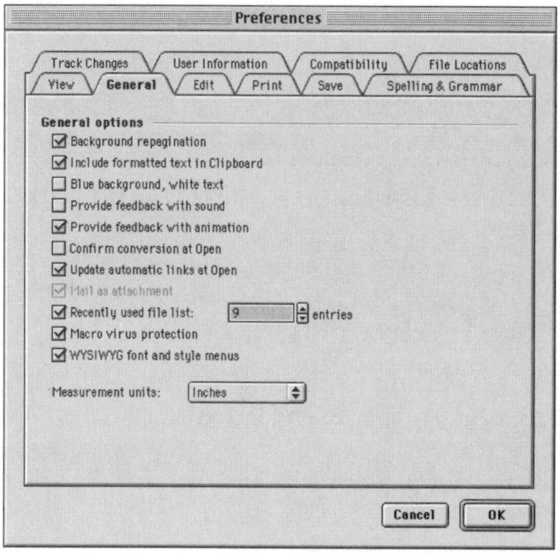

Preferences

Track Changes / User Information / Compatibility / File Locations
View / **General** / Edit / Print / Save / Spelling & Grammar

General options

☑ Background repagination
☑ Include formatted text in Clipboard
☐ Blue background, white text
☐ Provide feedback with sound
☑ Provide feedback with animation
☐ Confirm conversion at Open
☑ Update automatic links at Open
☑ Mail as attachment
☑ Recently used file list: 9   entries
☑ Macro virus protection
☑ WYSIWYG font and style menus

Measurement units: Inches

Cancel   OK

Figure 22-8:
The
Preferences
dialog box.

Use Word 5.1's Appearance

A large number of users never made the upgrade to Word 6.0, which received terrible reviews when it was released in 1994. These folks stuck with the venerable Word 5.1, which dates to 1992. To ease the shock of upgrading from Version 5.1 to Word 98, Microsoft has thoughtfully included a way to lend some of the appearance of the older version to Word 98. Choosing View⇨Word 5.1 Menus simplifies some of the menus and activates a toolbar that works like the old version's Ribbon.

Eliminate Automatic Grammar Checking

By default, Word 98 corrects your spelling and grammar as you type. If you find this feature to be annoying and would rather have the program check only when you ask it to do so, follow these steps:

1. **Choose Tools⇨Preferences.**

   The Preferences dialog box appears.

2. **Click the Spelling & Grammar tab.**

3. **Clear the check box labeled Check Grammar As You Type.**

4. **Click the OK button.**

Index

(continued)

IDG BOOKS WORLDWIDE
BOOK REGISTRATION

Register This Book and Win!

We want to hear from you!

Visit **http://my2cents.dummies.com** to register this book and tell us how you liked it!

✔ Get entered in our monthly prize giveaway.

✔ Give us feedback about this book — tell us what you like best, what you like least, or maybe what you'd like to ask the author and us to change!

✔ Let us know any other *...For Dummies*® topics that interest you.

Your feedback helps us determine what books to publish, tells us what coverage to add as we revise our books, and lets us know whether we're meeting your needs as a *...For Dummies* reader. You're our most valuable resource, and what you have to say is important to us!

Not on the Web yet? It's easy to get started with *Dummies 101*®: *The Internet For Windows*® *95* or *The Internet For Dummies*®, 5th Edition, at local retailers everywhere.

Or let us know what you think by sending us a letter at the following address:

...For Dummies Book Registration
Dummies Press
7260 Shadeland Station, Suite 100
Indianapolis, IN 46256-3945
Fax 317-596-5498

BUSINESS AND GENERAL REFERENCE BOOK SERIES FROM IDG

COMPUTER BOOK SERIES FROM IDG